The Heart of Biblical Narrative

Will & Zora,
For your morning
reflections, on rainy
days. Blessings,
Karl

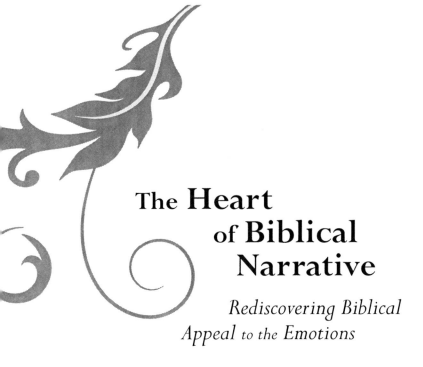

The Heart of Biblical Narrative

Rediscovering Biblical Appeal to the Emotions

Karl Allen Kuhn

Fortress Press
Minneapolis

For my daughter, Clare,
whose passion for life reminds us of its many blessings

THE HEART OF BIBLICAL NARRATIVE
Rediscovering Biblical Appeal to the Emotions

Cover image: © Erich Lessing/Art Resource, NY; © iStockphoto/Matt Knannlein
Cover and book design: Christy J. P. Barker

Library of Congress Cataloging-in-Publication Data
Kuhn, Karl Allen, 1967–
  The heart of biblical narrative : rediscovering biblical appeal to the emotions / Karl Allen Kuhn.
    p. cm.
  Includes bibliographical references (p.   ) and indexes.
  ISBN 978-0-8006-6338-4 (alk. paper)
  1. Pathos. 2. Bible—Criticism, Narrative. 3. Bible. N.T. Luke 1, 5-2, 40—Criticism, Narrative. I. Title.
  BS680.E4K84 2009
  220.6'6—dc22

                              2008039759

Manufactured in the U.S.A.

Contents

Contents

Acknowledgments

Several people have helped me shape this work into the form in which it now appears. Lakeland College colleagues Dr. Paul White, Professor Karl Elder, Dr. Meg Albrinck, and Professor Linda Tolman shared with me their insights on the relationship between emotion and literature. Their comments were very helpful as I began mapping out my own approach to the topic. Lakeland librarian Joe Pirillo graciously and ably processed scores of interlibrary loan requests for me, making my research of emotion and its relationship to literature much easier from our setting in rural Wisconsin. Five individuals served as my primary readers, each of whom carefully read and helpfully commented on the entire work: Rev. Dr. Mark Yurs, Rev. Becky Johnston, Rev. Kathleen Gloff, Rev. Bill Rishel, and Rev. Kathryn Kuhn. To them I owe great thanks for their generous gift of time, encouragement, and numerous insights that inspired many improvements in the work. I am also grateful to Fortress Press for the opportunity once again work with such a fine publisher, and especially to Neil Elliott, David Lott, and Marissa Bauck for their part in improving the work and shepherding it through the stages of publication. I give thanks for the many blessings I receive in my ministry of teaching and learning at Lakeland College, including a sabbatical leave in the fall of 2007, during which I wrote the bulk of the manuscript. As a college of the United Church of Christ with an undergraduate program in religion and a graduate program in theology, Lakeland has granted me many opportunities to shape my understanding of Scripture and faith in conversation with students, colleagues, and members of the wider church community. Above all, I give thanks to my wife, Kathryn, and our children, Joshua and Clare, whose support and love in this and many other endeavors are a source of tremendous blessing and joy.

Abbreviations

AB	Anchor Bible
Ant.	Josephus, *Antiquities of the Jews*
ATLA	American Theological Library Association
BAGD	W. Bauer, W. F. Arndt, F. W. Gingrich, and F. W. Danker, *A Greek-English Lexicon of the New Testament*
Bib	*Biblica*
CBQ	*Catholic Biblical Quarterly*
CTJ	*Calvin Theological Journal*
CurTM	*Currents in Theology and Mission*
EKKNT	*Evangelisch-katholischer Kommentar zum Neuen Testamentum*
HTKNT	*Herders theologischer Kommentar zum Neuen Testamentum*
JAMA	*Journal of the American Medical Association*
JBL	*Journal of Biblical Literature*
JETS	*Journal of the Evangelical Theological Society*
JSNT	*Journal for the Study of the New Testament*
JSNTSup	Journal for the Study of the New Testament Supplement Series
JTS	*Journal of Theological Studies*
Life	*The Life of Flavius Josephus*
NICNT	New International Commentary on the New Testament
NIGTC	New International Greek Testament Commentary
NovTSup	Novum Testamentum Supplements
NRT	*Nouvelle Revue Theologique*
NTOA	Novum Testamentum et Orbis Antiquus
NTS	*New Testament Studies*
OTP	*The Old Testament Pseudepigrapha. Edited by James H. Charlesworth.*
SBLDS	Society of Biblical Literature Dissertation Series
SNTSMS	Society for New Testament Studies Monograph Series
VT	*Vetus Testamentum*
WBC	Word Biblical Commentary
WUANT	Wissenschaftliche Untersuchungen zum Alten und Neuen Testament

Introduction

The Bible's
Neglected Heart

"So, how does this passage make you feel?"

Such a query in a roomful of biblical scholars would likely be met with irritable "harrumphs," amused titters, or nervous twitches. "How does this passage make us *feel*? Are you kidding? What do feelings have to do with it? We're interested in what a text *means*."

The Marginalization of Emotion

Biblical scholars have generally shown little interest in getting in touch with the affective dimension of biblical narrative. Only rarely has the emotional impact of literature on readers been engaged as a topic relevant to the critical study of biblical narrative. When one stops to think about it, this omission is remarkable. Emotion is basic to our experience of engaging other forms of narrative expression. When we read a novel or a dramatic work of nonfiction, view a play or movie, our affective faculties are often deeply engaged. Narratives cause us to feel. We all know that. Yet when it comes to the exegetical ruminations of biblical scholars, they typically lack any sense of a text's affective force. To be sure, scholars sometimes talk about the emotions displayed by characters within the text. At times they will express admiration for the artistry—rhetorically or stylistically—of a narrative, and one could perhaps infer from this that they have experienced some sort of affective connection with the passage. By and large, however, the emotive impact of a biblical narrative, either as intended by the author or experienced by the reader, is left unattended by those who devote much of their adult lives to this literature.[1]

1

Conversely, in other fields such as literary theory, psychology, philosophy, social science, and educational theory, it is widely recognized that emotion is integral to the function and experience of narrative, and the affective impact of literature is a subject of increasing attention. Patrick Colm Hogan, for instance, combines the fields of anthropology, literary theory, and cognitive psychology in his work on narrative and emotion. He explores how prototypical emotional experiences are given expression in narrative structures that are prevalent across cultures, what he terms "literary universals."[2] On the relationship between narrative and emotion in these literary universals and literature in general, he states:

> Literary stories, especially the stories we most admire and appreciate, are structured and animated by the emotions. Any coherent sequence of events might constitute a story. But the stories that engage us, the stories we celebrate and repeat—"paradigm" stories—are precisely stories that move us, most often by portraying the emotions or emotionally consequential events. Conversely, the emotive impact of verbal art cannot be discussed separately from its narrative structure.[3]

Those offering analyses of the psychological impact of narrative literature have also repeatedly demonstrated that imagination and emotional response are commonly integral to the experience of reading narrative. For instance, psychologist David Miall and colleagues point to studies showing that literary texts commonly invite affective responses in readers, which, in turn, influence their construal of meaning and also shape self-understanding.[4] Contributors to the volume *Empirical Approaches to Literature and Aesthetics*, among others, claim that readers' affective response to narrative contributes to their level of literary engagement and comprehension, citing studies devised to measure the phenomenon.[5] Based on still other studies, Keith Oatley argues that because narrative naturally engages the emotions of its audience, it can be employed to help readers explore their own emotional repertoires and become more aware of how emotions influence their perceptions of reality and their behaviors.[6] Similarly, the "education of emotions," which has become a major focus in educational circles, commonly makes use of narrative as a pedagogical tool.[7] Likewise, the use of storytelling as a form of psychiatric therapy designed to explore and shape emotion has become a common practice.[8]

In sum, numerous fields of study recognize the essential role emotion plays in the design and experience of narrative. This alone should commend more attention to the affective dimension of biblical narrative among interpreters. The stakes are even higher than this, however. Not only is affect crucial to the construction and experience of narrative, it is also essential to the *rhetorical* function and force of narrative. Allow me to unpack this a bit. First of all, narrative form is now commonly held to be essential to the way in which humans construe reality. With increasing frequency, psychologists, philosophers, and literary critics are recognizing that we conceive of our lives as "storied," *and that our emotions play an essential role in our narrative construals of ourselves and the world.*[9] When we say to one another, "Tell me your life story," we are not merely using a figure of speech. We tend to see ourselves and others as characters in an unfolding life saga, moving toward what we hope to accomplish, experience, or become. This insight is commonly held alongside another: that narratives, well-composed narratives at least, have the power to engage us deeply and mold our own story-formed perceptions of reality.[10] Many narratives, in other words, are essentially *rhetorical* in character. They call their readers to grasp "certain urgent claims" about the nature of the world and their own selves.[11] Similarly, Carol S. Witherall and her colleagues explain:

> Stories invite us to come to know the world and our place in it. Whether narratives of history, present experience, or the imagination, stories call us to consider what we know, what we hope for, who we are, and what and whom we care about. Stories have a certain engaging power—a ring of truth. . . . Narratives can also serve as an interpretive lens for reflecting the storied nature of human lives, for understanding the complexities of the human condition, and for enabling classrooms to expand their borders as interpretive communities. A good story engages and enlarges the moral imagination, illuminating possibilities for human thought, feeling, and action in ways that can bridge the gulf between different times, places, cultures, and beliefs.[12]

Likewise, Martha Nussbaum speaks of the "potential space" narrative—in this case tragedy—provides for exploring certain conceptions of the world and our place within it. She also notes the important role affect plays in energizing and shaping a reader's response to tragedy's rhetorical force:

> I have said that the "potential space" of aesthetic activity is a space with which we investigate and try out some of life's possibilities. In responding to a tragedy with pity and fear we are grasping certain urgent claims, not only about the characters but also about the world and about ourselves: not only that Oedipus is coming to grief through no fault of his own, but also that it is possible for us to do so. In this way, the reader or spectator of a literary work is reading or watching the work, but at the same time reading the world, and reading her own self.[13]

These insights on the storied nature of our worldviews and the rhetorical power of narrative have not been lost on some biblical scholars, especially those interested in engaging the Bible as a normative resource for believing communities. As stated by Joel Green:

> The biblical narrative is present as an alternative framework within which to construe our lives, and so challenges those who would be Christian by calling for a creative transformation of the stories by which we make sense of our lives and the world. If we all live story-formed lives, then we are confronted with the question, "What stories will shape us?" For Christians, the answer is non-negotiable: Our task is to make our lodging the Genesis-to-Revelation narrative so that our modes of interpretation are conformed to the biblical narrative, so that this story decisively shapes our lives.[14]

I believe Green has it right. The biblical story is to be for Christians that narrative, that chief "paradigm story," to use Hogan's phrase, which decisively shapes (to borrow from Witherall et al.) "what we know, what we hope for, who we are, and what and whom we care about." However, our accounting of how biblical narrative is to become our story and thereby shape our lives is almost devoid of any discussion of its affective character and potential emotive impact. This omission is significant, for it hampers our ability to appreciate fully the rhetorical character and religious power of biblical narrative. Emotions play a major role in our reading of a narrative, our engagement of its claims about the world, and our willingness or not to recast our own storied worldviews in response to that encounter. Good authors know this, either consciously or implicitly. *Affective appeal in varying forms is the means by which narratives compel us to enter their storied world and entertain out the version of reality they present.* Accordingly, James E. Gilman wisely notes that "whereas [biblical] narratives are tools by which the community opens itself to possible worlds, educating and reeducating its emotions and emotional habits, emotions provide the transformative power for appropriating possible worlds, for practicing the true meaning of God's kingdom."[15] The problem, simply stated, is this: at the same time we turn to biblical narrative as that normative guide which is to transform our worldviews, we commonly bracket out of our discussion that crucial element—emotion—that empowers Scripture's rhetoric and compels readers to embrace its portrait of the way the world should be.

Mark Allan Powell has documented contrasting reading tendencies between ordained clergy and lay folk that further illustrate the tendency of biblical scholarship to neglect the affective dimension of biblical narrative. In his *Chasing the Eastern Star: Adventures in Reader Response Criticism*, Powell reports on several "real reader response" studies he has conducted.[16] With one group of fifty clergy and fifty laity, he asked them to respond to the question, "What does this story mean?" in reference to John's fiery preaching in Luke 3:3-17. The vast majority of the clergy answered the question "in highly cognitive terms that attempt to identify the point or message that is conveyed," in other words, what the passage is saying about God, the kingdom, or discipleship.[17] The lay readers, on the other hand, were much more inclined to answer the question in terms of the effect or impact the story had on them—how it moved them emotionally: "This story reassures me," "It always amuses me," "I'm embarrassed," "This is annoying," and so forth. This was even the case in another study (involving different participants of fifty clergy and fifty laity) when Powell asked both clergy and laity to read Mark 7:1-8 (a controversy dialogue between Jesus, Pharisees, and scribes) and respond to the question, "What does this passage mean *to you?*" In this case the laity again overwhelmingly responded by indicating the story's personal and emotional impact. Yet "even when clergy were prompted to answer the question this way, very few told me how the story *affected* them."[18]

Powell's studies, by his own admission, engage only a small number of participants. However, the clear contrasts he finds between clergy and lay responses are yet one more indication of the scholarly propensity to marginalize the affective dimensions of biblical narrative.[19] If we treat the emotionally engaged responses of the lay readers as providing a "baseline" reading, how most "normal" readers would respond to these stories, then the question arises, "What would cause clergy to read these texts so differently, to distance themselves from the emotional elements of the text?" The answer: it must be how they have been trained. The education in biblical scholarship provided by most seminaries, for all of its substantial benefits, is teaching clergy to set aside the natural tendency—clearly reflected in laity—for affective engagement with the text.[20] Fortunately, some astute pastors are able to overcome this deficiency in their training and pursue the affective dimension of biblical texts in their preaching and teaching. But how clergy could be helped if biblical scholarship became a bit more engaged in the heart of biblical narrative! Perhaps even more lay folk would pick up and read a work of a biblical scholar or two. As scholars, we may like to think that the neglect of our work by laity is due to its erudition. But it may also be due to the fact that we don't have much to offer that really matters to them. We may do well in expounding the literary artistry of these texts and articulating their profound theological import, but when it comes to describing and reflecting upon their affective elements, which are especially relevant to the encouragement and transformation of believers, we are strangely silent.

Emotion and Narrative in Antiquity and the Bible

Some may fear that in calling for greater awareness of the affective dimension of biblical narrative, I am imposing a modern fascination with emotion upon ancient texts that were not designed to bear that burden. It is easy to see that modern novels and even nonfiction narratives commonly "pander to our emotions," but is this really a dimension of biblical narrative? Are we in danger of allowing pastoral concerns for the spiritual formation of laity to lead us to look for something in the text that might not be there?

Greco-Roman Rhetoric and Drama

The wedding of narrative, rhetoric, and emotion is not only a proclivity of modern literature and modern literary theory. As is commonly known, Greco-Roman handbooks on rhetoric, beginning with Aristotle and continuing on into the first century of the Common Era with Quintilian, commonly identified *pathos* (emotional appeal) alongside of *ethos* (appeal to the character of the speaker) and *logos* (use of reason) as the three main forms of rhetorical persuasion.[21] While the comments of ancient rhetoricians apply most directly to the composition of speeches, these and other principles of rhetorical persuasion influenced written discourse as well, such as treatises and letters. Accordingly, many have profitably applied Greco-Roman rhetorical theory to Paul's epistles, with some focusing on Paul's use of pathos and ethos.[22]

Yet the use of pathos was not confined by the ancients to speeches, persuasive treatises, or letters. Aristotle's *Poetics* examines how the dramatic elements of plot, character, and language in Greek tragedy combine to produce the emotional responses of pity and fear. This work provides us valuable testimony from a brilliant and influential thinker regarding how the relationship between emotions and the components of narrative form could be conceived in a period that may extend as far back to the composition of much Old Testament narrative and many centuries into the future.[23] Moreover, we also must be careful not to draw a hard and fast distinction between rhetorical oratory and narrative form, since the latter was commonly employed in rhetorical discourse. For instance, judicial, or forensic, rhetoric typically included a *narratio* near the beginning of the speech in which the circumstances of the case were relayed to the court. Among Roman rhetoricians, these came to be highly interpreted versions of the "facts" oriented toward the advantage of the speaker's client, with some rhetoricians freely employing emotional appeal to shape audience response. Speaking to this point, Quintilian complains that some among his colleagues neglect this use of affective appeal: "I am therefore all the more surprised at those who hold that there should be no appeal to the emotions in the narration. But why, when I am instructing the judge, should I refuse to move him as well?"[24]

Accordingly, Quintilian, following his mentor, Cicero, emphasized that "there is scope for an appeal to the emotions . . . in every part of a speech," and that "the prime essential for stirring the emotions of others is, in my opinion, first to feel those emotions oneself."[25] Quintilian goes on to describe the technique for eliciting such emotional arousal, one that essentially amounts to dramatic storytelling. Citing Quintilian, Mario M. DiCicco explains:

> In order to generate these emotions, he uniquely suggests the practice of vivid imagination resulting from "certain experiences which the Greeks call φαντασίαι, and the Romans *visions*, whereby things absent are presented to our imagination with such extreme vividness that they actually seem to be before our eyes." Through this power of the mind, the orator can visualize the scene and circumstances of a murder, for example, and experience "the blood, the deathly pallor, the groan of agony, the death rattle." In this way, the orator will stir up the appropriate emotions as if one were present at the actual occurrence.[26]

What these examples affirm is that within the socio-literary milieu of both the Old and New Testament texts, the use of emotional appeal for rhetorical effect was common in both nonnarrative and narrative forms of persuasion.

The Old and New Testaments

More importantly, the contention that storytelling was commonly viewed as including an affective dimension during the times when the Christian Scriptures were composed is verified by the Scriptures themselves. There are numerous occasions in the Old and New Testaments when the recitation of events—expressly or implied—was clearly meant to elicit an emotional response among characters within a narrative and/or recipients of the biblical text. The following is a list of representative examples to illustrate the point, to which many more could be added.

- Judah's plea to Joseph, which recounts the story of Jacob's frailty due to his grief for Joseph and Benjamin, is more than Joseph can bear, and he breaks down before his brothers (Gen 44:18—45:3).

- The entire book of Deuteronomy is framed as an exhortative sermon that calls not simply for the people's obedience but for the devotion of their whole selves to Yahweh. Accordingly, Moses often employs emotionally laden appeal in his recitation of God's saving acts on behalf of the people. For instance, in Deuteronomy 4, Moses alternates between recounting the dire consequences suffered by those have rejected Yahweh and wondrous blessings enjoyed by those who "held fast to the LORD" (v. 4). The unfaithful have been destroyed (v. 3), while the faithful now enjoy life (v. 4). More than that, "For what other great nation has a god so near to it as the LORD our God is whenever we call to him?" (v. 7). Moses reminds them that "the LORD has taken you and brought you out of the iron smelter, out of Egypt, to become a people of his very own possession, as you are now" (v. 20). And yet the people are extolled not to "forget the covenant that the LORD your God made with you. . . . For the LORD your God is a devouring fire, a jealous God'" (vv. 23- 24). Still, Yahweh is one in whom the people are called to "take heart," knowing that "the LORD is God in heaven above and on the earth beneath; there is no other" (v. 39).

- Joshua's speech in Joshua 24 similarly reviews the history of God's relationship with Israel, beginning with Abraham and continuing on through the conquest, and concludes with an exhortation for the people to devote themselves to Yahweh, closing with the stirring proclamation, "As for me and my household, we will serve the LORD!" (v. 15). The people respond with the insistent, "We will serve the LORD!" (vv. 16-18, 21).

- Nathan's parable about the poor man and his lamb after David has committed adultery with Bathsheba and murdered Uriah is skillfully composed to throttle David with emotion and to make plain to David the depravity of his own egregious actions (2 Sam 12:1-15).

- Ezra's impassioned prayer of confession on behalf of the Israelites who had taken foreign wives reviews the recent history of Israel, including Israel's unrelenting sin, God's judgment, and gracious restoration of the exiles. The prayer leads to remorse among the congregation of returned exiles: "While Ezra prayed and made confession, weeping and throwing himself down before the house of God, a very great assembly of men, women, and children gathered to him out of Israel; the people also wept bitterly" (Ezra 10:1).

- Perhaps most revealing on this point are the Psalms. Throughout the psalter, the psalmist responds in emotively charged tones to the remembrance of God's saving deeds for Israel and/or for himself (see, for example, Pss 78; 105; 106; 135:8-12; 136). As paradigms of faith and piety, the Psalms champion the affective dimension of devotion to and trust in God as elicited by the story of God's care for Israel.

- Few would question that the prophetic oracles are empowered by an engaging poignancy meant to move their hearers to shame and repentance for their past or hope for their future. Some such oracles that readily come to mind are Isaiah's song of the vineyard (Isa 5:1-7); Jeremiah's temple sermon (Jeremiah 7); Hosea's oracle of judgment in 6:1-6 and that of Micah in 3:1-12, followed by his oracle of restoration in 4:1-5; Ezekiel's disturbing and offensive (intentionally so, I think) account of Israel as God's faithless bride in Ezekiel 15; Isaiah's oracles of restoration in 11:1-9 and 40:1-5.

- The Gospels are filled with emotion and emotional characters. Emotional reactions (both positive and negative) to the announcement of Jesus' birth in Luke's and Matthew's infancy narratives, Jesus' miracles, Jesus' teaching about the kingdom of God, and the reality of Jesus' resurrection reveals that from the evangelists' perspective emotion is a fundamental dimension of human response to the in-breaking of God's reign in Jesus: "I tell you, if these [disciples] were silent, the stones would shout out" (Luke 19:40). Peter's Pentecost sermon in Acts 2:14-36 recounts in kerygmatic form the story of God's salvation in Jesus, in response to which those gathered are "cut to the heart" (κατενύγησαν τὴν καρδίαν; v. 37). Similarly, Peter's report to the church at Jerusalem regarding the conversion of Gentiles and their reception of the Holy Spirit is met first with stunned silence and then praise (11:18). Conversely, Stephen's testimony to Jesus and rebuke of the members of the Sanhedrin incites a murderous rage among his accusers (9:54-60).

What these representative examples reveal to us is that those composing the biblical writings and the audiences to whom they wrote understood affective response to the story of God's will and interaction with humanity as both common and appropriate. Now, I know this point teeters on the obvious, but it is worth noting since it joins with other evidence from antiquity making it apparent that biblical authors would have shaped their narrative also expecting and *intending* that they would have an emotional impact on their readers. This, too, underscores the deficiency in the way in which these same writings are now commonly engaged. If we don't, as scholars and pastors, begin asking how the recitation of these stories in Scriptures is meant to move those who hear them, then we will continue to bracket out of our analysis of these texts an important dimension of their function, and our exegesis will be the poorer for it. Since the dawn of historical-critical analysis following the Enlightenment, we have had the tendency to marginalize certain dimensions of biblical narrative in the name of "scientific" and "objective" analysis. We pushed to the periphery of our study, or neglected altogether, the function of biblical narratives as literary works and their confessional character as sources of proclamation for believing communities. Throughout the latter half of the previous century, our guild has managed to take deliberate steps in recognizing and reclaiming these fundamental dimensions of biblical narrative. Now we need to go one step further. We need to explore how biblical narrative is intended to function as skillfully composed, confessional literature that is affectively engaging.

Plan of the Work to Follow

The discussion presented here will be guided by the following premise, which was stated in a similar form above: *affective appeal in varying forms is the means by which narratives, including biblical narratives, compel us to enter their storied world and entertain the version of reality they present.* As a means of both testing and further illustrating the usefulness of this premise in guiding our engagement of biblical narrative, we will explore the use of affect in a number of Old and New Testament narrative texts. This will include a detailed investigation of how Luke employs emotional appeal in his infancy narrative to serve his rhetorical ends. Before we get to that analysis, however, we would do well to pursue a preliminary task. Emotion is a somewhat slippery and difficult phenomenon to define, and has itself become a topic of focused debate within various fields. Thus, the first chapter reviews the broad contours of this discussion and then presents my own understanding of emotion that will be operative in the chapters to follow. Then we move to the main concern of the work, as chapter 2 identifies particular narrative devices that authors of biblical narrative use to engage their readers' emotions, drawing from both the Old and New Testaments (chapter 2) to illustrate these techniques. Building on these insights, chapters 3 and 4 apply an "affective-rhetorical" analysis to Luke's infancy narrative, demonstrating how a full-fledged application of the approach advocated here might work. The conclusion reviews the findings of this study, reflecting on the exegetical advantages provided by an approach sensitive to the affective dimensions of biblical narrative, and offers some suggestions on the how our attention to the affective dimension of biblical narrative can serve as an important resource for Christian communities.

Part One

Approaching
the Heart of the Bible

Chapter 1
On the Emotions

Managing our emotions is, for most of us, a tricky affair. The epistle of James talks about the difficulty of taming the tongue (James 3:1-12). The same could be said of the emotions, which are certainly the impetus behind the tongue's irascible behavior. Perhaps the more disciplined among us manage to keep their emotions in check, but only *most* of the time. Even the most stoic eventually fail in their vigilance. Suddenly, unexpectedly, an emotion is there, demanding our attention, churning our insides, urging expression and action. Emotions quickly turn reasoned discussions into bitter, heart-frazzled arguments, or they can move us to spontaneous rejoicing in a seemingly ordinary moment, such as a child's laugh, a sunset, or a snow-blanketed dawn. Nearly all that we find meaningful and blessed in life is enriched by our emotions. Nearly all that we disdain or find threatening is darkened all the more so by their affective accompaniment. My, how they can be troubling—the sparks that light and winds that fan the ember—as James warns us. But how wonderful they can be! And for as much trouble as these powerful vagaries of the heart cause, I doubt that any of us would find life much worth living without them.

What Are the Emotions, Exactly?
The Broad Contours of the Debate

As difficult as it is for us to control the emotions, it has been equally difficult for us to figure out what, exactly, they are, and their place in the workings of the mind. Post-Enlightenment discussions of emotion commonly regarded anything having to do with affective response (moods, feelings, emotions) as nonrational, if not irrational, and primarily physiological reactions to stimuli. As a result, emotions were typically denigrated as noncognitive, low-level, even animalistic reflexes and held in sharp contrast to the higher activity of human reason. As Martha Nussbaum summarizes it, this view—which is still popular in some forms today—holds that "emotions are blind animal reactions, like or identical with bodily feelings, that are in their nature unmixed with thought, undiscriminating, and impervious to reasoning."[1]

One major contributor to the study of the human mind often cited as promoting this view is William James. Writing about a century ago, James claimed, "If we fancy some strong emotion and then try to abstract from our consciousness of it all the feelings of its bodily symptoms, we find that we have nothing left behind, no 'mind stuff' out of which the emotion can be constituted, and that a cold and neutral state of intellectual perception is all that remains."[2] "In short," states Antonio R. Demasio, "James postulated a basic mechanism in which particular stimuli in the environment excite, by means of an innately set and inflexible mechanism, a specific pattern of body reaction."[3] In other words, the mind—the "thinking" mind at least—has little to do with affective response. Emotions were simply physiological reflexes in response to environmental stimuli.[4] Such an understanding of emotion found a welcome home in the behaviorism of B. F. Skinner, which similarly viewed the psyche of animals and humans alike as functioning according to a stimulus-response mechanism. Dominating the psychological landscape of much of the twentieth century, behaviorists believed that psychology should be only concerned with external behavior as a reaction to environmental triggers and should not try to analyze the workings of the mind that underlay this behavior.

Behaviorism's fall from prominence in the latter third of the twentieth century resulted in a renewed interest in the relationship between emotion and cognition. This has led to an explosion of study and debate on emotion in recent decades, involving fields as diverse as cognitive psychology, developmental psychology, social science, neuroscience, and philosophy. Of key interest to participants in the debate are the processes initiating and shaping emotional response. Other observers have offered fine overviews of debate, reviewing in detail the work of its major contributors, and I do not intend a survey of similar precision here.[5] Instead, I will summarize the broad contours of the discussion, noting some of its key voices, and then present my own working understanding of emotion that informs the interpretive work on biblical narrative to follow.

Emotions as Intentional and Conscious Value Judgments

The idea that emotion involves cognition, and not simply a physiological response to certain stimuli, is a common element in most contemporary studies of emotion. There is widespread disagreement, however, on the nature of that cognition and therefore the actual character of emotion. One major branch of thought, beginning as a reaction to behaviorism, holds that emotions are states arising from cognitive activity that often involve high-level reasoning about the value of particular events or objects in relationship to one's self and worldview. In 1976, philosopher Richard C. Solomon announced that modernity's "myth of the emotions" is failing, and argued that emotions are no longer considered to be "the dumb forces beyond our control but judgments we make."[6] Writing later in 1986, he summarized his own theory and three books on emotions, stating, "Emotions are essentially a species of *judgment*. They are learned and intelligent, even if they are not always accurate."[7] Solomon's early work was followed by that of another philosopher, William Lyons, who promoted a "cognitive-evaluative" theory of emotion and similarly defined emotion as "a physiologically abnormal state caused by the subject of that state's evaluation of his or her situation."[8] Like Solomon (among others), Lyons stressed that emotions are evaluative judgments "of some object, event or situation in the world about me in relation to me, or according to my norms."[9]

Paralleling and often informing these philosophical discussions was the study of emotion by cognitive psychology. This field also developed in reaction to behaviorism, which, as stated above, viewed the psyche as functioning according to a stimulus–response mechanism and invested little effort in exploring cognitive activity. In contrast, cognitive psychology argues that cognitive processes (at times complex, intentional, and rational) kick in following the stimulus and direct the response. Shortly after it established itself in the 1970s, cognitive psychology was criticized for its "cold" approach to cognition (as computation) and seemed ill equipped to account for the "hotter" tendencies of emotion. Yet correctives were forthcoming, and numerous cognitivist studies on emotion have been produced.[10] Richard Lazarus provided one of the earliest treatments, claiming as did the philosophers reviewed above that emotions are integrally connected to conscious appraisals of the "person-environment relationship."[11] Following Lazarus's study, Andrew Ortony, Gerald L. Clore, and Allan Collins presented their seminal work on emotion, the *Cognitive Structure of Emotions*.[12] The authors state as their working hypothesis that "emotions arise as a result of the way in which the situations that initiate them are construed by the experiencer," and their main goal is "to present an approach to the study of emotion that explains how people's perceptions of the world—their construals—cause them to experience emotions." Accordingly, they define emotions as "valenced reactions to events, agents or objects, with their particular nature being determined by the way in which the eliciting situation is construed."[13] In short, intentional appraisal is an integral dimension of emotion.

Integrating numerous fields of study in her philosophical assessment of emotions and their role in ethical theory, Martha Nussbaum similarly claims that emotions are essentially "judgments of value."[14] More specifically, they are comprised of four basic elements: (1) emotions are about something; they have an object toward which one's thoughts are directed; (2) the object is an *intentional* object, that is, it is perceived through the lens of "one's own window," or through the lens of one's own vested interest in the object; (3) emotions embody beliefs—often very complex—about the object and how they impact one's vested interests; and (4) they are concerned with *value*, they see their object as invested with value or importance. In regard to this fourth element, Nussbaum goes on to claim that the value assigned to an object as reflected and amplified in an emotion is not simply self-centered in character, but is rather "eudaimonistic" ("goodness seeking").[15] Drawing on ancient Greek ethical theory, she explains that *eudaimonia* need not refer simply to the pursuit of one's own happiness or pleasure as the supreme good, as the concept is often understood today under the influence of utilitarianism. Rather, she takes *eudaimonia* as "inclusive of all to which the agent ascribes intrinsic value," including his or her place and role relative to others and the greater good.[16]

The field of social science has also weighed in on the discussion of emotions, investigating the different ways emotions are expressed in various cultures. Not surprisingly, social scientists have promoted the claim that emotions are culturally conditioned, defined as they are by one's social setting.[17] Summarizing this view, John Corrigan states, "the emotional lives of people—thought by some to be part of an inaccessible interior of self—are in fact socially dictated performances, social scripts as it were, grounded in shared understandings about the meanings of social events and actions. . . . As notions of self vary from one culture to another, so too does the practice of emotional life."[18] That emotions may be at least in part socially determined underscores the role of intentional cognition in shaping and expressing emotion. As Nussbaum explains, "If we hold that beliefs about what is important and valuable play a central role in emotions, we can readily see how these beliefs can be powerfully shaped by social norms as well as by an individual history; and we can see how changing social norms can change emotional life."[19]

Emotions as Primarily Unconscious Processes

As we have seen, one major stream of thought argues that emotions consist of or result from conscious appraisals of a situation, object, or event in relationship to one's values and interests. Many others, however, have argued that emotions consist of or arise from processes taking place in the realm of the subconscious.[20] Practitioners from the fields of neuroscience and developmental psychology in particular have often forwarded this view.

Neuroscientist Joseph LeDoux, for example, argues that the subjective states of awareness essential to emotional response are unconscious in character, only entering into the consciousness *after* the emotion has been fully engaged and begins to be processed by the conscious mind.[21] Adopting an evolutionary perspective on affective function, he treats emotions as "special adaptive behaviors that are crucial to survival."[22] Accordingly, he presents as his working hypothesis the theory that "different classes of emotional behavior represent different kinds of functions that take care of different kinds of problems for the animal and have different brain systems devoted to them." Then, focusing on fear to illustrate his theory, he cites numerous findings demonstrating that once animals are conditioned by a frightening stimulus, that fear will likely reemerge, and *uncontrollably so*, when anything resembling the stimulus presents itself either consciously or *subconsciously*. His work and the evidence he marshals in support of it offer a clear challenge to the understanding of emotion as resulting from conscious, intentional, value-laden judgments. On this point, LeDoux concludes:

> If emotions are triggered by stimuli that are processed unconsciously, you will not be able to later reflect back on these experiences and explain why they occurred with any degree of accuracy. Contrary to the primary supposition of cognitive appraisal theories, the core of an emotion is not an introspectively accessible conscious representation. Feelings do involve conscious content, but we don't necessarily have conscious access to the processes that produce the content. And even when we do have introspective access, the conscious content is not likely to be what triggered the emotional responses in the first place. The emotional responses and the conscious content are both products of specialized emotion systems that operate unconsciously.[23]

Developmental psychologists have similarly sought to demonstrate that "there are certain emotional states that are inbuilt in humans which do not appear to require cognition."[24] Robert Zajonc, often cited as a leading figure in this pursuit, has conducted several of his own experiments, and pointed to those conducted by others, showing that affective response can occur without any prior cognitive appraisal.[25] These experiments in varying forms explored the subconscious processing of human test subjects and repeatedly demonstrated subjects' preferences for objects that had been subconsciously associated with positive stimuli. In other words, the affective response in the subjects took place without any conscious, value-laden assessment.

Emotions Involve Both Unconscious and Conscious Appraisal

Up to this point, I have simplified the debate to some degree by presenting these two major streams of thought as opposing perspectives. The relationship between these two views is more nuanced than this, however, since many participants in the discussion do not hold to absolute versions of their respective positions. Rather, while still arguing for the primacy of their own view, many allow in varying forms that, depending on the situation, emotions can involve *either* unconscious or conscious appraisal, or *both* unconscious and conscious appraisal. This mediating tendency was anticipated by Nathaniel Brandon in the late 1960s, who argued that

> the sequence of psychological events is: from perception to evaluation to emotional response. On the level of immediate awareness, however, the sequence is: from perception to emotion. A person may or may not be consciously aware of the intervening value judgment. A separate act of focused awareness may be required to grasp it, because of the extreme rapidity of the sequence. . . . That a person may fail to identify either the judgment or the factors involved in it, that he may be conscious only of the perception and of his emotional response, is the fact which makes possible men's confusion about the nature and source of emotions.[26]

Similarly, neuroscientist Antonio Damasio offers assessments of emotion processing that identify conscious appraisal as a precursor for at least some affective responses, while still focusing his attention on unconscious processes. In previewing his work to follow, Damasio states:

> In this perspective, feelings are the sensors for the match or lack thereof between nature and circumstance. And by nature I mean both the nature we inherited as a pack of genetically engineered adaptations, *and the nature we have acquired in individual development, through interactions with our social environment, mindfully and willfully as well as not.*[27]

Damasio's study focuses on two cases of brain-damaged individuals who, as a result of their injury, developed personalities in stark contrast to their respective emotional and behavioral tendencies before being injured. Both men retained the ability to perform all sorts of higher cognitive functions; standard IQ tests revealed a superior intellect for one of them. However, both men demonstrated an *acute affective detachment* from real-life situations coupled with an inability to relate events going on around them to their own self-interest.

On the Emotions

Based on Damasio's research and discussion, Nussbaum concludes, "Damasio's research confirms the work of Lazarus, Ortony, and Oatley: emotions provide the animal (in this case human) with a sense of how the world relates to its own set of goals and projects."[28] Damasio's own statements about the import of his work—offered in response to James's physiological theory of emotion cited above—concur with Nussbaum's assessment and fill out his understanding of the relationship between conscious and unconscious emotional processes:

> In many circumstances of our life as social beings, however, we know that our emotions are triggered only after an evaluative, voluntary, nonautomatic mental process. Because of the nature of our experience, a broad range of stimuli and situations has become associated with that stimuli which are innately set to cause emotions. The reaction to that broad range of stimuli and situations can be filtered by an interposed mindful evaluation. And because of the thoughtful, evaluative filtering process, there is room for variation in the extent and intensity of preset emotional patterns.[29]

Nussbaum has sought to meet the challenge that the reality of unconsciously triggered emotions poses to her own view by pointing out that many of our emotional responses are part of a longer emotional history, including emotional triggers of which we are not consciously aware. However, she argues that such unconscious appraisals are also intentional in nature: even emotional triggers that develop in infancy are oriented toward a particular object and desire a particular end.[30] In arguing thus, however, Nussbaum highly nuances the meaning of "intentional appraisal," qualifying and thus limiting the force that it otherwise possesses throughout her study. Fittingly, she goes on to offer this eloquent concession:

> The roots of anger, hatred, and disgust lie very deep in the structure of human life, in our ambivalent relation to our lack of control over objects and the helplessness of our own bodies. It would be naïve to expect that projections of these negative emotions onto other people will not take place—although we may certainly hope to moderate their number and intensity.
> My view, then, urges us to reject as both too simple and too cruel any picture of character that tells us to bring every emotion into line with reason's dictates, or the dictates of a person's ideal, whatever that is. Given human ambivalence and neediness, and the emotions that have grown out of that, this is simply not a sensible goal to prescribe; and prescribing an unachievable norm of perfection is the very thing that can wreak emotional havoc. . . . If Aristotle's view entails that the good person can and should

21

demand emotional perfection of herself, so that she always gets angry at the right person, in the right way, at the right time, and so forth, then Aristotle's view is tyrannical and exacts of us more than humanity can deliver.[31]

After her own detailed review of the debate over emotions, Jenefer Robinson follows LeDoux in arguing that "at the core of emotion will always be physiological responses caused by automatic [unconscious] affective appraisal and followed by cognitive monitoring." Like Damasio, however, she allows that "more complex cases of emotion in human beings might involve affective responses not to a perception but to a thought or belief, and the cognitive monitoring may be correspondingly sophisticated."[32] Similarly, in his more recent work, Lazarus concludes that "there are two different modes of appraisals: one *conscious, deliberate and under volitional control*, and the other *automatic, unconscious, and uncontrollable*."[33]

Some Proposals

So then, what are the emotions? And, in light of the interest of this study, what role do they play in shaping and giving expression to one's worldview, and how might they be stimulated by authors to promote their narrative construals of reality? I consider myself nothing more than a novice to the study of emotions, an outsider looking in at the discussion. However, I offer the following proposals so that you will know the understanding of emotion that informs my discussion to follow, and so that you can also see how my thoughts on the matter are informed by current study on the topic by those who are the experts in the field. Several of the proposals below address matters raised in the preceding review; the remaining address still other issues common to the ongoing discussion of emotion.

1. *Emotions are complex phenomena of variable origins.*
After engaging numerous discussions in the field, it seems apparent to me that any theory that confines emotion to a single process will neglect to account for important features of affective response. The evidence that exists showing that emotions arise from unconscious triggers stimulating physiological response, as well as the commonsense view arising from the evidence of everyday experience that at other times emotions result from our conscious, reasoned engagement with the world, commend those theories noted above that take both types of evidence to heart. It also seems likely to me that emotions may not always be one or the other, but a combination of unconscious trigger and

reasoned appraisal leading to the redirection and nuance of an emotion. Still, the ongoing debate over emotion shows, as many of its participants admit, that we have a long way to go toward understanding these upheavals of the heart.

2. Many emotional responses are instigated and/or shaped by our conscious appraisal of events, objects, or persons and their relationship to what we value.
To build on my immediately preceding comments, the evidence from everyday experience in support of this claim is overwhelming. Let's say, for instance, that I am in the kitchen cleaning up after breakfast, and I hear my five-year-old daughter, Clare, scream from out in the yard. Now, my daughter frequently screams and nearly always for reasons that I do not deem sufficient to merit such an outburst, and so my first reaction is to stomp to the patio door in frustration and upbraid her for her disruptive behavior. Yet as I glare out the door, this scene presents itself: my nine-year-old son, Joshua, is chasing the rooster around the chicken yard with a shovel! My emotion changes from the irritation directed at my daughter to astonishment at my son's behavior. Then my powers of reasoning engage and my appraisal is reformulated: Clare screamed because Joshua is trying to kill the rooster. My astonishment now mixes with anger at my son's seemingly ruthless actions. Fumbling with the door, I rush outside toward the chicken yard and yell, "Joshua! What on earth are you doing?" Joshua halts his pursuit. Turning red-faced and panting for breath, he points to his sister. I now notice that Clare has scratches on her legs and arms, and tears streaming down her face. With a rare stroke of perspicuity, I finally manage to assess the situation correctly: the rooster attacked Clare, and Joshua, in an admirable display of courage and brotherly concern, fended off the vicious fowl. My emotional roller coaster makes yet another sharp bend and settles on concern for my daughter and admiration (not anger) for my son and righteous indignation at (not concern for) the rooster. After tending to Clare's wounds, still other thought-induced emotions emerge: remorse over the need to protect my children from future attacks by this rooster, and the anticipation of homemade chicken soup for supper.

While there may be some unconscious triggers contributing to my affective responses to the situation (perhaps in response to Clare's scream or the shocking image of Joshua wielding a shovel), they were not—in this instance at least—the most determinative factors influencing my emotions. It was my conscious appraisals of the situation, the value I placed on the animals in our care and higher value I placed on the well-being of our children, that directly led to the emotions I experienced. Once the appraisal was altered, the emotions transformed accordingly.

3. *Accordingly, our emotions are a gauge of what matters most to us—they are a window into our worldviews.*

Jesus knew this: "Where your treasure is, there your heart will be also" (Matt 6:21). Jesus may be talking about wealth here in Matthew 6, but the context makes it clear that he is also referring more broadly to anything we might value more than our trust in God: "But strive first for the rule of God in your lives and his righteousness and all these things will be given to you as well" (v. 33; my translation). This teaching was intended to help his disciples take stock of what it is that matters most to them, what it is that they have their hearts set on. I believe Jesus (as well as Nussbaum, Solomon, Ortony et al., and others) has it right. When we take a look at what it is that really moves us, what it is that consistently has us fuming or tied up in knots or erupting in praise, then we will begin to get a sense of what we really value and what we really believe about the world. Our emotions are often shaped by and give expression to our worldviews, our understanding of what matters most. Astute authors, of course, can use this to their advantage. They often play off of the perceived commitments and values of their readers to create an emotional response to certain characters or events, and thereby draw their audience more deeply into the story they tell. Authors can also use characters readers will admire, identify, or sympathize with to reshape or even challenge other values or per-spectives held by those same readers.

4. *Our emotions are, to some extent, culturally conditioned.*

This, as Nussbaum observes above, follows from the previous two points. Our culture and social location can play a significant role in shaping our view of the world and what it is that we value. Persons and groups can be counter-cultural, and emotions often play a key role in motivating and sustaining these movements. Still, it is helpful to appreciate that many of our values as well as many of the ways we display our emotions are to some extent scripted by our societies, shaped as they are by certain physical conditions, cosmological or religious beliefs, practices, language, economy, and politics. This is especially important to keep in mind when engaging texts arising from cultures that are in many ways very different from our own. Our knowledge of that culture's values, norms, and expectations will greatly enhance our ability to understand how a text intends to engage its readers affectively.

5. *Emotions are universal (for the most part).*

Within the wider discussion of emotion, the extent to which certain emotions are consistently experienced in response to similar situations across cultures is a hotly debated issue.[34] Many hold fast to opposite ends of the "universal vs.

24

culturally determined" spectrum, though some participants in the debate promote a moderate view that allows for both universal and socially constructed
dimensions of emotion. But what does it mean to claim the emotions are universal? Few would disagree with the judgment of Ortony and his colleagues
that "emotion is one of the most central and pervasive aspects of human experience."[35] Our lived experience and powers of observation confirm at least
this. But are there certain emotions that are universal, and are there at least
some types of situations that will evoke the same emotions in persons from
widely different times and places? One of the problems in addressing this
question is that the term *universal* implies a very high degree of consistency in
the manifestation of a phenomenon. Yet in any given circumstance, and with
any given person, the diversity of variables involved makes it precarious to say,
"In such and such a situation this person will *certainly* respond with emotion *x*."
It is also unwise to say, "If this person is behaving in this way, he *must* be experiencing emotion *x*," since different emotions can cause similar physiological
and behavioral reactions.[36] At the same time, there is good evidence to suggest
that *in general* people across time and place are able to recognize and effectively
express a rather large array of *very similar* emotional experiences, and that *in
general* many people across time and place will infer from certain situations
and behaviors that a particular range of emotional response is *likely*. Perhaps
the most important and relevant evidence we have to support this contention
is literature:

> It is apparent that writers can reliably produce in readers an awareness of
> a character's affective states by characterizing a situation whose construal
> is assumed to give rise to them. This suggests that writers use an implicit
> theory that individual emotions can be specified in terms of our personal or
> interpersonal situational descriptions that are sufficient to produce them.
> Thus, writers do not always have to state what emotions a character is expe-
> riencing because if the described situation contains the *eliciting conditions* for
> a particular emotion, the experience of that emotion can be inferred. The
> fact that millions of readers, often over decades and even centuries, all infer
> similar emotions from described situations suggests that the implicit theory
> cannot be too far wrong.[37]

What Ortony's compelling example suggests, along with our personal experience, is that most of us possess an emotional repertoire (for reasons both bio-
logical and social, it seems to me) that is similar enough to that possessed by
others across time, place, and culture that we can recognize in one another and
talk about with one another the experience of many different emotions. These

recognitions are certainly not foolproof, but they are likely "on the right track" most of the time.[38] The witness of literature to the conventional character of emotion also commends our confidence as students of biblical narrative that we can identify patterns in the text that are intended by its authors to lead to an emotional response on the part of its readers. This must be done with care, considering also the cultural context in which these narratives were constructed and their relationship to their surrounding literary context. But we share enough with the writers of these narratives—biologically, psychologically, spiritually, and affectively—that we can make educated guesses on how they intended their storytelling to impact their audience not only cognitively but also emotionally.

6. *Our emotions can be evaluated and altered, just as our beliefs about the world can be evaluated and altered.*

Without a doubt, it is normal for us to experience all sorts of emotions, some of which (as we saw above) may be beyond our ability to prevent. But if we agree with the claim that many of our emotions are shaped by and give expression to our worldviews, then it is also beneficial for us to ask whether the emotions we display, and especially those we encourage in ourselves and others, are in keeping with what we hold to be true. As people of faith, we do well to consider that our emotions are a measure of what we really believe, what really moves us. Just as our beliefs can be cultivated and nurtured so that they more clearly reflect what God is revealing to us, so, too, can our proclivities of the heart. We will return to this point in the concluding chapter as we consider how attentiveness to the affective dimension of biblical narrative may challenge believers to assess and seek to reframe their own affective responses to the biblical story.

7. *Our emotions are integrally connected to and excited by our imagination.*

The relationship between emotion and the imagination is a centerpiece of the lively discussion among philosophers, literary critics, and psychologists concerning our affective responses to fiction.[39] In brief, the debated issue is why and how we become emotionally involved in stories we know not to be true. Why do I care whether Frodo makes it to Mount Doom and destroys the ring, saving Middle Earth from the evil tyranny of Sauron? It's not a *real* story. Why should it matter to me that Romeo and Juliet never have the chance to live happily ever after? It's just a play (well, a very good play). We do care and it does matter to us because our emotions are excited by our imagination. As we noted in the previous chapter, good stories, even some bad ones, are able to gather us into their narrative world and entice us to dwell there. We become the characters in the story or imagine ourselves their companions and take part in the action and circumstances of the tale. Their story becomes our story, at least for a time.

Our imaginations are not only at work when reading (or viewing) fictional tales, however. As we also discussed in the previous chapter, psychologists and others are recognizing with increasing frequency that we conceive of our lives as "storied." More to the point, we tend to see ourselves as characters in an unfolding life, moving toward what we hope to accomplish or become. Our imagination is *always* actively at work in shaping our understanding of ourselves in relationship to others, the world, what we value and believe to be true. This, it seems to me, explains why we find it so easy to get caught up in and affectively engaged by fictional tales. For when we encounter these stories, we practice very similar processes of thought as when responding to the "nonfiction" world. As Solomon helpfully notes:

> It is typically argued that an emotion [induced by a fictional work] is vicarious and therefore not a real emotion because its object—what it is about—is not real. Now in this sense very few emotions are "real," since almost all emotions—love, hate, anger, or simple compassion—involve a certain subjective reshaping of their objects. . . . To say that an object of an emotion is fictional (and known to be so) is therefore not necessarily to say that the emotion is not real. To insist on this absurdity would be either to limit the range of "real" emotions to a pathetic and extremely timid group of realistic attitudes, or to deny the reality of emotions altogether.[40]

Thus, the line between "How does this (real) event affect me?" and "How would this (fictional) event affect me if I were there or if I were so and so?" is an easy one for us to cross. For all of our construals of the world—fiction and nonfiction alike—involve our use of emotively charged imagination to fit persons, objects, events, and situations into their storied roles. This realization helps us to appreciate all the more our vulnerability to narrative worlds and what makes all good stories so powerful and rhetorically effective (as advertisers and charitable organizations well know!).[41] Stimulating our imaginations and playing on our emotions, well-crafted stories subtly and even subversively gather us into their worlds, enticing us to see reality through the eyes of their authors and to adopt the values they promote or disdain those they disparage.

Implications: Reading with Mind *and* Heart

The understanding of emotion I have sketched here, including the relationship between emotion, cognition, worldview, imagination, and narrative, anticipates our transition to the main concern of this book: how we might read biblical narrative paying greater attention to how its authors employ affect to gather us up into their narratives and cultivate within us their understanding of the world. Biblical commentators, especially in recent decades with the emergence of narrative critical methods and a resurgence in theological interpretation, often do very well in describing how the plotting and various literary devices of a text "tell the story," and thereby provide valuable insights into the theology proclaimed by the text. Yet in their focus on the "message" of the text—what the story says about God, or Jesus, or the reign of God—commentators often leave its affective dimensions unearthed and fail to consider how pathos may be employed by the biblical author in the shaping of the narrative.

Perhaps biblical scholars presume that reflection on the emotional import of biblical texts is the domain of pastors: "Leave the serious scholarship to the experts, let the preachers exploit whatever emotional appeal they can imaginatively wring from biblical texts for their congregations." Indeed, preachers may have no other choice but to shoulder the load if the "experts" continue to neglect pathos as an important dimension of biblical study. Building on my comments in the introduction, I would claim that there are at least three reasons why scholars should enter the emotional fray of biblical narrative. First, investigating the pathos of a biblical text may help us better understand its literary and rhetorical function within the wider narrative. As I will seek to show in the chapters to follow, pathos is a dimension of biblical narrative that can have significant exegetical import. Second, many pastors are seminary trained, and are thus immersed in and tend to adopt the reading strategies of current biblical scholarship. They also continue to use resources produced by biblical scholars. If these scholars are not engaging the affective dimensions of the text, then (as we saw with Mark Powell's findings) many pastors likely won't as well. Finally, by virtue of their training in literary/narrative criticism and rhetorical theory, scholars are especially well positioned to discern how pathos may be employed by biblical writers and to teach others how the biblical author's use of pathos is reflected in the shaping of the text.

How scholars (and pastors) may go about such analysis is the task to which we now turn.

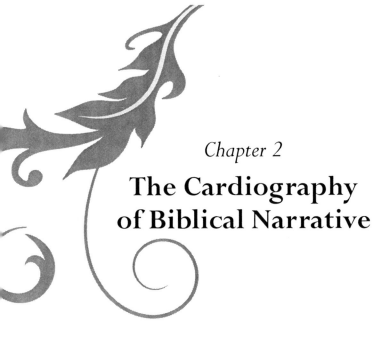

Chapter 2

The Cardiography of Biblical Narrative

Literature is in league with the emotions. Readers of novels, spectators of dramas, find themselves led by these works to fear, to grief, to pity, to anger, to joy and delight, even to passionate love. Emotions are not just likely responses to the content of many literary works; they are built into their very structure, as ways in which literary forms solicit attention.

—Martha C. Nussbaum[1]

Martha Nussbaum, among other philosophers and literary critics, champions the view that the emotional engagement of readers is a fundamental aim of writers, both ancient and modern, that it is, one might say, woven into the very fabric of storytelling itself. These thinkers are not alone in their assessment. One of the earliest surviving discussions of "poetics," or literary art, dates back almost two and one-half millennia to Aristotle. Aristotle claimed that the goal of tragedy—not simply a consequence or ancillary objective, but its goal—is to evoke the emotions of pity and fear in its audience, and in doing so to lead the audience to a more complete understanding of those emotions and the nature of life in general. He defines tragedy as follows:

> Tragedy is an imitation of an action that is admirable, complete and possesses magnitude; in language made pleasurable, each of its species separated in different parts; performed by actors, not through narration; effecting through pity and fear the purification [*katharsis*] of such emotions.[2]

How was the evocation of pity and fear to be accomplished? All of the six component parts of tragedy Aristotle identifies were oriented toward this goal, but chief among them was plot, the sequencing of a connected series of

events that imitates action and life: "So the events, i.e. the plot, are what tragedy is there for, and that is the most important thing of all" (4.3). The feature
of tragedy Aristotle regards as second in importance to plot, and to which it is
integrally connected, is character, what we commonly call "characterization."
As Aristotle states: "So plot is the source and (as it were) the soul of tragedy;
character is second. . . . Tragedy is an imitation of an action, and on account
above all of the action it is an imitation of agents" (4.4).[3] Scholars debate the
fine points of how Aristotle defines the role of characters (see 8.1), but Malcom Heath provides a summary representative of many: "Tragic characters
should be virtuous, but not outstandingly so. They are like us, in that they fall
short of the moral perfection whose downfall we would find outrageous; but
they still tend to the better rather than the worse."[4] In brief, these characters
were to be ones to whom we could relate. It was their likeness to the members
of the audience that enabled the tragic consequences of their lives to be felt
and in some measure experienced by those viewing the drama.

Scholars examining the emotive force of literature, and narrative literature
in particular, continue to focus on plot and characterization as that which drives
the affective dimension of narrative. Nussbaum argues that emotional responses
typically evoked by tragedy (and other forms of narrative) "are built into the
work itself, into its literary structures. Thus it involves no neglect of the literary form to conclude that a work is rich in emotive content; indeed one cannot
well describe the form or structure of a tragic work without mentioning this."[5]
According to Nussbaum, it is the plot structuring the work that provides the "suf-
ficiently attuned" reader with the opportunity to enter into the story and experience a range of emotions gravitating around the pitiable and fearful elements
of the tragedy unfolding in the narrative. Along with the sequencing of events,
characterization is commonly recognized as playing an equally critical role in the
emotional engagement of readers. In fact, the study of reader identity, sympathy,
and empathy for characters has become a primary means by which literary critics
and psychologists explore the emotional impact of literature, and the relationship
between affective response and reader comprehension and interpretation.[6]

The few studies that have investigated the affective dimension of biblical
narrative have also focused on the role of plot and character portrayal in evok-
ing emotional response. For example, Ronald J. Allen argues that the story
form is "peculiarly well adapted" for embodying feeling, and points to both
plot and characterization as essential to the ability of narrative to draw readers
into the narrative and evoke pathos:

> Story gives complex feelings a concrete form: we get a picture of the way
> someone feels. The story helps us envision reality as another person sees it.

> By joining the flow of the narrative, we can experience new ideas and feel-
> ings as if we were "there." . . . Stories, like art, have the capacity to open
> unfelt reaches of human experience to us. As we hear them, the experience
> they describe is, in some way, kindled in us.[7]

Likewise, Robert Baker seeks to show "how John has structured the Gospel in
order to inculcate the Christian affections of love and fear [awe] in the actual
reader."[8] He also describes how the evangelist's portrayal of Jesus in response
to the events in the narrative evokes these emotions. Cornelia Cross Crocker
focuses on Mark's depiction of character emotion in response to the plotted
events of the narrative. She proposes that "as readers are drawn into some of
the highly emotional scenes in Mark's narrative, they may similarly be moved to
answerability and to acts of faith in their own lives, and as a result, they may also
be able to perceive the apparent incongruities of Mark's gospel in a new light."[9]

The recognition that plot and characterization are essential ways narratives convey pathos is important for two reasons. First, by pointing out and
even demonstrating the emotional freight of plotting and characterization,
psychologists and literary critics have shown that the affective dimension of
narrative is integral to the function of narrative itself. This is why Nussbaum
states above that one cannot explain the form or structure of a literary work
without also commenting on its emotive content. Second, this observation is
significant in that it leads us to look for pathos in these essential elements of
the text. It gives us a place to begin and an idea of what to look for.

At the same time, the exploration of emotive arousal in these broad components of narrative often results in a type of analysis that seems to me rather
limited in terms of its "exegetical toolbox." Among both secular literary critics
and the few interpreters that examine the affective dimension of biblical narratives, the emotional impact of plotting and characterization is often described
without any further specification of what *particular* techniques of plotting or
characterization may be especially well suited to stimulating reader emotion.
The method of analysis is most often one of simply summarizing how develop-
ments in the narrative or certain features of a character have likely moved the
reader to some sort of emotional response.[10] For instance, here is a portion of
Baker's short summary of John's plot and its affective impact on the reader:

> As the readers create the narrative world, following the actions and words
> of Jesus through the story, they arrive at his death with an understanding
> that Jesus is on the cross yielding his life because they, the readers, are the
> objects of Jesus' love. Jesus' predictions and teachings are the main sources
> for forming such an understanding. In 6.50-51, Jesus makes an allusion to

his death as the offering of his flesh and that those who partake of his flesh will never die. In 10.11-18 Jesus teaches that he lays down his life because he knows and cares for his sheep. It becomes increasingly clear to the reader that whatever Jesus does, it is on his or her behalf. . . .

As Jesus suffers the humiliation of arrest, trial, crucifixion and death, the reader understands the cross as the ultimate expression of love for him or her. As the reader stands there with the others and together they see him offer up his life, they love and worship him. They see Jesus as worthy of all their life and all their love.[11]

In a similar vein, Walter Reinsdorf explains how the evangelists guide readers into identifying emotionally with Jesus by portraying Jesus as one who deemphasizes his divinity and embraces suffering:

To be seen as human, Jesus himself de-emphasizes his divinity by performing miracles reluctantly, by requesting silence from the healed, by avoiding Jerusalem as long as possible, by referring to himself in the third person, using the title "Son of Man", not "Son of God." . . . On the cross he seemingly despairs, as described by both Matthew and Mark. At Gethsemane, he prays for the cup to pass. Finally, at the climax, his crucifixion, he is mocked as King of the Jews whose God will not save him. Here on the cross he fully establishes his identity with us.[12]

My point here is not that there is anything deficient in this type of summary analysis in and of itself. Often it serves well in articulating how the plotting of a biblical narrative in conjunction with characterization has the potential to evoke an emotional response in its readers. In what follows below, however, I also seek to identify specific techniques of plotting and characterization, and other features of narrative artistry that strike me as geared toward stimulating not only the cognitive but also the affective faculties of readers. This will, I hope, provide a little more methodological backbone to the investigation of the affective function of biblical narrative. The point here is not to replace summarizations of plot and characterization, but to supplement them with additional tools for examining the biblical authors' use of pathos.

How Biblical Narratives Move Us

What I discuss below are some relatively common literary techniques employed by the writers of biblical narrative that are at least in part intended to evoke pathos among their readers. The following account is far from exhaustive. I hope readers more perceptive than I will identify and describe still other techniques, but I trust that what I provide below is enough to move the discussion forward in exploring the affective tendencies of biblical narrative. I have gathered these techniques into three categories: those that are part of the narrative's plotting, those that serve the function of characterization, and other techniques that do not fall neatly into either of those two.

Plotting

Plotting, the sequencing and presentation of events and actions is, as we have said, one of the defining elements of narrative. The sequencing is not random; the events described typically involve some sort of temporal, causal, or teleological relationship to one another. The plot revolves around problems to overcome or goals to accomplish by its leading characters. The sequencing is often artfully composed and rhetorically charged.

One advantage narrative possesses over other types of literary form, and which enables it to engage its readers deeply, is that (as already noted) we commonly conceive of our lives and the lives of others as "storied." For this reason many of us are easily drawn into a narrative as if "we are there." Thus, our participation in the story requires no major alteration in our normal mode of thought. We read the story with the same set of eyes with which we read our own lives and the lives of others. But, as we all know, there are stories that are told well and others that are not, and it is the good stories that gather us deeply into their storied world. In ways that are often subtle yet deeply engaging, these stories sequence and "set up" the events they narrate in order to compose in us an experience that moves both our minds and our hearts.

But how, exactly, do narratives do this? How does the plotting of the story draw us in, cause us to feel, and perhaps even lead us to affirm or reconsider our understanding of the world as we "try out" the portrayal of reality authored by the writer? In what follows I describe five common, "rhetorically affective" moves that biblical narratives employ as a means of gathering readers into their narrative.

Leading Readers to Threshold Moments

Narratives are, of course, filled with "threshold moments," those liminal states when what is sought by leading characters stands on the edge of achievement or failure. In certain instances, however, it is clear that the narrator invests significant effort in shaping the story so that it will draw readers deeply into a threshold moment, teetering them on the brink as they eagerly await climactic resolution, whether for good or for ill.

In Luke 24, for instance, the evangelist presents a highly structured account as he brings the Gospel to its culmination. The good news of the resurrection is, to be sure, the centerpiece of the chapter, as several themes and story lines are brought to resolution in light of this event. Among those story lines is the disciples' inability to understand Jesus' passion predictions concerning his death and resurrection. This story line becomes the focus of Luke 24 as it depicts the disciples' transformation from those who misunderstand and doubt to those who understand, believe, and proclaim the good news of Jesus' resurrection.[13] Throughout the narrative the reader has been repeatedly shown and told that the disciples have been unable to grasp Jesus' disclosure of his death and resurrection (9:43-48; 18:31-34; 22:14-30). But now, with the resurrection, the time for understanding has come. Luke composes a series of three accounts in which disciples cross the threshold from misunderstanding to understanding and become witnesses to God's salvation in Jesus: the women at the tomb (24:1-12), the Emmaus story (24:13-35), and Jesus' appearance to the Eleven and other disciples (24:36-49). Each of those accounts is structured according to a disclosure—misunderstanding—corrective instruction—understanding—proclamation pattern:

Women at the Tomb (24:1-12)

disclosure	"They found the stone rolled away . . ." (vv. 1-3)
misunderstanding	"While they were perplexed about this . . ." (v. 4)
corrective instruction	"'Why do you look for the living among the dead?'" (vv. 5-7)
understanding	"Then they remembered his words . . ." (v. 8)
proclamation	". . . they told all this to the eleven and to all the rest" (vv. 9-12)

Emmaus Story (24:13-35)

disclosure	"Now on that same day two of them . . . and talking about all these things that had happened" (vv. 13-24)
misunderstanding	"But we had hoped that he was the one to redeem Israel . . ." (vv. 21-24)[14]
corrective instruction	"Oh, how foolish you are!" (vv. 25-30)
understanding	"Then their eyes were opened . . ." (vv. 31-32)
proclamation	"That same hour they got up and returned to Jerusalem" (vv. 33-35)

Jesus Greets and Commissions His Disciples (24:36-53)

disclosure	"While they were talking about this, Jesus himself stood among them" (v. 36)
misunderstanding	"They were startled and terrified, and thought that they were seeing a ghost" (v. 37)
corrective instruction	"'Why are you frightened?'" (vv. 38-44)
understanding	"Then he opened their minds" (vv. 45-47)
proclamation	"'You are witnesses of these things . . .'" (vv. 48-53)

The threefold repetition of this pattern creates an extended threshold moment, or series of threshold moments, leading to a final iteration in which doubt is finally resolved and the disciples are sent forth by Jesus as witnesses. Why extend the threshold moment to this degree? One of the evangelist's motivations was likely to emphasize that the death and resurrection of Jesus could only be grasped after these extraordinary events took place, and their significance only fully understood when explained to the disciples by the risen Jesus himself. It was one more way Luke could underscore the pivotal role of Jesus' resurrection and ongoing ministry in God's designs for humanity. Yet another reason also seems likely. The extended threshold moment also enables Luke to underscore the disciples' repeated inability to grasp the reality of Jesus' resurrection: (1) the disciples disregard the women's witness as an idle tale (v. 11); (2) the disciples heading to Emmaus—ironically, and even comically—fail to recognize the significance of the events they narrate (vv. 18-24); and (3) despite being told by the Emmaus disciples and others that "the Lord has risen indeed," when Jesus appears the disciples think they are seeing a ghost (vv. 36-37). Thus, Luke leads his readers to experience (along with Jesus—see v. 25!), more fully than they otherwise would, frustration at the disciples slowness to understand and believe. In effect, Luke cultivates within his audience a keen, emotively charged awareness of the disciples' foolishness for not believing sooner. What's the rhetorical payoff? Through his shaping of this threshold moment Luke invites his audience to recognize and push aside such foolish doubt within themselves, to embrace the reality of Jesus' resurrection and ongoing ministry, and then also to join the disciples in living lives of joyous praise and witness (vv. 44-49, 50-53). The affective dimensions of Luke's portrayal serve his rhetorical and pastoral ends.

Consider also the example of Jacob's reunion with Esau in Genesis 32–33. The narrative leading up to these chapters has informed us of several matters relevant to the story: Jacob has stolen Esau's blessing, Jacob fled his homeland because Esau threatened to kill Jacob, Jacob is a scoundrel, and despite all this

God has promised to be with Jacob and has called him to return to the land of his family. So at the start of Genesis 32, we find Jacob on the road heading toward home. He sends messengers ahead as part of an initial attempt to appease Esau whom he still fears, and receives word that Esau himself is coming to meet him *with four hundred men*. Trembling with trepidation, Jacob immediately goes into crisis mode. He divides his massive company of livestock and servants into a series of droves that he drives ahead of him as a present for Esau (32:6-9). He then offers a desperate and self-centered prayer to God (notice that Jacob's reference to women and children in 32:11 comes only after "Deliver me please, from the hand of my brother, from the hand of Esau, for I am afraid of him," as if his concern for them is an afterthought). Yet it is clear that Jacob takes no heart in the prayer or Yahweh's earlier promise to be with him, for he continues to send waves of his company ahead of him in a vain attempt to put as much bodily (and evidently dispensable) mass between himself and Esau (32:13-21). We see his cowardice sink to even greater depths when on the eve of his meeting with Esau, he even sends his own family ahead of him, a final offering to save his own skin (32:22-23). It is in the midst of this desperate and depraved scenario that we encounter one of the more mysterious and powerful threshold moments in Scripture.

Left alone, Jacob is attacked by an unknown assailant and wrestles until daybreak (32:22-32). Mystery surrounds the scene, but this much is clear: Jacob, the coward, though no match for his superior opponent, courageously and somewhat miraculously wrestles him to a draw. At some point in the night, he senses that his opponent is none other than God. He comes to recognize the worth of *God's* blessing and will not let go without it. The divine stranger eventually acquiesces and blesses Jacob, granting him and the people that will come forth from him a name and identity: Israel—*those who struggle with God and one another, and yet persevere*. But the startling and mysterious nature of this event makes it unclear how it is going to alter, if at all, Jacob's encounter with Esau. Will Yahweh intervene? Will Jacob change his cowardly course? Will blood be spilled between brothers again? Notice how the narrator teases us in the immediately following verses (33:1-2):

> Now Jacob looked up and saw Esau coming, and four hundred men with him. So he divided the children among Leah and Rachel and the two maids. He put the maids with their children in front, then Leah with her children, and Rachel and Joseph last of all.

The reference to Jacob seeing "Esau coming, and four hundred men with him" is certainly meant to remind the reader of Jacob's fearful response the last time this reference was made (32:6), and the reader is now on edge waiting to see how Jacob responds. And much to the reader's dismay, Jacob once again starts fiddling with his remaining drove, once again, it seems, risking all in order to save his own skin. At this point I imagine the reader moaning in disgust: "Oh no, he's doing it again! How could he after what happened?" But then comes the following verse, and our revulsion toward Jacob's action and character is suddenly revised into relief and perhaps even admiration:

> *He himself went on ahead of them*, bowing himself to the ground seven times, until he came near his brother. (v. 3)

The creative, if not downright devious, shaping of these verses serves no other purpose, it seems to me, than to heighten the suspense of this threshold moment and increase its affective charge. Why take such efforts to invite this level of emotional response? I believe it is because the author saw this as a crucial moment in the narrative, and indeed, in Israel's history, disclosing an essential truth about God's people and faith. Thus, he employs pathos to deeply etch this moment and the truth it conveys into the hearts and minds of his audience: when Israel (as represented here by Jacob) trusts in God and clings above all else to *God's* blessing, then they shall live into their calling as God's people and persevere with both God and with others. Affirming this reading is the discovery in these verses that Isaac's blessing, stolen by Jacob, has become largely inefficacious: the blessing destined the recipient for great prosperity and rule over his brothers: "Be lord over your brothers, and may your mother's sons bow down to you," Isaac proclaims (Gen 27:27-29). But here it is Jacob who repeatedly prostrates himself before Esau, repeatedly addresses Esau as "lord," and repeatedly urges him to accept a significant portion of his possessions (vv. 3-15). It is not Isaac's blessing that will lead Jacob to the prosperity and success for which he was truly destined. That blessing is undone as another takes over and guides Jacob down a different path moving toward goals larger than his own gain. To be sure, Jacob's transformation may not be complete. His conniving still continues (vv. 12-16). But we have seen a change, and this pivotal moment puts before us in affectively charged fashion the fundamental biblical claim that Israel's well-being in its struggle with God and others will depend upon what and whose blessing it is to which they cling.

Sequencing That Draws Connection and Comparison

Scholars have long noted the tendency of biblical narrative to sequence or arrange material in order to color the reader's perception of particular events or the actions of characters. Bracketing, framing, or enveloping is one common arrangement employed in order to help the reader see connections between parts of the narrative. The narrator constructs this device by placing similar material at the beginning and end of a narrative unit, either large, small, or in between. Its specific narratological effect varies. At times it may be used to draw connections between the beginning and end of a narrative unit. For example, the bracketing provided by the reference to the rendering of the heavens and proclamation of Jesus as the Divine Son in Mark 1:11 and the similar reference to the rendering of the temple curtain and proclamation of Jesus as the Divine Son in Mark 15:39 serves to inform the reader that despite—and, indeed, because of—the crucifixion, Jesus' identity as God's beloved Son will now be known by humanity as well. It is one of several ways in which Mark emphasizes that Jesus' true identity, known previously only to God and the divine realm, can only become known to humanity from the far side of the cross.

At other times, a bracketing technique called "sandwiching" calls the reader to see two stories in close relation to one another. Mark is well known for these sandwich constructions in which he (or his source) has seemingly taken one story, pulled it apart, and inserted another story within it. Consider, for instance, the intercalated stories of Jairus's daughter and the woman suffering from hemorrhaging in Mark 5:21-43. While Jesus is on his way to heal Jairus's daughter, the woman approaches, touches Jesus, is healed, and is commended by Jesus for her faith. Then Jesus resumes his course to Jairus's house and heals the young girl. There are other details in these accounts that also invite the reader to draw comparisons between them: the girl is twelve years old (v. 42) and the woman has been suffering from her ailment for twelve years (v. 25); both are regarded as a beloved daughter, the girl by Jairus (v. 23) and the woman by Jesus (v. 34); both are restored because of faith, the woman by her own (v. 34), and the daughter by that of her father (v. 36).

Still another way biblical authors draw a connection between different parts of the narrative is by sequencing episodes in such a manner that the reader's perception of one event is colored by events preceding it. Of course, this commonly takes place when there is a clear causal relationship between events or when a particular event has been foreshadowed in some fashion. But what I am referring to here are connections more subtly drawn by the author in order to cast an event or situation in a particular light, leading to a more highly charged response from readers than would normally be the case. Consider, for example, Mark 6:1-6. Taken in isolation, the focus of the passage is the rejection of Jesus by his hometown folk because they cannot believe that one of their own, one whom they know, would be filled with wisdom and power. But when viewed in light of the narrative that has come before, including the miracle-laden section immediately preceding it in 4:35—5:43, the Nazarenes' rejection of Jesus takes on added dimensions. Jesus, the Divine Son, has displayed mastery over the forces of nature (4:35-41), Satan (5:1-20), incurable disease, and even death (5:21-43). Jesus emerges from this section of the narrative as a larger-than-life figure, possessing powers and a pedigree that suggest he is no mere mortal. And yet when he arrives in his hometown, this amazing figure, embodying the eruption of God's rule on earth, is dismissed as a fraud and offense: "What is this? Jesus a prophet? Jesus a teacher of wisdom and worker of mighty deeds? Ha! He's a carpenter! We know him. He's Mary's son! What lunacy!" In the view of Jesus' hometown folk, this carpenter of lowly estate is reaching well beyond the status determined by his parentage. This scene, colored by all that has come before it, underscores that those who think they know Jesus best of all, really—and tragically—do not know him at all (cf. Mark 3:20-21, 31-35). They, unlike the faithful depicted in the immediately preceding section, depend on conventions of status and identity that are ill equipped to make sense of who Jesus really is. They fall back on what they know, the familiar and prudent, because they lack the faith to see in Jesus the in-breaking of God's reign among them.

In speaking to these formal conventions, commentators rightly assume that Mark intended his readers to notice them and thus to draw the connections between the elements of the story held in view. These connections, however, are nearly always understood by interpreters as solely cognitive in character; their affective dimensions are rarely explored. But note, too, that these sequencing strategies may also increase the dramatic effect of the stories. This certainly seems to be the case with the examples from Mark we've glanced at, in which the sequencing joins with other dramatic elements to enrich both the cognitive and affective stimulation of the reader. In Mark 15, the parallels to Mark 1:11 help the reader to appreciate both cognitively *and* affectively the significance of what transpires with Jesus' death. Thus, the pity and horror evoked by this tragic scene is intermingled with amazement (and perhaps puzzlement) that this moment of suffering, humiliation, and death should be the moment when Jesus' identity as the Divine Son—announced by God at the very beginning of the narrative—should first be grasped by a human character. Or perhaps the reaction will be awe and wonder, the reader coming to see that what takes place here at the tragic end of Jesus' ministry is somehow of a piece with his commissioning by God during the baptism and the announcement of salvation at the Gospel's beginning (1:1-3, 14-15). With the stories of the two daughters joined together, the reader is led to consider that the healing of God's kingdom is made available not only to a daughter among the religious elite, but also to one outcasted and without *pater* or patron. Each contain poignant elements of characterization (more on this later). But the affective impact of their characterization is amplified by the intercalation of their shared vulnerability and the need for faith that courageously looks beyond the reality of the moment. Such plotting invites both sympathy from readers and joy that a new future is made possible for these two women, and thus perhaps also for themselves, by God's reign in Jesus. Finally, the example of unbelief provided by the hometown folk of Nazareth joins with others helping the reader understand that conventional status norms are inadequate for reflecting on Jesus' identity. But wouldn't we rather have them be proud of their hometown son? And doesn't readers' experience of the narrative leading up to this scene prompt them to feel more keenly—along with Jesus—the disappointing and even the tragic nature of the Nazarenes' lack of faith?

> And he could do no deed of power there, except that he laid his hands on a few sick people and cured them. And he was amazed at their unbelief. (6:5-6)

Withholding Resolution

Aristotle's description of plot as having a "beginning, middle, and end" has long been basic to the definition of plot offered by literary critics. Aristotle further defines the end as "that which does itself naturally follow from something else, either necessarily or in general, but there is nothing else after it."[15] We do well to keep in mind that Aristotle is discussing the genre of tragedy in particular in *Poetics*, a narrative form that leads to a tragic end "with nothing else after it." However, the phrase "that which does itself follow from something else, either necessarily or in general," would seem to have broader application to any literary form governed by plot. In other words, narratives are expected to "go somewhere," to move toward a resolution, which in some clear manner follows from the beginning and middle of the plot. Most biblical narratives, both on a large and small scale, follow this teleological recipe for plotting. But on rare occasions the biblical authors deviate from it and leave us hanging, staring blankly at the final line of a story and asking, "Surely, there is more!"

One notable instance of withheld resolution receiving much attention in recent scholarship is the ending of Mark's Gospel (16:1-8). A common assertion since the critical study of Mark began has been that the original ending of the Gospel was lost when the end of its papyrus roll was torn. This view is still maintained by some, but the majority of scholars now hold that the evangelist truly ended his Gospel with 16:8.[16] Yet with 16:8 as the Gospel's ending, the evangelist draws the plot to a close (or fails to) by reporting the scene of the women encountering the empty tomb and describing their response. On the day after the Sabbath, they arrive at the tomb to anoint Jesus' body, only to discover that the stone has been rolled away. Entering the tomb, they come upon a young man dressed in a white robe, and the women recoil with alarm.

> But he said to them, "Do not be alarmed; you are looking for Jesus of Nazareth, who was crucified. He has been raised; he is not here. Look, there is the place they laid him. But go, tell his disciples and Peter that he is going ahead of you to Galilee; there you will see him, just as he told you." (vv. 6-7)

The angel's announcement of Jesus' resurrection clearly recalls Jesus' passion predictions throughout the Gospel, as well as his disclosure to his disciples that even though he will be crucified and they will all fall away from him, he will rise from the dead and meet them in Galilee (14:27-28). Given the plotting that has led up to this point, we'd expect the women to recognize the connection between the angel's announcement and Jesus' earlier teaching, and to share this, good albeit, amazing news with his other followers (such as we find in Matthew, Luke, and John). This, it seems, would be the ending "that which does itself naturally follow." But instead, the Gospel concludes:

> So they went out and fled from the tomb, for terror and amazement had seized them; and they said nothing to anyone, for they were afraid. (v. 8)

Indications that this abrupt ending is not simply an offense to modern sensibilities but was also regarded as unsatisfactory by early Christians come from Matthew and Luke, who borrowed heavily from Mark's account but end their Gospels very differently, as well as the secondary endings that accrued around the Markan text. For some time now, interpreters have sought to understand the ending with respect to the larger designs of Mark's Gospel and its setting within a community facing persecution or at least the threat of it. Many argue that Mark leaves the reader hanging with this most incomplete and disappointing ending in hopes that it will inspire Christians of his (and perhaps a later) time and place to pick up where the women left off, and to choose faith and hope over fear.[17] As stated well by Mary Ann Tolbert:

> Each individual who hears the word sown by the Gospel of Mark, the word that human corruption and suffering will now be finally abolished by the glory of God's kingdom, is given the opportunity—as have all the characters in the story—to respond in faith or fear. The problem posed by the epilogue

[15:40—16:8] in strong rhetorical terms through the unfulfilled expectations raised by the named women is, If these followers will not go and tell, who will? In the end, Mark's Gospel purposely leaves each reader or hearer with the urgent and disturbing question: What type of earth am *I*? Will *I* go and tell? Indeed, one's response to the seed sown by the Gospel of Mark reveals in each listener's heart, as did Jesus' earlier preaching, the presence of God's ground or Satan's.[18]

In this sense, then, the ending of Mark's narrative serves as an "invitation to finish the story" as readers respond with surprise, dissatisfaction, and even dismay to its lack of resolution. But note how interpreters—uncharacteristically—address the affective nature of this rhetorical appeal, as here we find a rare instance in which commentators encourage reflection on the emotional dimension of a biblical narrative. Readers are, as Tolbert states above, led to the urgent and disturbing question: "What type of earth am I?" Similarly, David Rhoads, Joanna Dewey, and Donald Michie add:

The narrator's characterization of the disciples leads the reader to develop ambivalent feelings towards them. The reader probably identifies with the disciples more than any other characters and wants them to succeed. Readers can easily put themselves in the situation of the disciples: the privilege of being called by Jesus, being surprised by his acts of power, being frightened by the prospect of death by crucifixion, and eager to flee rather than be arrested. The positive and readily understandable characteristics of the disciples maintain the reader's interest in hopes that, despite their failures, the disciples will succeed in becoming faithful followers of Jesus. Some inside views even evoke sympathy for the disciples, for example, when they are awed by Jesus' authority over the storm, when their eyes are so heavy at Gethsemane, and above all when Rock [Peter] lurches off "sobbing" after his denials of Jesus. . . . The narrator has depicted the disciples as afraid, with little faith or understanding, concerned to save their own lives, and preoccupied with their own importance, but, nonetheless, leaving all and persevering in following Jesus. In the end, however, they fail to prepare adequately for death by persecution. Yet the reader is to learn from the failure of the disciples. If the disciples can fail again and again and Jesus still promises to go ahead of them, the reader can do the same. The thrust of this portrayal poses questions to the readers: "What will you do when faced with death for Jesus and the good news? Can you remain faithful? And can you, if you fail, begin again?"[19]

The dissatisfaction invited by Mark's ending is quite apparent, but in assuming that this was a rhetorical technique not lost on Mark's readers or unique to Mark, it provides a precedent for finding similar though perhaps less obvious occurrences of incomplete or unresolved plotting. Other possibilities may include the end of Deuteronomy, with the Israelites on the cusp of the promised land while the urgent reminders of Moses echo in their ears; the ending of Acts, with the results of Paul's fate unreported;[20] or smaller narrative units within a larger narrative, such as the potential followers of Jesus in Luke 9:57-62; or the rich man who "was shocked and went away grieving" in response to Jesus' call for him to sell all his possessions in Mark 10:17-22.

Astonishing Inversion of the Expected

Unexpected shifts and turns are common to narrative, but at times these shifts and turns are to such an extreme that it seems likely they are designed to elicit astonishment and wonder in an audience. Aristotle referred to this narratological move as "reversal," involving "an astonishing inversion of the expected outcome of some action," but "not at the cost of necessary or probable action."[21] (I will borrow Aristotle's phrase "astonishing inversion of the expected," to refer to this technique, and reserve the term *reversal* for a different narratological move I describe below.) At times, the reader has been prepared beforehand for such turns in the narrative, and thus the focus is on the astonishment experienced by the characters in the narrative, such as with Jesus' crucifixion ("We had hoped that he was the one to redeem Israel" [Luke 24:21]) and his resurrection ("The Lord has risen indeed!" [Luke 24:34]). At other times, however, the reader appears to be the target of unexpected inversions in the plotting. The Joseph story, for example, provides several. Joseph's brothers, caught in a fit of jealous annoyance, sell him into slavery and thus put into motion an astonishing series of events. Joseph's honor and faithfulness to his master, Potiphar, land him in prison, an unjust consequence that in turn plays a crucial role in Joseph's ascent to power, resulting in his exaltation over his brothers, all of Egypt (save Pharaoh), and much of the Mediterranean region, finally leading to the pathos-filled climax in which Joseph and his brothers are reunited and reconciled to one another. The engaging power of the story relies in part on these moments of twist, surprise, and reversal of fortune as they underscore the story's abiding theme of God's provision for Joseph, his family, Israel, and the world, even in and through the dysfunctions of humanity.

Another telling example occurs in Exodus 32:1-4, where Israel's breathtaking betrayal of Yahweh is met, ultimately, with astonishing grace. Among the many biblical accounts that portray the descendants of Abraham turning away from God and God's ways, the story of the golden calf affair (Exodus 32–34) stands out as one of the most thickheaded and egregious. The narrator's artistry in leading us to appreciate the utter depravity of the people's actions in Exodus 32:1-6 is apparent in the plotting leading up to this scene (and here we find the technique of sequencing employed as well). The opening chapters of Exodus tell the story of Yahweh hearing the cries of God's oppressed people, Israel, and with a mighty hand delivering them from their slavery to Pharaoh. God leads them out of Egypt by cloud and fire, through water and desert to Mt. Sinai. In God's own words, "I bore you on eagles' wings and brought you to myself" (Exod 19:4). There, God announces God's intentions to renew God's covenantal relationship with them (19:1-6). Of all the peoples of the earth, they are to be God's "treasured possession," a "priestly kingdom," and a "holy nation," a nation set apart (holy) for a particular purpose: to serve as priests for the rest of the world, bearing witness to God and God's ways. They need only to trust God's voice and keep God's statutes. The Decalogue comes next, spoken by God directly to the people. The commands begin with what is most central: "I am the LORD your God who brought you out of the land of Egypt, out of the house of slavery; you shall have no other gods before me" (20:2). This is followed by the command to "not make for yourselves an idol . . . you shall not bow down to them or worship them" (20:4-5). After God gives Israel the Ten Commandments, Moses goes back up the mountain to receive other instructions from God, statutes that were to guide the people into living rightly with God, one another, and also creation (Exodus 20–23).

In Exodus 24, the time for ratifying the covenant is at hand. Moses comes down from the mountain to give the instructions to the people. The narrator is careful to note the unanimity of the people's devotion: "and all the people answered with one voice, and said, 'All the words that the LORD has spoken, we will do'" (24:3). After final preparations are made for ratifying the covenant, Moses once again reads the book of the covenant to the people, and once again the people affirm, "All that the LORD has spoken we will do, and we will be obedient" (24:7). Moses then departs from the people and ascends Mt. Sinai to receive detailed instructions from God on the construction and maintenance of the tabernacle, the portable sanctuary that Israel will take with them through the wilderness embodying God's presence with the people (Exodus 25–31). God's instruction is painstakingly precise, emphasizing the sacredness of the tabernacle and the importance attached to its purpose: Yahweh dwelling among them. Moses is with God on the mountain for forty days and nights (24:18).

Thus, the background is set for the golden calf affair. This people, the descendants of Abraham, have just been delivered by God from Egypt. Yahweh, the Lord of the universe, the God who covenanted with their ancestors, has heard their cries and led them out into the wilderness to be God's treasured possession. God has instructed them on how to walk rightly in relationship with God and one another. The people pledge their devotion to God. The marriage is enjoined, and now God is helping them to prepare a place where God's very presence will dwell among them. All seems to be going so well. If at this point in the story you were to ask, "What would be the most outrageous thing the people could do to threaten their renewed relationship with God?" it would be difficult, I think, to come up with something more destructive than what happens next. The people tire of waiting for Moses to return from the mountain. They now command Aaron, "Come, make gods for us, who shall go before us; as for this Moses, the man who brought us up out of the land of Egypt, we do not know what has become of him" (32:1). Aaron, without a hint of resistance to the people's demand, collects gold from them (part of their plunder from Egypt) and forms it into an image of a calf. Then comes the line that really stings. With the golden calf before them, the people bow down before it proclaiming, "These are your gods, O Israel, who brought you up out of the land of Egypt!" (32:4).

Perhaps Aaron tries to salvage some semblance of devotion to God when he announces, "Tomorrow shall be a festival to the LORD" (32:5). But the "reveling" that characterizes the people's "worship" (32:6; see also vv. 18-19) clearly indicates that the Yahweh they had come to know as Savior has—*in essence if not in name*—been co-opted by a new god, and one designed according to the worst angels of their nature.[22] Remember the people's words the very last time they spoke in the narrative. They devoted themselves to the covenant, saying, "All that the LORD has spoken we will do, and we will be obedient!" (24:7). They couldn't even get past the first two commandments! Yet not only are the people transgressing these commands, in doing so they are also rejecting and betraying everything that God has revealed God's self to be. It is Yahweh, not Pharaoh or any other god, who is Lord of the universe. Yahweh has delivered them from Egypt and from this time onward is to be known to them as Savior. Yahweh has "brought them to myself" and renewed the covenantal relationship with them. But they get tired of waiting for Moses, cast away their special relationship with Yawheh, Lord of all, and bow down before a lump of gold. In one of the worst and most astonishing ways imaginable, they betray Yahweh, their Creator, Savior, and Lord, who desires to dwell with them.

Yahweh's initial response is one of rage and threatened wrath. God immediately distances God's self from the people, in effect disowning them. Yahweh commands Moses, "Go down at once! *Your* people, whom *you* brought up out of the land of Egypt, have acted perversely" (32:7). After relaying a full account of the people's actions to Moses, culminating in their cry. "These are your gods, O Israel, who have brought you up out of the land of Egypt!" Yahweh pronounces their doom: "I have seen this people, how stiff-necked they are. Now let me alone, so that my wrath may burn hot against them and I may consume them; and of you I will make a great nation" (32:9).

Yahweh's response of judgment may strike some readers as a little over the top. Yet from the perspective of the biblical writer—as indicated by the way in which he carefully situates this story in the sequencing of the narrative—I think we are meant to see God's response as justly commensurate with the people's crime. So egregious is their betrayal, so warped have they revealed themselves to be, that their destruction, and God's attempt to begin again with a new people, seems the only fitting option. The people, from the perspective of the biblical author, deserve no more. They have completely forfeited any covenantal claim that could be made on their behalf.

Noting this, I think, not only helps us to understand the harshness of Yahweh's response to the people, but also helps us rightly hear Moses' words to God as both bold and outlandish. Moses, in effect, calls Yahweh to abide by the covenant promises even when the people—in a most incredible manner—have failed to do so.

> But Moses implored the LORD his God, and said, "O LORD, why does your wrath burn hot against your people, whom you brought out of the land of Egypt with great power and with a mighty hand? Why should the Egyptians say, 'It was with evil intent that he brought them out to kill them in the mountains, and to consume them from the face of the earth'? Turn from your fierce wrath; change your mind and do not bring disaster on your people. Remember Abraham, Isaac, and Israel, your servants, how you swore to them by your own self, saying to them, 'I will multiply your descendants like the stars of heaven, and all this land that I have promised I will give to your descendants, and they shall inherit it forever.'" (32:11-13)

Moses reminds Yahweh of Yahweh's own intentions in delivering Israel from Egypt. One intention was to reveal to Egypt and the rest of the world that Yahweh, not Pharaoh, is Lord of creation (see, for example, Exod 5:1-2; 9:14; 15:11; 18:10-12). Moses now says to God, in effect, "What will the Egyptians and the rest of the world think of you if you destroy this people? Will anyone want to follow you?" But God's primary intention was to act on the promises God had made to Abraham and his descendants, to call out this people as God's own, to grant them provision, security, and land, so that they may multiply and eventually be a source of blessing for all the peoples of the earth (see

Gen 12:1-3; Exod 3:1-17). Knowing this, Moses calls Yahweh to take back the people and to claim them once more as God's own: "O LORD, why does your wrath burn hot against *your* people, whom *you* brought out of the land of Egypt with great power and with a mighty hand? . . . Turn from your fierce wrath; change your mind and do not bring disaster on *your* people" (32:11-12). In light of how the narrator has carefully crafted the narrative to highlight the depravity of the people's betrayal, it seems to me that the response the narrator is expecting from the reader at this point is along the lines of heart-panged incredulity intermingled with awe-struck hope that such might be possible: "Forgive them? How could God? There's just no way! Is there?" Then come those astonishing words: "And the LORD changed his mind about the disaster he planned to bring on his people" (v. 14).

This is remarkable. Divine intention is reversed by human intercession. And yet in the very next chapter we see God change God's mind once again. God commands Moses and the people to leave Mt. Sinai and to resume their journey to the promised land (33:1). He tells Moses, "Go, leave this place, you and the people whom *you* have brought out of the land of Egypt," using the second-person singular pronoun again to signal that Yahweh still refuses to reclaim the people. Although an angel will be sent before them to drive out the inhabitants of the land, Yahweh will not go with them, "or I would consume you on the way, for you are a stiff-necked people!" (33:3). Once again, Moses intercedes, this time appealing to the intimate relationship that he and Yahweh share, and again urging Yahweh, "Consider too that this nation is *your* people" (33:12-13). Yahweh relents once more and assures Moses, "My presence will go with you, and I will give you rest" (33:14).

To be sure, judgment is also a part of this story. In 32:35 we learn that "the LORD sent a plague on the people, because they made the calf—the one that Aaron made." But this reference to the judgment God imposes is mild in comparison to what God had initially threatened and also pales in comparison to Moses' actions preceding the plague. Upon coming down from the mountain after interceding on behalf of the people, Moses sees with his own eyes the Israelites reveling before the calf. He smashes the tablets written by God's hand, grinds the idol into powder, spreads the dust into the water, and makes the Israelites drink it (32:19-20). When the people still run wild with idolatrous frenzy, Moses gathers the sons of Levi around them and tells them to take up their swords: "'Go back and forth from gate to gate throughout the camp, and each of you kill your brother, your friend, and your neighbor' . . . and about three thousand of the people fell on that day" (32:27-28). Readers disagree on whether Moses' drastic actions were commanded by God. That Moses claims to act on God's behalf is clear: "Thus says the LORD, the God of

Israel, 'Put your sword on your side . . .'" (32:27). But in nearly every other case in which Moses speaks with divine authority, the narrator tells us that Yahweh has directed Moses to do so. Here, we are never told that God issues such a command. Instead, we go from Yahweh relenting from anger and the threat of destruction to Moses, once he sees for himself how bad things have gotten, responding with bloody vengeance. The point of the contrast seems to be that Moses, despite his great love for and loyalty to the people, was incapable of the mercy that Yahweh displays. Such astonishing forgiveness and forbearance is something that is only possible for God. Fittingly, this narrative unit, beginning with the golden calf affair, ends with God's own self-disclosure:

> The LORD, the LORD, a God merciful and gracious, slow to anger, and abounding in steadfast love and faithfulness. (34:6)

That this story deeply left its mark, theologically and emotionally, on its early hearers, is indicated by how and how often it was remembered. From this point on in the biblical story, God is known as "merciful and gracious, slow to anger and abounding in steadfast love and faithfulness." This disclosure becomes an oft-recited confession of faith identifying these traits as fundamental dimensions of God's character (Num 14:18-19; Neh 9:17, 31; Pss 77:7-8; 86:15; 103:8; 116:5; 145:8, 13; Isa 30:18; 63:7; Lam 3:20-32; Jonah 4:2; Joel 2:3). And even though this story contains instances of God's wrath, whenever the account of the golden calf affair is remembered in subsequent Old Testament traditions, it is not remembered as a story of judgment, but is celebrated as a story of God's forgiveness and mercy (Neh 9:18-19; Pss 78:36-38; 103:7-8; 106:19-23). It is likely that the astonishing nature of both the people's betrayal and Yahweh's forgiveness profoundly moved those who heard it and deeply inscribed this story into the collective memory of Israel.

Composing Conflict

Still another element related to plotting that serves both a cognitive and emotional function in narrative is the composition of conflict. So ubiquitous is conflict throughout Scripture that we hardly need to illustrate it. Some reflection on its dramatic and affective function may be helpful, however. By reporting and staging conflict, authors of biblical narrative are able to accomplish a variety of aims. They are able to present conflict as something that is basic to the human experience, a manifestation of the depravity miring the human condition (for example, Cain and Abel, David and Absalom). The portrayal of conflict draws attention to opposing commitments, with one party often representing a perspective consistent with that of the biblical author (Samuel vs. Jezebel and Ahab; Jeremiah vs. the false prophets; John vs. Herod; Jesus vs. the Pharisees). In many such cases, the authors imply that the conflict portrayed goes beyond the individual actors and is part of the larger conflict between the ways of God and the ways of Israel and/or the world, and even the spiritual realm (story of Jacob; Herod's massacre of infants; Paul's arrest and impending trial; Jesus' exorcisms). In still other cases, the way in which a character instigates or responds to conflict may serve the author's purposes of characterization (for example, Samson, David, Jesus).

That the portrayal of conflict is meant to draw the reader into the narrative and elicit an affective response of rhetorical import would seem to need little argument. Conflict between characters, competing cultures, or worldviews, the forces of nature and human intention or well-being, form the core of most story lines coursing through our literature and all other forms of storytelling. How many of us do not commonly, as a matter of course, find ourselves choosing one side over the other when we engage a good story, pulling for the "good guys," despairing the victory of evil, loathing those who clothe themselves in cruelty, greed, or destructive ignorance? By employing conflict and pairing it with characterization, authors create moments pregnant with tension and angst that lead readers to invest themselves emotionally in the tale, respond in certain ways to its characters (positively or negatively), and align themselves with perspectives that are consistent with the views of characters who are in the right, portrayed as brave, noble, or just.

Characterization

The casting of characters is among the most powerful rhetorical tools available to an author of narrative. Well-composed stories introduce us to characters that we come to know, perhaps even just as, if not more, intimately than close friends or members of our own family. While biblical narratives often (but not always) lack the level of characterization we commonly encounter in modern novels, biblical authors also play upon our emotional connections or aversions to characters in order to draw us into their narratives. They also use these affective techniques to lead us—subversively at times—to embrace their versions of the world.

Inviting Sympathy and Empathy

As mentioned previously, reader sympathy and empathy has been a topic of recent interest among psychologists and literary theorists participating in the wider discussion of the impact of characterization on readers. Reader sympathy is typically defined as a reader's wishes for a character to achieve a beneficial state or to be delivered from some sort of threat or suffering. Reader empathy, in contrast, occurs when a reader becomes so intimately engaged with a character that the reader actually experiences the same or similar emotions as the character, as those are either expressly stated or implied by the author or imagined by the reader.

To be sure, the extent to which readers sympathize or empathize with a character is dependent upon a whole host of factors relevant to the reader and beyond the control of the author (e.g., the reader's personality, reading skill, personal experience, gender, social location, etc.). But the likelihood that readers will sympathize or empathize with a particular character is greatly enhanced by the amount of attention and complexity the author gives to a character. In general, "round" (multidimensional) as opposed to "flat" (one-dimensional) characters are more likely to capture our attention. These are characters we encounter in a variety of situations. We see their struggles, strengths and weaknesses, triumphs and failures. We get a sense of what moves them, their hopes for themselves and others. In other words, we have the opportunity to "get to know them." There are numerous biblical characters sketched in such detail: several of the patriarchs and matriarchs, Moses, Joshua, Samson, Hannah, Samuel, Ruth, Naomi, Ahab, Elijah, Elisha, David, Solomon, Jeremiah, John, Mary, Elizabeth, Zechariah, Jesus, the Twelve, Nicodemus, Peter, Mary Magdalene, James, Stephen, Paul, and so on. At the same time, characters with only small parts in the biblical drama may also draw out our sympathy, especially if we encounter them in emotionally charged settings of injustice or vulnerability, such as Uriah or Naboth, the infants massacred by Herod, or those experiencing disease and illness, such as Jairus's daughter or the woman suffering from hemorrhaging.

Inviting Reader Identity

Reader identity has to do with the extent to which a reader considers him- or herself similar to a character in the narrative. To be sure, reader identity can play an important role in enhancing reader sympathy or empathy, but not necessarily so. In fact, some readers may identify with characters for which they have little or no sympathy or empathy. For example, in reading through Jesus' controversy dialogues with the Pharisees and scribes, I may come to the unpleasant realization that I am in some ways like Jesus' opponents, that I share some of their attitudes and values, and even engage in similar behaviors. But I can grudgingly make this connection without liking the Pharisees and the scribes, or wishing them well in the pursuit of their goals or relief from Jesus' sharp rebuke. By presenting a wide range of characters, authors of narrative provide readers with multiple opportunities for identifying with at least some of those characters or some elements of their characterization. This feature of narrative draws readers more deeply into the story, as the reading of characters becomes a reading of one's self in relation to others and the world. Affectively, identity may lead readers to develop a sense of solidarity with characters, resulting in sympathy or even empathy, especially when these characters are at least in some ways admirable. When readers identify with characters that they don't admire, this creates opportunities for self-reflection that are far from affectively benign: I really don't like the fact that I see myself in these Pharisees! And such emotion can serve to empower transformation.

Inviting Admiration or Disdain

Still another common technique used to elicit an affective response to characters is portraying qualities that invite either admiration or disdain. Justice, faithfulness, superior wisdom, power over threatening forces, compassion, courage—these and other qualities typically lead readers to admire the characters who possess them in large measure. Conversely, those displaying narcissistic self-interest, cruelty, ignorance, conceit, cowardice, or lack of mercy are typically disdained by readers. The rhetorical import of this technique is worth noting. Through such characterization, an author may lead us to admire certain characters and then use these characters to promote ideas the author wishes us to adopt. Conversely, the author may identify those we disdain with a competing worldview he or she would have us reject. In doing so, the author employs the rhetorical force of pathos and ethos in order to persuade us, perhaps so subtly that we don't know it, to entertain and even embrace the view or reality he sets before us.

At still other times, the author may seek to elicit mixed feelings for certain characters in order to lead readers to "affective dissonance." This is rhetorically effective as well, since readers will likely be affectively stimulated by negative actions or qualities attributed to characters they otherwise find admirable. The dissonance creates discomfort, may even be jarring, and focuses attention on the negative attributes or actions assigned to the characters. Biblical narrative is filled with such characters: the patriarchal narratives contain numerous examples of those who display both remarkable trust in God, moments of anxiety and doubt, and sometimes the deplorable treatment of others. These are followed by others, such as David, Solomon, Zechariah, the disciples, even Israel and the church as "corporate" characters, to name a few.

Other Techniques Inviting an Affective Response

Besides those that are clearly connected to plotting and characterization, authors of biblical narrative make use of still other techniques inviting affective response.

Essential Relevance

This may be too obvious to merit mention, but well-composed narratives that revolve around matters essential to human well-being and fulfillment are likely to gain the attention of their readers. The "stuff that really matters" throbs with pathos, calling readers to feel not only for the characters in the narrative but for themselves as well. Thus, as readers envision characters experiencing the deprivation or achievement of that which is central to blessing, they are likely moved not only for the sake of the characters in the story but in response to the same realities readers are invited to envision as possible for themselves. Consequently, the decision of characters in the narrative whether to heed Moses' urgent pleas for trust and obedience or to embrace Jesus' call to follow is not their decision alone. The choice between life and death, blessing and cursing, is also one put before the reader.

Paradox

Paradox is the assigning of seemingly disparate attributes to a particular person or situation. For example, Mark—followed by the other Gospel writers—presents Jesus both as the divine and powerful Son of God whose coming inaugurates the long-awaited rule of God, and also as the humble, human, suffering one who is rejected and suffers the excruciating shame of the cross. This technique is not limited to characters but can be applied to events or circumstances as well. In the Joseph story, Joseph characterizes all of the trial and injustice he experienced as part of God's plan to save his family and indeed much of the Mediterranean world.

Such mixing of seemingly incompatible categories creates cognitive dissonance in readers, leading them to question established ways of seeing the world and perhaps to discover some truth about the ways of God. Yet the mental energy stimulated by this technique is not only cognitive in character. Especially when addressing matters deemed essential to human well-being and fulfillment, paradox is also meant to encourage affective dissonance. The confounding of categories we use to order our view of reality is not only cognitively jarring but emotionally stressing. The security we enjoy when all is "in order" with our construal of the world and our perceived place in it most of us zealously guard. Consequently, we often respond to challenges to essential elements of our worldview with emotionally charged defenses or an angst that heightens our recognition that something pivotal is at stake. That the biblical authors recognized the affective dimension of paradox (and reversal—see below) and intended this for their readers is implied by their portrayal of characters responding to paradoxical realities. For example, Peter's confession of Jesus as the Messiah in Mark 8:27-30 is followed by the first of Jesus' passion predictions (and this is the first of several sequences in which Jesus' exalted character is juxtaposed with predictions of his shameful suffering and death). The cognitive dissonance this creates in Peter is clear, but so too is Peter's emotional tumult: "And Peter took him aside and began to rebuke him" (v. 32). Jesus' scathing response to Peter further underscores the paradoxical nature of his mission (to wish for Jesus' earthly rule and well-being is to align one's self with the evil one) while also amplifying the emotional energy of the scene: "Get behind me, Satan! For you are setting your mind not on divine things but on human things" (v. 33). While not directly stated by the evangelist, it is obvious that Peter, as the recipient of Jesus' passion prediction and vehement retort, is filled with both cognitive and affective dissonance at this point in the narrative.

Reversal

Here I use "reversal" not to refer to sudden changes in the action of the narrative or unexpected consequences of a character's actions ("astonishing inversion," as described above), but to the inversion of culturally endorsed norms and worldviews. Reversal is similar to paradox in that it undermines established notions and compels readers to respond to a revised understanding of reality that challenges the ways of the world. In fact, paradox may well be categorized as a type of reversal. Yet reversal does not always depend upon the sharp juxtaposition of two disparate realities assigned to a particular character or event, but can also be accomplished by revealing in various ways how those who are regarded as powerful and wise in the eyes of the world are instead impotent and foolish when confronted with the rule and wisdom of God. Conversely, those whom the world often disregards as of little worth or as disruptive rabble-rousers are instead celebrated as the righteous or heroes in the faith. The midwives' foiling of Pharaoh's attempt at population control in Exodus, the tracing of David's ancestry back to a Moabite great-grandmother in Ruth, God's regard for the vile people of Nineveh in Jonah, the account of the magi and Herod's desperate yet unsuccessful scheme to slay God's Messiah, the Beatitudes among countless other sayings of Jesus, Jesus' calling of the sinful and outcast, and the exaltation of a crucified enemy of the state as resurrected Savior of humankind, are just a few of many examples of reversal in biblical narrative.

As with paradox, these other forms of reversal challenge readers to redress their understanding of what truly matters, to see the world and adopt values that are consistent with the profession that Yahweh rules. As such, they may seem to be primarily, if not exclusively, cognitive in character. Yet it also seems to me that reversal—especially when dramatically portrayed and accompanied by other narrative techniques enticing emotional engagement—evokes both a cognitive yet affectively laden response as readers react to or embrace the reshaping of reality it presents. That biblical authors understood reversal as inviting emotional response is (as with paradox) indicated by the fact that they frequently portray or imply the affective response of characters (both positive and negative) in response to the announcements or occurrence of reversal within the narrative. For instance, recall the religious authorities' response to Jesus' embrace of marginal persons, or the ways in which Jesus recast the Law of Moses. One example should suffice:

> Again he entered the synagogue, and a man was there who had a withered hand. They watched him to see whether he would cure him on the sabbath, so that they might accuse him. And he said to the man who had the withered hand, "Come forward." Then he said to them, "Is it lawful to do good or to do harm on the Sabbath, to save life or to kill?" But they were silent. He looked around at them with anger; he was grieved at their hardness of heart and said to the man, "Stretch out your hand." He stretched it out, and his hand was restored. The Pharisees went out and immediately conspired with the Herodians against him, how to destroy him. (Mark 3:1-6)

The evangelists knew what the psychologists among others we surveyed in the previous chapter emphasized: that emotion and worldview are integrally connected. When someone messes with our understanding of reality and our place in it, we tend to emote with fear, anxiety, anger, or—depending on our perceived place in the true order of things—perhaps jubilation.

Nostalgia

The authors of biblical narrative are masters at weaving into their accounts allusions to other, most often past, biblical events and characters. This recognition is, of course, basic to any serious engagement of biblical narrative.

But scholars commonly overlook the fact that such allusion is often freighted with emotional appeal. Through these intertextual echoes, biblical authors transport some of the affective force of earlier stories (and what they have come to represent for their audience) into their own accounts in order to foster expectation, renew hope, color readers' perceptions of contemporary characters or events, and to heighten readers' perceived significance of what is taking place in the narrative. One might suspect that nostalgia is in play whenever one encounters an intertextual echo, but perhaps it would be best to focus on those instances when nostalgia appears to play a significant role in shaping reader response. For instance, we noted earlier in chapter 1 that biblical authors frequently present recitations of major events in Israel's history as leading to some sort of emotional response on the part of characters in the narrative. It is also likely that these biblical "summaries" (Josh 24:1-15; Ezra 9:5-15; Neh 9:6-37; Acts 7:2-50) were meant to function in a nostalgic manner (sometimes positively, other times negatively [as in Acts 7]) for intended readers, leading them to commit themselves all the more to the ways of blessing God provides for the characters in the story as well as for themselves. The use of nostalgia is exceedingly common in the New Testament's casting of Jesus as the fulfillment of Jewish hopes and expectations, as we will have ample opportunity to see in our discussion of Luke's infancy narrative.

Contrasting the Beautiful and the Ugly, the Desperate and Hopeful

Still another technique employed by biblical writers to evoke an affective response from readers is the juxtaposition within a scene of two sharply contrasting dispositions that represent the extremes of which humanity is capable. For example, the story of Solomon judging between the two women both claiming an infant as their son juxtaposes the sacrificial love of one woman with the callous, self-serving cruelty of the other (1 Kgs 3:16-28). David's heart-wrenching angst over the death of his rebellious son Absalom movingly displays his paternal love for a troublesome child that sought David's own life and yet also recalls David's own cruel sin against Uriah: "Now therefore the sword shall never depart from your own house" (2 Sam 12:9-12). Jesus' cry on the cross, "*Eloi, Eloi, lema sabachthani?*" captures both the desperation and hope embodied in Psalm 22 as a whole, while Stephen's heavenly vision and echo of Jesus' grace-filled words on the cross, "Father, forgive them for they know not what they do," while he meets his own end dramatically contrasts Stephen's confident hope in Jesus with the fearful, stiff-necked rejection of God's Messiah and his followers by those who stone him (Acts 7:54-60).

Affective Rhetoric and Exegesis

The discussion provided in this chapter has aimed to specify and illustrate some of the common techniques biblical authors employed to engage the emotions of their readers. Yet my interest in doing so is not simply aesthetic. Underlying this analysis and that to follow is the premise adopted in the introduction: *affective appeal in varying forms is the means by which narratives, including biblical narratives, compel us to enter their storied world and entertain the version of reality they present.* In short, authors of biblical narrative seek to elicit emotion for their rhetorical ends.

Still, it is one thing, some may argue, to recognize that authors of biblical narrative often make use of emotional appeal, and another to specify what emotional response they are seeking from their readers in any given passage or larger unit. Indeed, emotions are highly variable phenomena, influenced by all sorts of factors, only some of which are under an author's (and even a reader's) control. Doesn't this make it rather precarious to say that an author can reliably appeal to certain emotional tendencies in order to advance his or her persuasive interests? Does it make good exegetical sense to claim that in a particular passage, the author is seeking to evoke the specific emotion x in order to have reader adopt belief y?

Dealing with the emotions is precarious business. To be sure, even very skilled, informed, and emotionally sensitive readers of biblical narrative will come away from passages with varying affective responses. As argued in the previous chapter, however, emotions and emotional triggers are universal "enough" that I believe we can reasonably speculate as to what types of affective response may be sought and elicited by an author's particular construal of narrative form. Thus, we will cautiously move ahead, presuming that an author may be after a specific emotional response (or a tight range of emotional responses) in a certain passage, and then seek to discern what that targeted affective response may be. Indeed, this interpretive endeavor will be fraught with guesswork and speculation, but in this at least it will not be so different from any other type of biblical exegesis! At the same time, we would do well to match this pursuit for specificity with the realization that in some and perhaps many cases the author may not be concerned to evoke a *specific* emotion. Instead, the author may be satisfied to draw out a more general positive or negative response to certain characters or events in order to keep us emotionally invested in the narrative and gradually cultivate our affective dispositions toward the worldview he or she promotes. Moreover, we also do well to recognize that the author likely expects that different readers will have somewhat different affective responses, especially if he anticipates that his audience will include both those who are favorably disposed toward the worldview he promotes and those who are not. One of the keys to the "affective-rhetorical" approach introduced here is to determine which kind of audience the author is targeting (favorable, unfavorable, mixed?) and how he shapes the narrative's use of affect accordingly.

What, then, should be the pursuit of exegesis that is interested in unpacking the affective freight of biblical narrative, and what could be some of the benefits of this interpretive endeavor? As will be clear in what follows, I do not intend to present this form of "affective-rhetorical" analysis as a stand-alone method. As I employ it, this approach participates in the historical-critical task of discerning the intentions of the biblical author or redactor who shaped the text into its final form, and as such it is meant to complement other critical techniques employed in pursuit of that goal (such as source criticism, form criticism, redaction criticism, social-scientific criticism, rhetorical criticism, and so on). At the same time, as is clear from the material presented in this chapter, this approach also relies heavily on the insight gained from various literary critical studies that attending to the literary dimensions of biblical narrative (the "narrative-rhetorical" devices discussed above and the relation of a text to its literary context) is also crucial to understanding a text's intended function. What an "affective-rhetorical" approach adds to the exegetical endeavor is attention to another, currently neglected, avenue for discerning the meaning "leading out of" a biblical narrative.[23]

More specifically, allow me to propose the goals and attending benefits of this type of analysis, which the chapters to follow will further seek to illustrate.

Goal 1: *Just taking note of the affective dimension of biblical narrative*
One goal is simply to begin taking note of the various ways in which authors of biblical narrative invite our emotional engagement. My sense is that we have a lot to learn about this dimension of biblical narrative, and our understanding of pathos as a rhetorical device will be enhanced as we keep an eye out for it. One way to enhance our understanding of the affective dimensions of biblical narrative is to assess critically how biblical authors may be using the narrative-rhetorical techniques outlined above to evoke pathos. This is the focus of the exegetical analysis of Luke's infancy narrative presented in the following two chapters, and I will say more about this below. Yet another way we can come to appreciate more the affective dimension of biblical narrative is by calling ourselves to reflect on how the text is moving us, affectively, as readers. Perhaps this "touchy-feely" manner of intuiting the affective function of the text will not sit well with many in our field. But as a supplement to our sober, scholarly

work, it just may well help us discover something else about the text that otherwise we would not see.

Goal 2: *Discerning how affective appeal is meant to impact the reader's response to a passage*

Including the exploration of pathos in our exegetical regimens may lead us to understand more fully the function of a passage within the larger work it resides. Pathos is a largely untapped datum in our interpretive work, despite the fact that emotion may play as significant a role in shaping reader response as any purely cognitive dimension of a passage. One important element of biblical narrative to which our study of pathos could contribute is the "voice" we give to a passage, or to characters within the passage. Are we to read character dialogue or narrator description with a hint (or heavy dose) of sarcasm, genuine concern, anger, heart-panged rebuke, resigned disappointment, or a touch of humor? As I tell my students, the tone we give to a passage when reading it aloud is a major interpretive decision, for it will greatly affect the way in which a passage is heard. By attending to the affective dimensions of a passage, we may be in a better position to discern the voice implied by the author. Moreover, as we work through a larger narrative attentive to its affective dimensions, we have the potential of developing an author's "emotional repertoire"—a set of emotions that seem to be invited in certain situations—which can also help us to discern the voice we should infer within individual passages.

Another important benefit our attention to pathos might offer is that our affective response to characters and events might help us fill in "narrative gaps" in a manner invited by the author. Since the form of narrative makes it inconvenient, indeed impossible, for an author to state explicitly everything we might need to know in order to make certain sense of an event or character, authors rely on us to make inferences as we read to fill in the resulting gaps. Frequently authors of biblical narrative are intentionally reticent, calling us to participate in "discovering" the portrait of an event or character that the author is sketching by being attentive to more subtle directions they offer. Pathos may often serve as one of those subtle directions the author provides and one more factor we can take into account, especially with the more troublesome gaps we encounter. As Jenefer Robinson explains,

> The gap-filling activities I've described so far are all *cognitive*: we fill in the gaps by making causal inferences or inferences about the way the world is. But in addition to making causal inferences, readers also fill in the gaps, I suggest, through their *emotional* responses. When we respond emotionally to a text, our attention is alerted to important information about character and plot that is not explicitly asserted in the text.[24]

Still another contribution our investigation of pathos can offer our exegesis is that when different readings for a passage are proposed, affective analysis can be employed to determine which reading is more consistent with the affective tendencies and rhetorical interests of the author. Our discernment of pathos and how it is being applied can be another important, even crucial, datum for deciding between competing interpretations of a text.

Goal 3: *Discerning how the author's use of pathos betrays his rhetorical goals for the entire work*
An author's repeated use of affective appeal can also serve as another indicator of the particular rhetorical interests guiding the composition of the work as a whole. Typically, we look to the prominence of certain themes, structuring features such as enveloping and chiasm, and (when plausible) redactions the author makes to his sources as indicators of what elements the author was especially concerned to emphasize in a particular passage or the work as a whole. Yet attentiveness to an author's employment of pathos throughout his narrative can also help us to affirm or adjust our understanding of what ideas or elements of faith the author is casting in especially sharp relief. If affective appeal signals an author's rhetorical aims, emotively charged narration will lead us to the worldview the author is urging readers to embrace.

Part Two

Reading with Mind and Heart

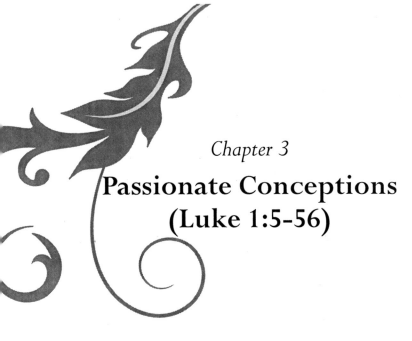

Chapter 3

Passionate Conceptions (Luke 1:5-56)

This and the chapter to follow will explore how Luke employs pathos in his infancy narrative to draw readers into his story and lead them to consider the world to which he bears witness.[1] The purpose of this investigation is to test and further illustrate the premise promoted in the preceding chapters: that is, *affective appeal in varying forms is the means by which narratives, including biblical narratives, compel us to enter their storied world and try out the version of reality they present.* If this is indeed the case, then it should follow that our attention to affective appeal can help us better understand the intended function of a particular passage and even the concerns of the work as a whole.

Why Luke's infancy narrative? Numerous features of these opening chapters suggest that they would be fertile ground for the kind of affective analysis I outlined in the previous chapter. The infancy narrative plays a crucial role in establishing the "ideological perspective" of Luke-Acts as a whole, bearing witness to fundamental claims about God, Jesus, and the salvation God is bringing to fruition, and introducing key motifs that course throughout the remainder of the Gospel.[2] If, as I have claimed, affective appeal is a primary means by which authors draw their readers into the narrative's storied world, then we should expect to find Luke employing pathos here as he sketches many features of the world he portrays. Moreover, these opening chapters would also seem to be ripe for examining affective elements in Luke's characterization. Numerous characters cross the stage in the infancy narrative, many of whom dwell there long enough for us to get a sense of their desires, inner thoughts, struggles, or triumphs. We also get to hear most of them speak, as character speech dominates these opening chapters. Such concentrated use of direct and indirect discourse leads the reader into close contact with the personalities and hopes of characters. Yet, for Luke, character speech also fulfills another crucial role in his infancy narrative: it serves as a primary means by which Luke introduces and emphasizes through consistent reiteration of themes the ideological perspective confessed by his Gospel and Acts.[3] These characters are spokespersons for Luke's view of faith and the world. And if we suspect that authors of biblical narrative might have attempted to forge an emotional connection between their readers and characters in order to facilitate their readers' embrace of the worldview these biblical authors promote, then Luke's infancy narrative would be a good place to start looking. Finally, I selected this section because in my own reading of these chapters—both critically and reflectively—I am often moved by them. I figure that if I—one of sober Germanic descent and emotionally challenged Midwestern stock—can recognize the affective power of Luke's infancy narrative, then so can most anyone.

The Ideological Landscape of Luke's Milieu

Before we get to our analysis of Luke's infancy narrative, it may be of some help to review—very briefly—the broad contours of the first-century Mediterranean's ideological landscape. What, in others words, might be some of the worldviews Luke is seeking to challenge in his narrative as he proclaims the story of God's salvation in Jesus? In suggesting the usefulness of this exercise, I am presuming that Luke "had something to prove" in the writing of his narrative, that he wrote his Gospel in order to address and sway perspectives he considered somehow less than fully formed by the truth he sought to convey, as he himself indicates in the prologue to the Gospel (1:1-4). As John A. Darr points out:

> While we may well find it advantageous to consider the audience open-minded and receptive rather than suspicious and antagonistic, it will hardly be helpful to construe it as already fully cognizant about and convinced by the "truth" (*asphaleia*, Luke 1:4) of Luke's narrative. If the audience were but a mirror image of the author's experience, knowledge, and values, then he would have little reason to write the highly rhetorical text we have before us.[4]

I will briefly describe four of the various perspectives dominating the ideological landscape of Luke's setting here and then refer back to them in the conclusion as I summarize the findings of our analysis and offer a tentative sketch of the alternative worldview that Luke is presenting in his narrative.

Caesar Is Lord

Many within the Roman world, especially those who were Roman citizens, embraced a highly structured, hierarchical view of reality in which all power, status, wealth, and privilege flowed from the throne of the emperor, who himself was the divinely ordained viceroy of the gods (and was held by some to be divine himself). The emperor was the *pater* (father) of an extended family that included the entire empire and even beyond. The Roman hierarchy was fueled by aggressive taxation and a mode of economic distribution in which nearly all wealth circulated upward toward the socially elite with much of it eventually reaching the emperor who then sanctioned or distributed the wealth others received. Figures vary, but it is commonly estimated that during Jesus' time the social elite made up 5 to 7 percent of the population and possessed 75 to 85 percent of the wealth. As a result, the vast majority of the population was living at or near subsistence level, many of whom worked as tenant farmers, artisans, or slaves. Redistribution of wealth to those of lowly estate existed on only a comparatively minor scale but took place as those of low social standing provided services or favors for wealthy patrons in exchange for goods or compensation. Commonly termed the "patron-client" relationship by scholars, it was an exceptionally meager form of "trickle-down" economics that ensured the privileged abundance and status of the elite and the precariousness of life for the vast majority.

Moses, Prophet of God's Torah

In Jesus' day and for several decades following, Palestinian Judaism was theologically and socially diverse, divided into various sects, such as the Essenes, Pharisees, Sadducees, Herodians, eventually Zealots, and likely several others. By the time Luke wrote his account (presuming a dating following the early 70s c.e.), Jews in Palestine had suffered the aftermath of the Jewish revolt and Judaism was becoming a far more unified tradition centered on the study and application of the Torah, eventually leading to what we know as Rabbinic Judaism. Of course, challenging this unity were groups of Jews who had embraced Jesus as the Messiah and his teachings as an authoritative recasting of the Mosaic law. In contrast, early Rabbinic Judaism denied that Jesus was the Messiah. It also reasserted the primacy of the Mosaic law over against Jesus' teaching and the revised understandings of law, salvation, temple, and the relationship between Jews and Gentiles promoted by Jewish and Gentile Christians.

On the Margins of the Christian Movement

Before and after Jesus' time, there were non-Jewish converts to Judaism, but more common were so-called God-fearers, Gentiles who were attracted to Judaism and participated in its religious life in varying degrees but did not undergo full conversion, including circumcision. Many have speculated that the Christian message may have been attractive to such God-fearers who were familiar with and favorable toward many elements of Jewish tradition but hesitant to adhere to all of the elements of the Mosaic law.[5] It is also likely that there were a fair number of Gentiles in Luke's day hanging on the margins of Christianity, those who found elements of Jesus and his teaching, or Christian community, engaging but had yet to take the full plunge of conversion. Reasons for this hesitation were presumably manifold. But one concern that likely held many on the periphery of Christianity, and one that many commentators believe Luke sought to address, was the legitimacy of Christianity and its professed origins in Judaism given that many of Jesus' own people failed to embrace him as God's Messiah.[6] Was Theophilus, Luke's apparent patron (see Luke 1:1; Acts 1:1), such a one?[7] Was he a God-fearer troubled by the realization that while Christians claimed Jesus as the Messiah many Jews rejected him?

Jesus Is My Lord . . . Right?

Or, was Theophilus one of these—one who had converted to Christianity but was now struggling—at least from Luke's perspective—with doubt and what it means to be a faithful Christian in the Greco-Roman world? Scholars have debated the precise meaning of Luke's own statement of his purpose in 1:4: "to write an orderly account for you, most excellent Theophilus, so that you may know the certainty/assurance/reliability/truth [ἀσφάλεια] concerning the things about which you have been instructed." It would seem that any of the common translations of ἀσφάλεια could lead us to understand Luke's Gospel as directed toward one (as described above) who may still be on the fringes of the Christian movement and need a little more convincing before committing to the faith. At the same time, the statement could also apply to one who was already a confessed Christian and active participant in a Christian community. Adopting this reading, Joel Green proposes that Luke's aim was to "strengthen the Christian movement in the face of opposition by (1) ensuring them in their interpretation and experience of the redemptive purpose and faithfulness of God and by (2) calling them to continued faithfulness and witness in God's salvific project."[8] If so, then Theophilus is (or represents) a recent convert who has some doubts concerning "the redemptive purpose and faithfulness of God." Perhaps the rejection of Jesus and Christianity by many Jews troubled both believers as well as those hanging on the margins of Christianity, thereby leading Luke to ground the Christian story thoroughly in the soil of Judaism as a means of stressing the connection between what God has done in Jesus and God's covenant commitment to Israel. Moreover, perhaps in Luke's view Theophilus and others like him do not realize the extent to which Jesus represents God in both his mission and person, explaining why Luke's project, as we shall see, takes on such a strong christological focus. Concerning faithfulness and witness, it may be that Theophilus also does not fully understand the full implications of what it means to be a disciple of Jesus. There were likely some, if not many, Gentile Christians who found themselves caught between the collision of competing worldviews. Could one be a Christian and still promote or participate in the systems of status, power, and wealth that sustained the Roman Empire? To what extent? Perhaps Theophilus's heart is divided and he is struggling to live out his confession that Jesus is Lord and Caesar is not.

This cursory listing of worldviews and notation of how some commentators see them addressed in Luke's narrative is somewhat simplistic. Still, I think it is roughly representative of the ideological terrain Luke potentially engages. Which ones of these worldviews was the evangelist's rhetorically charged narrative especially concerned to target, and in what manner? We now turn to our affective-rhetorical analysis of Luke's infancy narrative to see if the evangelist's use of emotional appeal might suggest a tentative answer.

The Evangelist's Use of Pathos in Luke 1:5—2:39

The investigation of Luke's infancy narrative will proceed in the following fashion. I will first provide an overview of each pericope, describing how it contributes to the broader portrait of God, John, Jesus, and God's salvation that Luke sketches. Then I will engage in an affective-rhetorical analysis of the text, sometimes focusing on particular interpretive issues presented by the passage in order to demonstrate the method's exegetical benefits. This analysis will examine the techniques Luke employs to engage the emotions of his readers and suggest how Luke intended his use of affective appeal to influence them.[9] Its goal will be to uncover the ideal affective response Luke is seeking from his readers in pursuit of his rhetorical ends. The discussion of each pericope will conclude by summarizing the findings of the affective-rhetorical analysis and, when relevant, indicating how the resulting interpretation differs from common scholarly assessments of the passage.

The Announcement of John's Birth (1:5-25)

[5] In the days of King Herod of Judea, there was a priest named Zechariah, who belonged to the priestly order of Abijah. His wife was a descendant of Aaron, and her name was Elizabeth. [6] Both of them were righteous before God, living blamelessly according to all the commandments and regulations of the Lord. [7] But they had no children, because Elizabeth was barren, and both were getting on in years.

[8] Once when he was serving as priest before God and his section was on duty, [9] he was chosen by lot, according to the custom of the priesthood, to enter the sanctuary of the Lord and offer incense. [10] Now at the time of the incense offering, the whole assembly of the people was praying outside. [11] Then there appeared to him an angel of the Lord, standing at the right side of the altar of incense. [12] When Zechariah saw him, he was terrified; and fear overwhelmed him. [13] But the angel said to him, "Do not be afraid, Zechariah, for your prayer has been heard. Your wife Elizabeth will bear you a son, and you will name him John. [14] You will have joy and gladness, and many will rejoice at his birth, [15] for he will be great in the sight of the Lord. He must never drink wine or strong drink; even before his birth he will be filled with the Holy Spirit. [16] He will turn many of the people of Israel to the Lord their God. [17] With the spirit and power of Elijah he will go before him, to turn the hearts of parents to their children, and the disobedient to the wisdom of the righteous, to make ready a people prepared for the Lord." [18] Zechariah said to the angel, "How will I know that this is so? For I am an old man, and my wife is getting on in years." [19] The angel replied, "I am Gabriel. I stand in the presence of God, and I have been sent to speak to you and to bring you this good news. [20] But now, because you did not believe my words, which will be fulfilled in their time, you will become mute, unable to speak, until the day these things occur."

[21] Meanwhile the people were waiting for Zechariah, and wondered at his delay in the sanctuary. [22] When he did come out, he could not speak to them, and they realized that he had seen a vision in the sanctuary. He kept motioning to them and remained unable to speak. [23] When his time of service was ended, he went to his home.

[24] After those days his wife Elizabeth conceived, and for five months she remained in seclusion. She said, [25] "This is what the Lord has done for me when he looked favorably on me and took away the disgrace I have endured among my people."

Overview

Following the highly stylized prologue (1:1-4) announcing Luke's intent to narrate the "matters that have been fulfilled among us" (my translation) (v. 1), the Gospel begins with the story of a most extraordinary birth announcement. Switching to a style of Greek reminiscent of the Greek translations of the Jewish Scriptures, Luke introduces a Jewish couple of impeccable pedigree and character: a priest of the order of Abijah, and his wife a descendant of Aaron. Zechariah and Elizabeth were "righteous before God, living blamelessly according to all the commandments and regulations of the Lord" (v. 6). Still, there was a problem. Their faithfulness was not matched with the blessing of offspring: "But they had no children, because Elizabeth was barren, and both were getting on in years" (v. 7).

In their time and place, barrenness was most feared and despised, perhaps only little less so than other physical maladies such as leprosy or physical deformation (see Luke 1:25, 36; cf. Gen 16:4; 29:32; 30:1; Deut 28:15, 18; 1 Sam 1:5-6; Pss 127:3-5; 128).[10] But in so introducing us to this couple, Luke calls to mind other extraordinary couples who were also faithful yet faced the bleak prospect of bearing no children (for example, Abraham and Sarah, parents of Isaac; Elkanah and Hannah, parents of Samuel [see 1 Sam 1:1-18]). When one takes note that Elizabeth and Zechariah were both "getting on in years" (v. 7), the couple that most prominently comes into view is Abraham and Sarah.[11] This allusion to the couple whose offspring were to become God's treasured possession (see Gen 12:1-3; 17:1-27; Exod 19:1-6) hints at what will soon be explicitly proclaimed. Another child will be born to a faithful, barren couple "getting on in years," and he too will play a major part in accomplishing God's will for Israel, and perhaps even all of humanity.

Right on cue, we quickly move from this introductory portrait to a scene that goes on to underscore Zechariah's righteousness and the grounding of this story in the soil of Jewish faith. Zechariah has been chosen by lot to perform the incense offering, an honor a priest will be called to perform only once or twice in his lifetime (vv. 8-9).[12] The people have gathered outside to lift up their voices in prayer to God (v. 10). And then the announcement the reader might have been expecting arrives. An angel appears before Zechariah, standing at the right side of the altar of incense, freezing Zechariah in terror, and says to him,

Do not be afraid, Zechariah, for your prayer has been heard. Your wife Elizabeth will bear you a son, and you will name him John. You will have joy and gladness, and many will rejoice at his birth, for he will be great in the sight of the Lord. He must never drink wine or strong drink; even before his birth he will be filled with the Holy Spirit. He will turn many of the people of Israel to the Lord their God. With the spirit and power of Elijah he will go before him, to turn the hearts of parents to their children, and the disobedient to the wisdom of the righteous, to make ready a people prepared for the Lord. (vv. 13-17)

Numerous elements of the angel's announcement identify the child to be born as one who will play a pivotal role in ushering in God's long-awaited salvation. He will be great in the sight of the Lord, he will live a life consecrated to God, he will be filled with the Holy Spirit, he will take up the vocation of the eschatological Elijah (cf. Mal 3:1; 4:5-6; Sir 48:10), and he will lead the people to repentance. Taken together, these descriptors present John as the long-expected prophetic figure whose mission is "to make ready a people prepared for the Lord." Thus, he will be a source of joy, not only for Zechariah and Elizabeth as their prayer for a son is answered, but for a multitude as their prayer for God's salvation is being fulfilled.

But then the most unsettling series of events transpires. Zechariah, so soon before trembling with terror before the messenger of God, now questions the veracity of the angelic claim: "How will I know that this is so? For I am an old man and my wife is getting on in years" (v. 18). The angel is not pleased. He identifies himself as none other than Gabriel, one who stands in the very presence of God, sent to deliver the extraordinary good news to Zechariah.[13] He rebukes Zechariah for not believing his words "which *will be* fulfilled in their time" (vv. 19-20). And so a sign is given to the disbelieving priest, but one that is punitive in kind: "you will become mute, unable to speak, until the day these things occur" (v. 20). When Zechariah finally stumbles out of the sanctuary and into the larger confines of the temple court where the people have been waiting, he tries to communicate in rudimentary sign language, but with little success. Luke reports that the people were able to discern that Zechariah had a vision, but no more. The multitude that should now be rejoicing in the angelic announcement of good news is left in the dark. In sharp contrast to Zechariah's silence and the crowd's ignorance, Elizabeth closes the scene celebrating God's gift of a child with words echoing the praise of her matriarchal ancestors of old: "This is what the Lord has done for me when he looked favorably on me and took away the disgrace I have endured among my people" (v. 25; cf. Gen 21:1 [Sarah]; Gen 30:23 [Rachel]).

Affective-Rhetorical Analysis

Luke's use of affective appeal to draw his readers into the story is apparent at numerous points in his shaping of the passage. Several of the techniques we reviewed in the previous chapter are found here: inviting admiration, inviting sympathy and perhaps even empathy, sequencing that draws connection and comparison, essential relevance, astonishing inversion of the expected, conflict, nostalgia, reversal, and even withholding resolution. Let us work through the passage again, focusing now on how these features accompany and illuminate the basic plotting of the passage and may be meant to affect Luke's audience.

In his impressive commentary on Luke, Green treats verses 8-23 as a unit distinct from, though closely connected to, verses 5-7 and 24-25. He further proposes a chiastic structure for verses 8-23:

(A) Service, Sanctuary, People (vv. 8-10)
    (B) Angel's Appearance and Zechariah's Response (vv. 11-12)
        (C) Announcement of "Good News" (vv. 13-17; cf. v. 19)
    (B') Zechariah's Objection and Angel's Response (vv. 18-20)
(A') People, Sanctuary, Service

Green notes that the chiastic structure presents "the weight of emphasis falling, as we might expect, on the angelic message concerning John's birth and role in salvation history."[14] Most commentators would concur with this assessment of Luke's emphasis, and it is difficult to argue against it. However, there may be more than one emphasis in a given passage, and the omission of verses 5-7 and verses 24-25 from Green's structuring of verses 8-23 obscures another important element Luke sought to convey in this pericope. Consider now the chiastic structure of the passage with verses 5-7 and verses 24-25 included:

(A) Faithful Couple, yet Barren Elizabeth (vv. 5-7)
    (B) Service, Sanctuary, People (vv. 8-10)
        (C) Angel's Appearance and Zechariah's Response (vv. 11-12)
            (D) Announcement of "Good News" (vv. 13-17; cf. v. 19)
        (C') Zechariah's Objection and Angel's Response (vv. 18-20)
    (B') People, Sanctuary, Service
(A') Pregnant Elizabeth Offers Faithful Praise

Of course, some may object that the chiasm as I present it does not preserve a balance of parallel elements, since Zechariah is included in (A) but not in (A'), where Elizabeth alone appears to give faithful praise and witness. But this imbalance is just my point, and Luke's, I think, as well. The pericope does not end as it began because something has gone wrong to disrupt how it was supposed to go: Zechariah doubted Gabriel's testimony and was rendered mute.

Attending to the affective and rhetorical dimensions of the passage helps us to recognize this element of the text as another Luke wished to emphasize, and prepares us for the imbalance we encounter at its ending.

How does Luke set up and prepare us for the passage's less than satisfactory ending? Verses 5-7 offer a textbook case of an author inviting both admiration and sympathy. Zechariah and Elizabeth are both celebrated by Luke as upstanding, God-fearing, righteous Jewish folk. For any of his readers with connection to Jewish tradition, including those on the margins of the Christian movement, the intent of Luke's introduction of the couple is clear: Elizabeth and Zechariah are to be admired. They are the epitome of Jewish faithfulness. The quality of their character makes the abruptly introduced plight they face all the more surprising and even distressing.[15] The righteous in Israel's past are usually blessed with offspring. Why is God withholding children from Elizabeth's womb? Thus, not only admiration, but also sympathy is invited from the reader. But in the consideration of their plight there is still another reason for the astute reader to admire the couple and become more deeply engaged in their story. "Wait a minute. Where have I heard this story before? That's right, why, Zechariah and Elizabeth are just like Abraham and Sarah!" Cued in by this nostalgic allusion, the reader begins to suspect that something astonishing is going to take place. The elderly, barren couple—just like Abraham and Sarah—is going to be blessed by God with a child. The reader is also likely to suspect that this child, as did Abraham and Sarah's offspring, is going to play a momentous role in the history of God's people.

Filled with this sense of admiration, sympathy, nostalgia, and anticipation, the reader then turns to the opening scene of Zechariah in the temple. Once again Zechariah's faithfulness is stressed, as he fulfills his priestly duties and is now blessed with the special privilege of offering the incense in the temple. The potential significance of this moment not only for Zechariah but for all of Israel is hinted at by Luke's emphatic description: "the *whole* assembly of the people was praying outside" (v. 10). Then an angel appears, as the reader likely expected to happen at some point (recalling birth announcements preserved in the Jewish Scriptures), and good news of extraordinary significance for Zechariah and Israel is revealed. A son will be born, set apart for God's service, who will "make ready a people prepared for the Lord" (vv. 13-17).

This is indeed a crescendo moment in the story. Sympathetic readers can't help but to experience the joy and rejoicing awaiting Zechariah and Elizabeth (vv. 13-14a), as they feel it on their behalf (empathy). But note how Luke affectively ups the rhetorical ante. Through nostalgic allusion and Gabriel's words, readers are also invited by the evangelist to see the joy that God was

72

working in the lives of Zechariah, Elizabeth, and Israel as potentially applying to their own lives as well: for *"many will rejoice at his birth"* (v. 14b). With
this the reader is led to wonder how this story is or could be related to his or
her own life story: this is not only good news for Zechariah and Elizabeth,
"for I too am (or could be) one of the many who rejoice in the birth of this
extraordinary babe." By inviting readers to admire Zechariah and Elizabeth, to
sympathize with their plight, and to rejoice alongside them with the news of
their blessing by God (vv. 13-14a), Luke leads readers to the very edge of also
embracing the full account of why this news is so good not only for Zechariah
and Elizabeth but for all the people (vv. 14b-17), including themselves. Thus,
at the same time Luke's portrayal reinforces the origins of God's salvation
among the most faithful of Israel and its rootedness in Judaism, the evangelist
hints that all readers are called to join the story.

A kinder author would allow readers to bask in the glow of this jubilant,
blessed scene for just a bit and gently lead us through its resolution by recounting Zechariah's own joyous response. At this point in the story, I would very
much like to see Zechariah, nervously trembling with excitement—yet still
solemnly—complete the incense offering, and then rush wildly out of the
temple whooping through the streets of Jerusalem and running home to tell
his beloved Elizabeth the good news as they passionately embrace and together
erupt in a psalm of praise for all to hear. But Luke is not so kind, at least not
here. Instead, he confronts the reader with an astonishing inversion of the
expected, as the admirable, faithful, and now wonderfully blessed Zechariah
doubts the heavenly messenger and asks for a sign: "How will I know that this is
so?" Then, picking up the narrator's own words from verse 7, he protests, "For
I am an old man, and my wife is getting on in years" (v. 18). Zechariah's questioning also forgoes any reference to the wider significance of John's birth; his
attention is limited only to his and Elizabeth's condition, as though he got stuck
on the angel's opening words and failed to hear the rest of the annunciation.
The content of Gabriel's rebuke makes it clear that this was not the response
for which he was hoping, and we are likely meant to hear it in a solemn yet
scathing tone. Zechariah's doubt is an offense to Gabriel's authority and even
that of God (v. 19), and is regarded as nothing less than a lack of faith: "Because
you did not believe my words . . ." (v. 20). The faithful Zechariah, blameless
in his adherence to God's law, is now deemed faithless at the moment when
God's will for him is most incredibly, transparently, and engagingly relayed.
His son is to be one who "makes ready a people for the Lord." But John's father,
thus far, is not ready for the extraordinary good news Gabriel announces.[16]

On one level, Zechariah's doubt is understandable. This really is unusual
news. Even Abraham questioned the workings of the divine promise when

years went by and Sarah produced no heir (Gen 15:1-3; see also 17:7), and asked for a covenant commitment from Yahweh when he was told that he would possess the land of Canaan (Gen 15:8). But the author of Genesis still emphasizes Abraham's trust in God's promise: "And he believed the LORD; and the LORD reckoned it to him as righteousness" (Gen 15:6). Such is not the case with Zechariah here in Luke. We have been told in Gabriel's opening line that Zechariah has been praying for a son all along (v. 14). Yet he now doubts God's ability to bring it to pass. Elsewhere in the Gospel requests for a sign are also consistently interpreted negatively (11:16, 29-30; 23:8).[17] Moreover, the attention Luke gives to Zechariah's inability to speak (note the redundancy in v. 22), and the resultant inability of the people to learn of and rejoice in the tremendous good news that has just been announced, further underscores the disappointing character of Zechariah's response. Zechariah's proclamation of the good news—at least for now—has been put on hold. The people discern that a vision has taken place, but so much is left unsaid. Silence and incomprehensible gesturing replace what should have been a raucous celebration, and Zechariah's service ends in quietude. Thus, as we move to the end of the unit, we find Elizabeth alone rejoicing in God's gift of a child (vv. 24-25).

The interruption readers experience in their admiration for Zechariah is jarring. Emotional ambivalence, accentuated with disappointment and even frustration, is the affect that Luke likely intends. The conflict that ensues between Zechariah and Gabriel (and also God), including Gabriel's scathing rebuke, underscores the seriousness of Zechariah's failure to trust, and further contributes to the reader's sense of discomfort. What rhetorical purpose would this emotional freefall serve? At the very moment Luke leads readers to consider that the good news for Elizabeth, Zechariah, and all the people may also be good news for themselves, he provides for them a striking, negative example of disbelief. While Zechariah's faithful service and impeccable adherence to the regulations of the law are sources of admiration, Luke immediately puts his audience on notice that this alone is not sufficient to embrace the eruption of God's salvation in their midst. Another act of faith, consistent with Zechariah and Elizabeth's admirable piety and devotion to the temple, but not guaranteed by these idealized markers of Jewish identity, is also needed. This is further emphasized by Luke's use of sequencing that invites comparison. Zechariah's lack of faith is followed by Elizabeth's praise, marking the first instance of a pattern often repeated throughout the infancy narrative: promise (Gabriel's announcement that Elizabeth will conceive) → fulfillment (Elizabeth's conception) → praise (Elizabeth's thanksgiving).[18] The wife gets it right, and the priest does not, and so Luke also prepares the reader for the reversal that will become more pronounced in the very next episode and beyond. Indeed, the passage ends on a note of praise, and in this there is hope and expectation that the message will spread. But the chorus that should have included many is now comprised of only one. Moreover, Elizabeth offers her praise in seclusion and is at this point unaware that her personal blessing of a child is really good news for all. The scene thus ends with a lack of resolution, with a priest that has so much to say and tell, but whose testimony is silenced by little faith and lack of voice. For many readers, this is unacceptable, and they eagerly await the moment of John's birth when Zechariah might then believe, have his tongue loosed, and offer his belated praise. In (subversively) shaping the narrative this way, Luke already has readers rooting for the acceptance and proclamation of the good news by the characters in the narrative, thereby preparing "the way of the Lord" within the readers themselves.

Summary

The affective dimensions of the passage, including inviting admiration, sympathy and empathy, essential relevance, astonishing inversion of the expected, conflict, nostalgia, sequencing that draws comparison (between Zechariah and Elizabeth), reversal, and withholding resolution, draw readers into the story and lead them not only to learn but also *emotionally participate in* the significance of what takes place both for the pious couple and perhaps even for themselves. A child will be born to Zechariah and Elizabeth. This is good news for the admirable couple, and Theophilus and others are invited to rejoice in God's gift of offspring for the elderly parents to be. Yet readers—having themselves been "prepared" by their connection to and happiness for Elizabeth and Zechariah—are also invited to take the next step and rejoice for themselves, for the birth of this Jewish child in the heart of Judaic identity and hope is to lead to the celebration of many. Do they dare trust this good news, or do they (like Zechariah) respond with doubt?

By tracking the affective appeal of the passage, we have also been led to a reading that helps us to affirm and account for the imbalance apparent in the episode's structure and to speculate as to its rhetorical function. Without attending to Luke's use of pathos, we would likely overlook the significance of the passage's disappointing denouement with Zechariah's failure to believe and instead focus on its proclamation of salvation. This is a tendency typical of commentators, as few identify Zechariah's lack of faith and comparison to Elizabeth as a prominent concern of the passage.[19] In fact, a common explanation scholars offer for Zechariah's disbelief and resulting muteness is that it allows for the celebration of John's significance to be delayed until the *more fitting* moment of his birth.[20] Thus, according to this view, the reader is to see Zechariah's unbelief and punitive sign of silence as ultimately fortuitous and in accord with God's initial designs! But this hardly squares with the affective tenor of the passage as sounded by the jarring and disheartening character of Zechariah's unbelief, Gabriel's sharp rebuke, and the passage's imbalanced structure. It also runs counter to a prominent motif coursing throughout the infancy narrative and the entirety of Luke-Acts: when the good news of God's salvation is announced, faithful response is portrayed as one of belief, rejoicing, and witness. Zechariah's lack of faith is fortuitous not because it ensures a fitting delay in his response of praise. Rather, the stunning disappointment and voluminous silence that result serves Luke's emotionally and rhetorically charged ends. It challenges doubting readers by showing them that those who fail to hear Gabriel's announcement as the extraordinary good news it truly is participate in Zechariah's lack of faith and render themselves as having little worthwhile to say. For those readers already inclined to believe, it leads them to desire more deeply their own embrace, celebration, and proclamation of the good news.

The Announcement of Jesus' Birth (1:26-38)

[26] In the sixth month the angel Gabriel was sent by God to a town in Galilee called Nazareth, [27] to a virgin engaged to a man whose name was Joseph, of the house of David. The virgin's name was Mary. [28] And he came to her and said, "Greetings, favored one! The Lord is with you." [29] But she was much perplexed by his words and pondered what sort of greeting this might be. [30] The angel said to her, "Do not be afraid, Mary, for you have found favor with God. [31] And now, you will conceive in your womb and bear a son, and you will name him Jesus. [32] He will be great, and will be called the Son of the Most High, and the Lord God will give to him the throne of his ancestor David. [33] He will reign over the house of Jacob forever, and of his kingdom there will be no end." [34] Mary said to the angel, "How can this be, since I am a virgin?" [35] The angel said to her, "The Holy Spirit will come upon you, and the power of the Most High will overshadow you; therefore the child to be born will be holy; he will be called Son of God. [36] And now, your relative Elizabeth in her old age has also conceived a son; and this is the sixth month for her who was said to be barren. [37] For nothing will be impossible with God." [38] Then Mary said, "Here am I, the servant of the Lord; let it be with me according to your word." Then the angel departed from her.

Overview

Gabriel's announcement to Mary follows on the heels of the annunciation of John's birth. The brief introduction to the scene establishes important points

76

of continuity and difference between the two announcements. The mention of the "sixth month" (ἐν τῷ μηνὶ τῷ ἕκτῳ) of Elizabeth's pregnancy ties the two episodes together (see also v. 36), and provides initial indication that the events announced by the first annunciation are somehow related to what now takes place. Similarly, the repeated occurrence of an angelic visit by one who is again identified as Gabriel implies that the eschatological tenor that character- ized the first episode is to be seen as continuing in these verses. The description of Gabriel as ἀπεστάλη . . . ἀπὸ τοῦ θεοῦ ("sent from God" [v. 26]) reminds us that God is the originator of these events and reaffirms the truthfulness of Gabriel's testimony. Moreover, in addition to the inclusion of Gabriel in this scene, the mention of Joseph as "of the house of David" (v. 27) maintains the connection of these events to Israelite tradition and paves the way for Jesus to be portrayed as the Davidic Messiah (see also 1:69; 2:4). Finally, the passages, both of which follow the annunciation form, also unfold in a remarkably simi- lar manner and contain numerous verbal parallels.[21]

Despite these points of continuity, the narrative context of the present episode differs from that of the previous by being far removed from the main- stream of temple piety and the status normally associated with Jerusalem, the temple, and the priesthood. The locale of Nazareth places the annunciation in an obscure town with no known significance in Jewish tradition.[22] Moreover, the character of Mary, a betrothed virgin of yet-unmentioned family origin, contrasts sharply with Zechariah, a priest serving in the temple and of the house of Aaron. As pointed out by Green:

> [Mary] is portrayed as a young girl, not yet or only recently having achieved
> puberty, in an insignificant town in a racially mixed region. Joseph is a son
> of David, but Mary has not yet joined his household and thus has no current
> claims on inherited status. Mary's family is not mentioned. Indeed, she is not
> introduced in any way that would recommend her to us as particularly note-
> worthy or deserving of honor. In light of the care with which other charac-
> ters are introduced and portrayed as women and men of status in Luke 1–2,
> this is remarkable. Mary's insignificance seems to be Luke's primary point
> in his introduction of her.[23]

Yet the insignificance shrouding Mary's character is only momentary. With Gabriel's greeting the reader is called to a completely different assessment. The expression ὁ κύριος μετὰ σοῦ ("the Lord is with you")[24] and the clarify- ing statement of verse 30, εὗρες γὰρ χάριν παρὰ τῷ θεῷ ("for you have found favor with God"), which parallels κεχαριτωμένη ("favored one") in verse 28, both suggest that Mary is to be viewed as one who will play a key part in forwarding God's covenant relationship with Israel. Of the many instances of the several forms of the expression ὁ κύριος μετὰ σοῦ in the LXX, the overwhelming majority are predicated of individuals whom God calls to serve an essential role in fulfilling God's covenant promises to Abraham's offspring: Isaac (Gen 26:3, 24, 28); Jacob (Gen 28:15; 31:3); Joseph (Gen 39:2, 21); Moses (Ex 3:12); Joshua (Josh 1:5, 9, 17; 3:7; 6:27); Judah (Judg 1:19); Gideon (Judg 6:12, 16); Samuel (1 Sam 2:26); David (1 Sam 18:28; 2 Sam 7:3); Solomon (1 Kgs 11:38); Jehoshaphat (2 Chron 17:3); Jeremiah (Jer 1:8, 19; 15:20).[25] Similarly, forms of the statement εὗρες γὰρ χάριν παρὰ τῷ θεῷ also occur with respect to individuals at key moments in the history of the relationship between God and God's people: Noah (Gen 6:8); Abraham (Gen 18:3); Gideon (Judg 6:17). The use of this terminology for Mary places the young virgin in rather exalted company: she is to be counted among the leading figures in Israel's history as one called to help bring about God's desires for God's people.

Given the implications of Gabriel's greeting, it is surely understandable that Mary is "much perplexed" (NRSV) or "utterly confused"[26] by this address (v. 29). But she has little time to ponder "what sort of greeting this might be." Gabriel again affirms her favor before God and then presents a most unexpected announcement, "And now, you will conceive in your womb and bear a son, and you will name him Jesus" (v. 31).

Scholars have long noted that the annunciations of John's and Jesus' birth are to be seen in parallel relationship, with the result that Jesus emerges as the (much) greater child than John. Conceptual and verbal correspondences between the accounts draw direct connections between the two figures and reveal Jesus as the superior of the two, resulting in a "step-parallelism."[27] Many commentators are content to point out this feature of the text without providing any explanation for it other than simply Luke's intent to portray the superiority of Jesus with respect to John.[28] Others have sought to attribute Luke's use of step-parallelism between John and Jesus to an apologetic interest. For instance, Raymond Brown concludes that the early Christian concern to present Jesus as greater than John, as revealed in Luke and the other canonical Gospels, stems from the presence of a messianic sect proclaiming John as the Christ.[29] Still others follow Hans Conzelmann's lead in arguing that in Luke's Gospel John represents the Period of Israel. They claim that in his infancy narrative Luke shows this period as superseded by the Period of Jesus' ministry both by the fact that Jesus is revealed as the greater of the two and by the narrative's steady progression toward focusing exclusively on Jesus.[30] While it is plausible that Luke's shaping of the account may have been in part motivated by apologetic concerns, three elements of Luke's portrayal of John and Jesus in their paired annunciations and throughout the infancy narrative point to a more complete explanation for the step-parallelism he employs in Luke 1–2. In short, the point of the step-parallelism is not simply to portray Jesus as greater than John, but to compare Jesus' greatness with the greatness of God. Christology, not apologetics, is Luke's primary concern.[31] The evangelist, in other words, is not worried about how Theophilus views Jesus with respect to John, but how Theophilus views Jesus with respect to God.

First, Athalya Brenner has observed that biblical stories of birth are often cast as situations in which two mothers-to-be are placed in competition with one another, with the effect that "one of the newborn children (usually the first) will prove to be a 'false' hero; and only one, as time will tell, will be the 'real' hero who carries the divine promise."[32] But, as Brenner points out, such competition and "one-upmanship" are clearly not guiding patterns for Luke's presentation of Jesus and John, nor for Mary and Elizabeth.[33]

Second, the correspondences in Luke's portrayal of John and Jesus in the paired annunciations and throughout the infancy narrative not only reveal the differences between them but also serve to emphasize their common mission as well as the exalted significance of *both* of them. As Augustin George rightly points out, Luke's parallel presentation of John and Jesus shows that "it is the single and same design of God which they come to accomplish."[34] In fact, the very details that constitute the parallels between them present both Jesus and John as exalted figures crucial to the unfolding of God's plan: the advent of each is hailed as marking the fulfillment of God's awaited salvation; both are "great"; both are empowered by God's Spirit. These observations call into question the view that Luke's exclusive or even primary concern throughout the infancy narrative with respect to the relationship between Jesus and John is to show that John is inferior to Jesus.

A third factor indicating the need for an explanation other than those already suggested is the observation that throughout the infancy narrative Luke avoids directly stating that John prepares the way for Jesus. Instead, John is presented as the eschatological Elijah who prepares the way of the Lord *God* (1:15-17, 76-77). It is only by implication that members of Luke's audience are able to discern that Jesus is the one for whom John prepares. An adequate explanation of the relationship between Jesus and John must account for this feature of Luke's presentation.

In my view, the cooperative tone dominating Luke's account, the emphasis upon both John and Jesus as persons essential to the accomplishment of God's awaited advent, and the fact that Luke presents John as readying Israel for the advent of Yahweh *and* Jesus, together suggest that Luke is primarily concerned to portray the greatness of Jesus not vis-à-vis John who some have thought is the Messiah, nor vis-à-vis John as the representative of the Period of Israel, but vis-à-vis John as one who *prepares the way of the Lord*. This proposal helps us grasp two important functions served by the step-parallelism Luke composes between John and Jesus. First, it is Jesus' superior greatness and significance with respect to John as revealed in the step-parallelism Luke employs that sets him apart as the one for whom John prepares. Otherwise, Jesus' role in the unfolding of God's salvation becomes unclear: that is, if John prepares the way of the Lord God— and not that (also) of Jesus—then how does Jesus, who is greater than John and who is hailed Messiah and Son of God, fit into God's plan of restoration? By his portrayal of Jesus as greater than John, Luke implies that Jesus must be the one whose way John readies. At the same time, the seeming contradiction that this implication creates (how can John be directly said to prepare the way of the Lord God, while it is clearly implied by the narrative that it is Jesus for whom John prepares?) invites Luke's audience to consider that Yahweh's awaited advent and Jesus' coming are somehow one and the same. It also invites Luke's audience to reflect upon the nature of the relationship between Jesus and God.[35]

Second, the descriptions of Jesus' significance and person provided by Luke's characters not only provide a point of comparison between Jesus and John, *they are also the very details that suggest a convergence of mission and person between Jesus and God*. Thus, in the case of the paired annunciations, it is crucial to note that the attributes of Jesus' person and the description of his mission provided by Luke do not simply serve to reveal the superiority of Jesus (and thus imply that Jesus is also—somehow—the one for whom John prepares). Just as importantly, they are what cast Jesus in a manner that further leads Luke's audience to perceive that Jesus' coming fulfills Yahweh's awaited advent. In other words, Jesus is not simply greater than John and thus the one for whom John prepares. Jesus is greater than John and the one for whom John prepares because he represents Yahweh in his mission and person.

In the words of Gabriel, Luke assigns to Jesus features of mission and person that are typically predicated only of God in Jewish tradition: Jesus is, without qualification, "great" (v. 32)[36] and "holy" (v. 35).[37] Not only does Luke twice apply the titular designation "Son of the Most High/Son of God" to Jesus (vv. 32, 35), he also draws a direct connection between Jesus' designation as the Holy One, Son of God, and his conception by a creative act of the Holy Spirit: "The Holy Spirit will come upon you, and the power of the Most High will overshadow you; *therefore* [διό] the child to be born will be called holy; he will be called the Son of God" (v. 35). As Raymond Brown aptly puts it:

> But the way these ideas [Holy Spirit, conception, sonship] are combined in
> 1:35 takes us out of the realm of Jewish expectation of the messiah and into

the realm of early Christianity. The action of the Holy Spirit and the power of the Most High come not upon the Davidic king but upon his mother. We are not dealing with the adoption of a Davidid by coronation as God's son or representative; we are dealing with the begetting of God's Son through God's creative Spirit.[38]

What sets Jesus apart from someone as great as John is what sets him apart from all others: he is the Spirit-conceived Divine Son, called into existence not by a human union but by the very Spirit of God. Thus, an essential point of Luke's description of Jesus in the annunciation—and a point that must not be missed—is its emphasis on the very close relation between Jesus and God. This close relation is expressed both in terms of Jesus' accomplishment of God's promised salvation as God's messianic divine agent who will reign on Jacob's throne forever *and* his very person as the uniquely great, holy, and Spirit-conceived Divine Son. In sum, not only does Luke intend to present Jesus in comparison to John through his use of step-parallelism here, but also in comparison to God. The reason Jesus is greater than John, and thus the one for whom John prepares, is because Jesus participates more fully than anyone else in the greatness of Yahweh.[39]

While Luke's disclosure of Jesus' person and mission is an essential element of the passage, so too is Mary's response to her encounter with Gabriel and his extraordinary announcement. Mary's interaction with the annunciation is conveyed at the beginning, middle, and end of the passage: her puzzlement (v. 29), her question of Gabriel (v. 34), and her response of devotion (v. 38). The characterization that thus emerges in Luke's shaping of the pericope is of a girl initially overwhelmed by this most unexpected (good?) news, who struggles to comprehend it, and then impressively overcomes that fear and confusion to embrace what God has in store for her: "Behold [ἰδού], I am the servant of the Lord; let it be with me according to your word" (my translation).[40] Coming on the heels of John's birth announcement and opening with the conspicuous "Behold!" Mary's faithful response stands in sharp contrast to the doubting of Zechariah. Thus, the step-parallelism that exists between these two passages is not only between Jesus and John. It exists between Mary and Zechariah as well, with the Jewish girl embracing her even more incredible call with a humble trust that far outstrips the trembling doubt of the righteous priest.

Affective-Rhetorical Analysis

Again in this pericope, we find Luke employing a host of techniques designed to elicit an affective response from his audience: the amazing and paradoxical news of a virgin-born child whose person and mission mirror that of Yahweh, sequencing that draws comparison (in the form of step-parallelism) between John and Jesus and Mary and Zechariah, reversal, and characterization that invites reader sympathy and identity. As a means of exploring—in an economical fashion—Luke's use of affect to serve his rhetorical ends in this theologically dense passage, my analysis will revolve around Mary's question of Gabriel in verse 34: "How can this be, since I do not know a man?" (my translation). Mary's query presents two problems for interpreters. Why is Mary's question, unlike that of Zechariah, not regarded by Gabriel as an instance of unfaithful doubt? The second is more difficult. Why does Mary ask the question in the first place? As one who was betrothed and awaiting marriage, shouldn't she assume that her conception of Jesus would result from her union with Joseph?

Various solutions have been proposed. Darrell Bock helpfully summarizes six of the more common proposals.[41]

1. Mary questions Gabriel because she had already taken a vow of perpetual virginity.
2. Mary knows that Isaiah 7:14 teaches that the mother of the Messiah is a virgin, so she questions Gabriel on how the conception is to occur.
3. The question results from an awkward insertion of verses 34-37.
4. The question is simply a literary device to provide the opportunity for Gabriel to elaborate on his announcement.
5. The account Luke gives is not a verbatim account, so we should expect some inconsistencies in Luke's shaping of it.
6. The traditional view, still held by a few and endorsed by Bock, is that Mary understood the angel to be announcing an imminent pregnancy.

The view that has won the support of most recent commentators is that Luke uses the question as a literary device to set up the further disclosure of Jesus' person and mission in verse 35, including his conception by the Holy Spirit.[42] This solution is indeed plausible, but it ultimately leaves a gaping narrative gap unfilled by not offering an explanation of how Luke intended the question to be handled by a reader. Did Luke simply expect his readers to gloss over the disjunctive query? Did he get sloppy here? I believe Luke was a more conscientious author than this explanation suggests, and that by tracing how

Luke promotes his rhetorical aims in this account through his use of pathos we may be able to come up with a better solution.

What were Luke's rhetorical aims in this passage? It seems to me that Luke sets out in this story to present some pretty extraordinary ideas about the mission and person of Jesus. His notion of Jesus' divine sonship, eternal reign, and conception by the Holy Spirit were likely matters of heated contention between Christians and non-Christian Jews, and were perhaps even debated among Christians, with some holding to an adoptionist notion of Jesus' sonship that was more consistent with Jewish tradition.[43] As noted above, Mark Strauss likewise suggests that "Luke seems to be consciously opposing the view that Jesus' sonship is merely 'functional'—a special relationship with God by virtue of his role as king."[44] Luke, in other words, through his paradoxical portrait of Jesus, would be seen by many of his potential readers (including, perhaps, Theophilus) as pushing the christological envelope, even confusing the boundaries between Jesus and God, the human and the divine. As of means of leading readers at least to entertain the portrait of Jesus he presents despite the dissonance it creates, Luke presents Mary as an admirable, sympathetic character, whose own confusion is ultimately overcome as she responds to Gabriel's incredible words with startling faith.[45] Insofar as readers relate to Mary via the sympathy or reader identity Luke invites for her as one who is understandably unprepared for the wondrous announcement she receives, and admire her for the courageous trust she nevertheless exhibits at the end, they are also prodded to join Mary in responding to these extraordinary claims with their own bold devotion.

Allow me to unpack this with a few more specifics. The primary way Luke seeks to cultivate reader sympathy for Mary is to present her as a vulnerable, admirable character, favored by God, and yet completely befuddled by Gabriel's announcement. Luke employs the emphatic διαταράσσομαι (to be much perplexed or greatly confused) to underscore Mary's bewilderment and disturbance.[46] In addition, he diverges from the typical annunciation form by portraying Mary's reaction not as fear directed at the sudden appearance of the angelic visitor (as is standard; cf. 1:12), but as intense puzzlement *at his greeting*, which signals her important role in God's designs for Israel. Note too the redundancy (via synonymous parallelism) in verse 29 lest the reader miss this point:

But she was much perplexed by his words and pondered what sort of greeting this might be.

ἡ δὲ ἐπὶ τῷ λόγῳ διεταράχθη καὶ διελογίζετο ποταπὸς εἴη ὁ ἀσπασμὸς οὗτος.

The oddity of Mary's reaction and the intensity of her puzzlement—along with our attentiveness to its affective and rhetorical function—provide the cues we need for filling in the gap created by her seemingly out-of-place query in verse 34. To be sure, Luke likely has as a motive in composing the question his desire to say more about Jesus' manner of conception. But in terms of Luke's narrative portrait of the young virgin, the ill-aimed (but ultimately right-on) question also makes sense as another display of Mary's angst and confusion, which Luke has emphasized from the start. Mary, at this point in the narrative, is completely out of sorts with what Gabriel has just announced about her and the child she will bear. For her, unlike Zechariah, the problem is mental and emotional overload, not doubt. Accordingly, she does not ask for a sign as a test of God's faithfulness.[47] Rather, beside herself, she confusedly asks, "How is this going to happen?"

But why would Luke so emphasize Mary's bewilderment and portray it as continuing on into verse 34? Luke does it in order to maintain his audience's sympathy for Mary even as he then goes on to relay even more extraordinary claims about Jesus' conception and person. Moreover, readers are also likely meant to sense Mary's bewilderment continuing through Gabriel's response to her query. Using Mary's question as an opportunity to elaborate on the greatness of her child, Gabriel provides additional explanation (v. 35), an unrequested sign (v. 36), and a profession about God (v. 37). But note, the incredible explanation regarding the instigation of her pregnancy hardly seems to clarify the issue! Has a more mysterious and undefined manner of conception ever been conceived? In the reader's mind, Mary's perplexity is certainly understandable. Some readers may even identify with Mary's confusion and claim her as an ally, for these notions about Jesus and his manner of conception are in their minds just too strange to grasp.

But then, when Mary hears what God has done for Elizabeth, and the angel's profession about what is possible for God, Mary remarkably pulls out of her befuddlement and embraces Gabriel's words. Or, better said, perhaps we are meant to see her as putting faith in God despite her continuing uncertainty about the details concerning Jesus and his conception.[48] And in this Luke intends her to serve as an example for those who sympathize with her and perhaps even identify with her confusion. For the assurance Gabriel provides seems directed at doubting/confused readers as much as it is at Mary. Yes, this really is amazing, hard-to-believe stuff about Jesus and how he came to be, Luke admits. But recall what God has already done for Elizabeth, he reminds the reader. Then comes the poignant profession: "For *nothing* will be impossible with God" (ὅτι οὐκ ἀδυνατήσει παρὰ τοῦ θεοῦ πᾶν ῥῆμα). And the skeptical reader is invited to respond in a way that matches Mary's admirable trust and devotion: "Here am I, the servant of the Lord; let it be with me according to your word." All those long years, Zechariah prayed for what he is not willing to believe in. Mary believes what she could have never before imagined. Luke's audience is invited to follow her lead and do the same.

Summary

In this pericope, Luke seeks to elicit affective response from his audience in various ways: the drafting, in part through step-parallelism, of amazing and paradoxical news of a divinely conceived child born to a virgin, characterization that invites reader sympathy and identity, additional sequencing that draws comparison between Mary and Zechariah and in doing so composes reversal. By focusing on Luke's characterization of Mary as a means by which he invites the emotional engagement of readers to serve his rhetorical ends, we are led to see how the gaps created by Mary's question can be filled. Within the flow of Luke's narrative, Mary's question displays her ongoing confusion and provides readers further opportunity to sympathize with her or even to identify with the difficultly she is having grasping this incredible news. The answer Gabriel provides Mary and the reader as to the manner of Jesus' conception is more extraordinary still. But this is then immediately followed by a reminder of the remarkable things of which God is capable, an assurance that calls readers back to the heart of biblical faith: *nothing* is impossible for God. Wouldn't Theophilus and other readers want to be part of a world in which this is so? Wouldn't they want their doubt and confusion dispelled by the kind of trust Mary displays? *Nothing* is impossible for God, even something as strange as a divine-like savior conceived by the Holy Spirit and born to a virgin peasant girl. Luke invites his readers to embrace this good news about God and Jesus, and to welcome the outlandish, category-defying world God is fashioning among them.

Mary Visits Elizabeth (1:39-56)

[39] In those days Mary set out and went with haste to a Judean town in the hill country, [40] where she entered the house of Zechariah and greeted Elizabeth. [41] When Elizabeth heard Mary's greeting, the child leaped in her womb. And Elizabeth was filled with the Holy Spirit [42] and exclaimed with a loud cry, "Blessed are you among women, and blessed is the fruit of your womb. [43] And why has this happened to me, that the mother of my Lord comes to me? [44] For as soon as I heard the sound of your greeting, the child in my womb leaped for

joy. [45] And blessed is she who believed that there would be a fulfillment of what was spoken to her by the Lord." [46] And Mary said,

"My soul magnifies the Lord,
[47] and my spirit rejoices in God my Savior,
[48] for he has looked with favor on the lowliness of his servant.
Surely, from now on all generations will call me blessed;
[49] for the Mighty One has done great things for me,
and holy is his name.
[50] His mercy is for those who fear him
from generation to generation.
[51] He has shown strength with his arm;
he has scattered the proud in the thoughts of their hearts.
[52] He has brought down the powerful from their thrones,
and lifted up the lowly;
[53] he has filled the hungry with good things,
and sent the rich away empty.
[54] He has helped his servant Israel,
in remembrance of his mercy,
[55] according to the promise he made to our ancestors,
to Abraham and to his descendants forever."

[56] And Mary remained with her about three months and then returned to her home.

Overview

Mary's visit to Elizabeth further binds together the stories of John and Jesus, with the result that it continues to express three crucial elements that the narrative up to this point has thus far implied or emphasized: Jesus is the one for whom John is to prepare the way, the merging of Jesus' and Yahweh's mission and person, and the reversal that will characterize the manifestation of God's saving rule. Beginning with a temporal marker ("in those days") that is typical of Lukan style (see also 2:1; 4:2; 5:35; 6:12; 9:36; 23:7; Acts 1:15; 11:27), Mary is portrayed as journeying "with haste" (μετὰ σπουδῆς) to the house of Zechariah.[49] Her eagerness is likely meant to convey her obedience to the command to "go and see" implicit in Gabriel's giving of the sign (1:36) and demonstrates that her pledge to respond faithfully to the word of God (v. 38) is immediately honored.[50] Upon her arrival and greeting, the unborn John leaps (σκιρτάω) in Elizabeth's womb.[51] What Gabriel announced in 1:15 is now revealed as having come to pass: John is filled with the Spirit even before his birth, and from the womb he hails the advent of the eschatological age embodied in the one to come after him.[52] The sign given by the unborn John is then interpreted by Elizabeth as she too is filled with the Holy Spirit. Like Mary in the previous episode, Elizabeth is now granted a revelation of her own concerning Jesus' conception and significance. Moreover, John's leaping and Elizabeth's Spirit-led response mark the first of numerous occurrences throughout the birth narrative in which human characters are filled with the Holy Spirit and subsequently serve as spokespersons for God (see also 1:67; 2:27).[53] The bestowal of the Spirit upon a faithful Israelite also recalls the expectation that the Spirit would be poured out upon the righteous at the time of God's awaited deliverance.[54] The emphatic expression ἀνεφώνησεν κραυγῇ μεγάλῃ ("exclaimed with a great cry") characterizes Elizabeth's prophetic speech as an outpouring of unrestrained joy.[55]

In so bringing the two yet-unborn eschatological agents and their mothers together, Luke once again expresses the implied contrast between Jesus and John that was communicated in the previous episodes. Yet here, as before, Jesus is portrayed as greater not so much to indicate his superiority over John, but to reveal Jesus as the one for whom John prepares, even though it has been directly stated that John prepares the way for Yahweh (vv. 15-17). That this is a guiding impulse for the episode's presentation of John and Jesus is made clear by the immediate reaction of the unborn John upon Mary's arrival and its effect. It is John's Spirit-inspired leaping in the womb that puts the scene into motion and functions as the catalyst for Elizabeth's Spirit-inspired interpretation of that sign. Not only does the progression of the narrative in verses 41-42 show this, Elizabeth herself explicitly connects John's stirring (v. 44) with her recognition that Mary is the mother of "my Lord":

And why has this happened to me, that the mother of my Lord comes to me? For as soon as I heard the sound of your greeting, the child in my womb leaped for joy. (v. 43)

In effect, John has begun his ministry of "going before the Lord." His calling to hail the advent of Israel's awaited salvation begins in the womb and is given voice by his mother, who is moved by the same Spirit who stirs him. Already John is "announcing" the coming of one who is greater than himself (cf. 3:15-17), and that one is Jesus.

Moreover, that the intent of Luke's portrayal is not simply to portray Jesus vis-à-vis John, but also vis-à-vis God, is further indicated by Elizabeth's designation of Jesus as κύριος ("Lord") in verse 43. Interpreters have had difficulty assessing the significance of Luke's use of κύριος for Jesus here, while noting the evangelist's use of the same term of God immediately following in verses 45 and 46. The modification of κύριος in verse 43 by the possessive pronoun μου suggests to some that it may be functioning simply as a term of respect, as in "my lord" or "my master." Others point out that the expression could be taken as an allusion to Psalm 110:1 (cited by Luke in 20:41-44 and Acts 2:34) and thus a messianic designation (cf. 1:32-33).[56] Indeed, the pairing of χριστός with κύριος in 2:11 supports a meaning for "Lord" that is closely associated with Jesus' identity as the Messiah. However, Luke's portrayal of Elizabeth as "filled with the Spirit" and knowing details concerning Mary and her offspring (that except for the Spirit's inspiration she would otherwise not know) argues for an even more exalted sense to the expression. For Luke thus gives the impression that in being filled with the Spirit, Elizabeth knows all of what was announced by the angel Gabriel to Mary. Therefore, in discerning the meaning of "my Lord" here in verse 43, one must view it in connection to Luke's portrayal of Jesus in the preceding annunciation.

Beyond simply echoing a messianic allusion, the use of the title for Jesus further suggests what the preceding narrative has already disclosed: the very close relation between Jesus and God in both mission and person. Supporting this proposal is the repeated use of κύριος as a title both for God (1:6, 9, 11, 15, 17, 25, 38, 45, 46; 2:9, 15, 22, 23, 24, 26, 29) and Jesus (1:44; 2:11) throughout the infancy narrative, including 1:76 where it is unclear to whom it refers. It appears that Luke is inviting his audience to consider the close relationship between Yahweh and Jesus through his interchangeable and ambiguous use of the title. Furthermore, the pronouncement of Jesus as χριστὸς κύριος ("Messiah Lord") in Luke 2:11 parallels Acts 2:36, leading Joseph Fitzmyer to conclude that the understanding of Jesus as Lord in Acts has been retrojected back into the infancy account.[57] According to Fitzmyer and Larry Hurtado among others, the designation of Jesus as κύριος in Acts and throughout the New Testament reflects a confession widespread in early Christianity that in some sense regarded Jesus on a level with Yahweh (cf. Phil 2:5-11).[58] Indeed, the exaltation of Jesus as κύριος will be more straightforwardly expressed in the narrative to follow. Even so, Gabriel's annunciation of Jesus' conception by the Holy Spirit and his identity as the great and holy Son of God who will reign forever affirms the exalted sense of κύριος here in Elizabeth's greeting: Jesus comes as one not only representing God in his mission but also, as one uniquely related to God, he represents Yahweh in his person to such an extent that he, too, is rightly called Lord.[59]

Just as the amazing and paradoxical news of a divine savior carries over from the previous passage into Elizabeth's greeting, so too does the notice that the dawning eschatological age will be marked by reversal. In verse 42,

Elizabeth hails Mary as "blessed . . . among women" and "mother of my Lord." Brown notes that εὐλογήμενος ("blessed") is typically used to invoke the blessing of God upon an individual, "but in the present passage the Holy Spirit enables Elizabeth to recognize that the blessing has already been granted by God."[60] This recognition by the elder Elizabeth of God's greater blessing of Mary, when Elizabeth herself has also been extraordinarily blessed by God, leads to a striking inversion of social order. Joel Green aptly explains:

> Elizabeth first receives greetings from Mary. This is proper, for Elizabeth is clearly the superior, by normal canons at least. She is the daughter of Aaron, the wife of a priest, the elder of these two women. What is more, had she not received divine affirmation in the blessing of a child? What is surprising, then, is Elizabeth's greeting to Mary. Prompted by the child in her womb, filled with the Holy Spirit, she places herself in the servant's role, bestowing honor on her guest whom she now recognizes as "the mother of my Lord," "blessed . . . among women." Suddenly the tables have turned, and we have from Elizabeth a second testimony to the favored status of Mary first proclaimed by Gabriel (1:28, 30).[61]

In addition to the social reversal apparent in the portrayal of Mary and Elizabeth, the stark contrast drawn between Mary and Zechariah via Elizabeth's beatitude in verse 45 continues the reversal surrounding these two characters that began in the previous episode. Again, Mary, the young virgin, is cast as one whose faith far outshines the pious yet doubting Zechariah.

Elizabeth's Spirit-inspired and joyful greeting is met in response by Mary's equally jubilant hymn of praise. Some have thought that Mary's canticle is situated somewhat awkwardly in the narrative, leading to various source and redaction critical theories regarding its provenance and adaptation by Luke. Yet the Magnificat fits well within the context of Luke's infancy account. As a response to Elizabeth's greeting, it takes up but then moves beyond the celebration of Jesus' conception as an event that God has accomplished for Mary, to its celebration as a saving act that the Merciful and Mighty One has worked on behalf of all Israel. Throughout, the canticle is replete with references to God's deliverance, which themselves are rich with allusion to the Jewish Scriptures.[62] Such a close reduplication of many Jewish themes and expressions as Mary rejoices in Jesus' conception (v. 49) continues to reinforce Luke's claim that Jesus' birth is God's decisive act of restoration fulfilling God's long-standing promise to redeem Israel and dwell with God's people forever.[63]

From beginning to end, the Magnificat exclaims that the saving event at hand—the advent of Jesus—and the attending blessedness it brings to Mary

and Israel, emerges from God's sovereignty and will. So clearly and intentionally does the canticle burst forth with this proclamation that this point
may hardly seem to need further elaboration. Yet as the hymn celebrates God's
active role in what is now taking place among them, it emphasizes elements
of God's character that were more implicit in the preceding episodes.[64] At the
start, Mary rejoices in "God my Savior" (τῷ θεῷ τῷ σωτῆρί μου), echoing
a fundamental element of God's character professed in Jewish tradition. The
attribution also functions as a fitting introduction to the salvation described in
the verses to follow, for God's role as savior in the Jewish Scriptures is typically
associated with both God's merciful keeping of the covenant and his victory
over Israel's enemies.[65]

Repeated references to God's ἔλεος ("mercy": vv. 50, 54b) and the
hymn's closing lines announcing God's fulfillment of the covenantal promises
(vv. 54-55) repeat the long-standing claim of Israel's testimony that mercy,
or steadfast love, is an enduring feature of God's character and that which
sustains God's covenant with God's people. In further magnification of God as
savior, Mary's canticle also celebrates God as ὁ δυνατός ("Mighty One") and
who has done "mighty things" (μεγάλα), proclaiming the victory that God has
won over the δυνάσται (powerful) of this world by the strength of God's arm
(βραχίων, v. 52). With these expressions, Mary celebrates God's sovereignty
over all things. The title "Mighty One," with its allusions to the LXX, also casts
God as the Divine Warrior (Deut 10:17; Ps 23:8 [LXX]; Jer 39:18; Isa 10:21;
42:13; Zeph 3:17) who overthrows the enemies of Israel (here the δυνάσται
of the world). The expression ἅγιον τὸ ὄνομα αὐτοῦ ("holy is his name") in
verse 49b likely echoes Psalm 110:9 (LXX) and similarly carries overtones of
God's power and transcendence.[66]

The portrayal of God as merciful and mighty Savior-Warrior who acts
on behalf of God's people rehearses traditional Jewish notions about God
and God's will. Yet when Mary's praise is joined with Elizabeth's greeting
and the preceding episodes, these very traditional notions about Yahweh's
character take on a strikingly paradoxical hue. "For the Mighty One has
done great things for me, and holy is his name!" cries Mary (v. 49). In her
words we find the startling juxtaposition of God's immanence and transcendence, for the "great things" that the Mighty One has accomplished
with the "strength of his arm" begin with God's intimate involvement in
the lives of these two Jewish women, fashioning human life in barren and
virgin wombs. God is portrayed by Luke as immanent in the most private
and earthy of domains. Even more, their two children will grow to become
God's instruments in the accomplishment of God's long-awaited restoration of God's people and (as we later find out) all of humanity.[67] The saving

90

deeds of the sovereign Divine Warrior will be wrought by their hands. In fact, the second of the two is—beyond reason—to be known as "Lord." For in him, somehow and someway, God's presence and power will dwell so completely that he himself will represent Yahweh in both his mission and person.

Indeed, in countless Old Testament stories, we find Yahweh intimately engaged in the lives of God's human creatures. God blesses and calls them to faithfulness in hope that God's dreams for Israel and all of humanity will be realized. And, of course, this isn't the first time God has meddled in birth processes to bring forth offspring to lead God's people. However, the close proximity of the two miraculous conceptions to Mary's jubilant celebration of Yahweh as mighty Savior and Warrior, *and* the degree to which the second offspring will represent both Yahweh's own mission and person, presents a portrait of God whose transcendence is matched with an incredible immanence. In short, Luke presents "God my Savior," the sovereign and powerful Divine Warrior, as intimately at work in the womb and offspring of Elizabeth, and amazingly incarnate in the womb and offspring of Mary. The categories of human and divine are being pulled and stretched in remarkable ways.

The salvation that Mary proclaims as being accomplished with the conception of her child also turns the tables on established socioeconomic norms. In the previous episodes, Luke presented reversal through his portrayal of the characters who were first to receive the announcement of God's coming salvation, including Elizabeth's and Mary's faithfulness in contrast to Zechariah's slowness to believe. In the Magnificat, this reversal continues yet moves to a much broader character set and political scope as all of faithful Israel are held in opposition to those who counter God's will for humanity. Representative of God's people, the ταπεινοί (lowly) and the πεινῶντες (hungry) shall be exalted while the δυνάσται (powerful) and the πλουτοῦντες (rich) will be brought low. The notion of reversal of fortune is well represented in the Old Testament (1 Sam 2:7; Job 12:19; 22:29; Ezek 21:26; Sir 10:14, 11:4-6; Pss 17:28; 137:6; Prov 3:34) as is God's favor upon and exaltation of the lowly or poor, especially in the Psalms (see Pss 9:9; 12:5; 67:11; 81:1b-4; 108:31; 112: 7-8; 139:13; 144:14-16; 146:3 [all LXX]; Isa 25:4).[68] Concerning the portrayal of the poor in the psalter, Stephen Farris observes:

> There seem to be three closely related elements in the use of the language about the "poor": attitude, situation and national identity. The poor are not only the destitute; they are also those who depend utterly upon Yahweh. They are, however, also very often those who live in real affliction and cry to Yahweh because of their need. They are also recipients of salvation; God

sees their weakness and delivers them from it. Finally, the word can be a self-designation for Israel.[69]

Farris points out that each of the dimensions surrounding the portrayal of the poor in the psalter are relevant to the Magnificat.[70] Here, the "poor" are also presented as those who are opposite of the proud (v. 51), the "powerful" (v. 52a), and the "rich" (v. 53a). They are those "who fear God" (v. 50), the "lowly" (vv. 48a, 52b), the "hungry" (v. 53b), and ultimately, "Israel" (v. 54) for whom God has acted (vv. 51-54). Farris adds that in the Magnificat "that rescue of the poor which is so characteristic of God has been definitively achieved."[71]

In light of the stereotypical presentation of the poor in the psalter and throughout the Jewish scriptures, it may seem that the presence of this motif here in the Magnificat simply functions as another general expression of God's eschatological deliverance of Israel. However, the strong emphasis on reversal in the antitheses of verses 52-53 cautions against adopting a purely spiritualized reading of these verses, as does Luke's focus on social, political, and economic reversal throughout his two-volume work.[72] As recognized by most recent commentators, the exaltation of the poor announced in Mary's Song refers to both spiritual and socio-economic realities.[73] Concerning the terminology of verses 51-53, Green argues that these verses proclaim Jesus' conception as that which has set into motion the decisive, eschatological work of God. However, he goes on to explain:

> At the same time, that these verbs sponsor images of God's salvific work that are so concrete and this-worldly, and that they are set within a larger narrative world of foreign occupation and religio-political oppression, requires that we not relegate Mary's vision of redemption to some distant future or spiritualize it as though it were not concerned with the social realities of daily existence. The decisive event, the advent of God's kingdom grounded in the miraculous conception of Jesus, has already occurred. Hence, already in Mary's exaltation is the vision of her Song coming to fruition.[74]

Just as God's salvation is given birth through the conception of two children, so, too, does God's salvation have to do with the mundane realities of the present world order. The new kingdom John and Jesus are fashioning is incarnate in the world God is seeking to overturn.

Affective-Rhetorical Analysis

I imagine most readers of these verses (me included) have become so accustomed to the stories of Jesus' birth and Luke's infancy narrative in particular that we easily overlook the radical nature of what is here proclaimed. But when you stop and think about what is being said here and in the preceding episodes about God, Jesus, and God's saving reign, in light of the worldviews that dominated Luke's setting, it really is rather startling. I suspect that the reaction Luke was expecting among much of his audience, including some who were Christians or on the margins of the Christian movement, was astonishment and wonder, and perhaps even incredulity. I know that facial expression is not always a reliable gauge of emotion. But I picture Luke's readers or hearers, by the time they encounter these verses, responding with at least eyebrows highly arched, if not mouths agape, as the paradoxical and world-reversing claims made by Luke about God, Jesus, and God's salvation begin to sink in.

To be sure, Luke's narrative trades in images and ideas that were commonly known to Christians and Jews in his day. In fact, Mary's proclamation of what God is going to accomplish could not be more deeply rooted in Second Temple Jewish hope and expectation. The potential for nostalgia abounds, and Luke likely intends for his readers to wade—at least briefly—in these familiar waters. But Luke takes these common notions about God, Jesus, and salvation and redraws them in ways that compel his readers to discover more fully what the story of John and Jesus' birth—and the Gospel story itself—reveals about God and Jesus and what it means to be God's people. In other words, Luke combines and recasts these common elements in order to push the theological, christological, and soteriological commitments of his audience. Luke does not intend this as merely a cognitive and abstracted exercise, however. He also intends his readers to experience the discomfort of dissonance, the chafing of challenge, and the affection of allegiance, so that they may be all the more ready to embrace the incredible portraits of God, Jesus, and salvation he proclaims.

Luke continues in this episode to use characters as a means of emotionally connecting his readers to the narrative via admiration and sympathy. Both Elizabeth and Mary are drawn as engagingly admirable characters. Mary goes with haste to see her kinswoman and joins in the joy of her pregnancy. Elizabeth, moved by her enwombed child and filled by God's Spirit, proclaims the blessedness of Mary and Mary's offspring, and fittingly (though counterculturally) humbles herself in declaring, "And why has this happened to me, that the mother of my Lord comes to me?" (v. 43). Then she celebrates Mary's faith: "And blessed is she who trusted that the word spoken by the Lord to her would be fulfilled" (v. 45; my translation). Mary responds by offering her jubilant song of praise, rejoicing in the great works God has done for her and all of Israel in the conception of her child. Mary and Elizabeth, these two kinswomen, stand here as paradigms of faithfulness and joy-filled heralds of the good news unfolding in their very midst. Insofar as readers respond positively to these two women and their joy, they are also led by Luke to consider seriously the good tidings Elizabeth and Mary proclaim.

But these are strange tidings indeed, especially when viewed as a continuation of what has been revealed in the preceding episodes. The long-standing hope for Israel's deliverance won through the eruption of God's power and might is to be achieved through the conception, birth, rearing, and mission of these two children. But even more than that, Luke continues to present the paradoxical reality that the second of these children is to represent Yahweh in both his person and mission. The lines of distinction between them are so fuzzy that Jesus, like Yahweh, is to be claimed as holy, great, eternal, and even "Lord." Fundamental categories dividing human and divine are being blurred. Basic conceptions of reality are called into question. At the same time Luke compels his readers to embrace Mary and Elizabeth as admirable witnesses to and even agents of God's good news, he also keeps many of them reeling in cognitive and emotional dissonance in response to his paradoxical portrait of God and Jesus.

In Mary's hymn we also encounter world-defying reversal. Mary's Song brings to the fore the well-established notion in Jewish tradition that Yahweh acts on behalf of the oppressed, destitute, and outcast (as we noted above). Mary proclaims that the kingdom of God will bring about nothing less than a reversal of the social order itself, not simply the removal of those unfriendly to the aspirations of God's people. The proud will be scattered. The powerful will be brought down from their thrones, and the lowly exalted. The hungry will be filled, and the rich sent away empty. Long-standing social, political, and economic norms will rule the day no more. The status quo will be swept away by these two mothers and their children.

Through paradox and reversal, Luke is asking his readers to revise their understanding of divinity and society, two basic elements of their worldview. In doing so, Luke invites a cognitive and affective dissonance that many of his readers must have found difficult to tolerate. How would Theophilus, a man of some means as indicated by his ability to commission Luke's lengthy, two-volume work, respond to such reversal? Would he allow himself to be convicted by Mary's Song (and many similar statements to follow)? Would he tolerate a tale that names him as the odd man out? Would he dare show his expensive book to wealthy friends? Or how about those (including, possibly Theophilus) for whom Luke's portrait of Jesus—as somehow intimately connected to and representative of God—transgresses their notions of divinity? Does the evangelist lose these readers already at this early juncture in his story? Dare they read on? Luke is scribing a precarious line with his audience.

You have to admire his honesty; he's not pulling any punches. But wouldn't it have been safer, more tactful, to delay a bit before potentially pulling the rug out from under so many of his audience?

Perhaps this is where the two mothers-to-be come into play. Yes, Luke likely leads many of his readers to cognitive and emotional dissonance here as a means of challenging them to take a step further in their understanding of God, Jesus, and the world God is calling into being. But he also gives them hands to hold as he leads them down this uncanny path. Mary and Elizabeth, the admirable kinswomen who themselves participate in the reversal of God's saving reign, stand as witnesses to just how good this strange new world can be. If the likes of these are the ones whom we are called to adore and uplift as heroes, then perhaps the reversal and paradox they embody and proclaim may not turn out to be so bad. A little weird, maybe, to be esteeming a formerly barren and elderly mother-to-be and a young peasant girl who is somehow a virgin pregnant with a divine-like savior. But they are such good and faithful folk! For their sake, perhaps, some readers will hang on and dare to explore where the rest of the Gospel will lead. Perhaps the readers' dissonance will eventually turn into discernment and they will not only admire Mary, Elizabeth, and the many other folk who rejoice in this crazy good news, but decide to join them.

Summary

A jubilant greeting between two kinswomen leading to a heartfelt psalm of praise. Just how subversive could this be? Quite, for Luke utilizes this quaint and nostalgia-laden scene as a means of inviting his audience to consider further the paradoxical and socially undermining character of the good news he proclaims. Dissonance, cognitive and affective, seems to be Luke's primary aim in crafting the episode, challenging his readers to revise their understanding of God, Jesus, and faith. Yet the evangelist also gives his readers a reason to hang on. The two pregnant heroines, Mary and Elizabeth, not only nurture the embodiment of good news within themselves, through their admirable joy, boldness, and Spirit-filled witness, they also help to give birth to it in Luke's readers.

Chapter 4

Birth Pangs
(Luke 1:57—2:40)

We continue in this chapter to explore Luke's use of pathos, turning now to the stories recounting the births of John and Jesus and the early years of Jesus' life.

The Birth of John (1:57-80)

[57] Now the time came for Elizabeth to give birth, and she bore a son. [58] Her neighbors and relatives heard that the Lord had shown his great mercy to her, and they rejoiced with her.

[59] On the eighth day they came to circumcise the child, and they were going to name him Zechariah after his father. [60] But his mother said, "No; he is to be called John." [61] They said to her, "None of your relatives has this name." [62] Then they began motioning to his father to find out what name he wanted to give him. [63] He asked for a writing tablet and wrote, "His name is John." And all of them were amazed. [64] Immediately his mouth was opened and his tongue freed, and he began to speak, praising God. [65] Fear came over all their neighbors, and all these things were talked about throughout the entire hill country of Judea. [66] All who heard them pondered them and said, "What then will this child become?" For, indeed, the hand of the Lord was with him.

[67] Then his father Zechariah was filled with the Holy Spirit and spoke this prophecy:

[68] "Blessed be the Lord God of Israel,
    for he has looked favorably on his people and redeemed them.
[69] He has raised up a mighty savior for us
    in the house of his servant David,

⁷⁰ as he spoke through the mouth of his holy prophets from of old,
    ⁷¹ that we would be saved from our enemies and from the hand of all
        who hate us.
⁷² Thus he has shown the mercy promised to our ancestors,
    and has remembered his holy covenant,
⁷³ the oath that he swore to our ancestor Abraham,
    to grant us ⁷⁴ that we, being rescued from the hands of our enemies,
might serve him without fear, ⁷⁵ in holiness and righteousness
    before him all our days.
⁷⁶ And you, child, will be called the prophet of the Most High;
    for you will go before the Lord to prepare his ways,
⁷⁷ to give knowledge of salvation to his people
    by the forgiveness of their sins.
⁷⁸ By the tender mercy of our God,
    the dawn from on high will break upon us,
⁷⁹ to give light to those who sit in darkness and in the shadow of death,
    to guide our feet into the way of peace."
⁸⁰ The child grew and became strong in spirit, and he was in the wilderness until the day he appeared publicly to Israel.

Overview

Since Gabriel's announcement to Zechariah, readers have been waiting for this day to arrive. There's been a delay in Luke's reporting of John's birth, due to the intervening announcement and celebration of Jesus' conception and character. But God continues to fulfill God's promises as most of the events portrayed here—the birth, rejoicing of the people, naming, and loosening of Zechariah's tongue—are all things that Gabriel announced would take place (1:13-20). The absence of Zechariah from the account of John's birth and its initial celebration is notable (vv. 57-58) and reminds us of his disappearance from the narrative after its opening scene. Zechariah's reappearance and redemption are one of the dominant concerns of the passage, and his tardy but jubilant witness serves as its crescendo (vv. 64, 67-79).

The redemption of Zechariah is intertwined with another important dimension of the story that Luke features. Zechariah's absence from the opening of the scene is notable, but so, too, is the perfunctory fashion in which Luke recounts the actual birth: "Now the time came for Elizabeth to give birth, and she bore a son" (v. 57). An equally brief account of the ensuing celebration follows (also minus Zechariah), reminding readers of the tremendous blessing

God has bestowed upon Elizabeth and Israel, and the response befitting the manifestation of God's saving work among them (v. 58). Yet the moment of John's birth, while important to Luke, is not where he wants readers' attention to linger. Instead, he quickly ushers us through the birth scene and on to the day of circumcision, leading us to ponder the controversy over the naming of the newborn child.

> On the eighth day they came to circumcise the child, and they were going to name him Zechariah after his father. But his mother said, "No; he is to be called John." They said to her, "None of your relatives has this name." Then they began motioning to his father to find out what name he wanted to give him. He asked for a writing tablet and wrote, "His name is John." And all of them were amazed. (vv. 59-63)

There are several interpretive issues that impact one's understanding of the controversy and also play an important role in our affective-rhetorical analysis to follow. First, commentators differ over to what extent the convention of naming a son after the father was prominent in John's day, with many noting that the custom of naming a son after the grandfather is equally, if not better, attested.[1] The latter may account for the crowd's retort in verse 61, "None of your relatives has this name." However, what seems clear from Luke's account is that he understands the naming of a son after a father or other family member a convention of the time, and a rather important one at that, as indicated by the crowd's chagrin over its transgression. Second, the NRSV fails to capture the emphatic nature of Elizabeth's dismissal of the crowd's presumption that the child would be named after the father (vv. 59-60). The Greek οὐχί is an adverbial form of οὐ, likely emphatic when followed by ἀλλά, and used in response to questions when an affirmative answer is expected (see also Luke 12:51). Thus, it is better rendered "Not so!"[2] The emphatic nature of Elizabeth's response, coupled with the crowd's ensuing retort, "None of your relatives has this name," together draw out the conflicted character of the scene and also focus attention on the transgression of social custom as the point of dispute in the naming of John.

This observation helps us steer our way through another contested component of the passage: the precise focus of the witnesses' and well-wishers' amazement in verse 63 in response to Zechariah's naming of John. Nearly all commentators agree that their amazement is cast by Luke as a response to what they perceive as God's miraculous intervention. Although θυαμάζω can be used generally to express amazement at an occurrence not linked to a divinely ordained event (such as in 1:21; 7:9; and 11:38), in the overwhelming majority of instances in which it is used in Luke-Acts it refers to a response to events or revelation attributed either to God (2:18; 2:33; 24:12; Acts 2:7; 7:31; 13:41), Jesus (4:22; 8:25; 9:43; 11:14; 20:26; 24:4; Acts 3:12), or to the manifestation of God's power in Jesus' disciples (Acts 3:12; 4:13). Luke's own obtrusive summation in verse 66c ("For, indeed, the hand of the Lord was with him") confirms the evangelist's intent to portray the events surrounding John's birth as manifestations of God's intervention and as the source of the people's wonderment concerning John (v. 66ab).[3] What is less clear, however, is how Zechariah's naming of the child constitutes a manifestation of divine action that leads to the amazement of the crowd. Because Luke tells us that the crowd "began motioning to his father to find out what name he wanted to give him," many conclude that Zechariah was not only rendered mute by Gabriel's punitive sign but deaf as well. Accordingly, they propose that the crowd marvels at Zechariah's response because—since he could not have heard Elizabeth's insistence that the child be named John—his giving of the same name would have been such an extraordinary coincidence that it could only be attributed to God's miraculous intervention.[4]

In my view, this proposal fails for three reasons. First, it seems to me unlikely that if Luke intends us to see Zechariah as both mute and deaf he would have waited until this point in the narrative to indicate this to the reader and would have chosen to do so in such an indirect fashion.[5] What Luke has instead repeatedly and singularly emphasized as the consequence of Gabriel's punitive sign is Zechariah's inability to speak (vv. 20, 21, 22), including here in verses 63, 64. Consequently, a more plausible explanation is that Luke intends us to view the crowd's motioning to Zechariah not as an attempt to communicate in rudimentary sign language because Zechariah is deaf, but simply their attempt to get his attention so that they may inquire of him concerning the child's name. This is consistent with the meaning and use of ἐννεύω, which basically means to gesture or signal with the hands.[6] Narratologically, it functions to bring Zechariah in from the periphery of the account and now place him at its center. Second, the proposal requires that we fill in the narrative gap created by Elizabeth's naming of John by concluding that she must have come to this decision independent of her husband.[7] To be sure, when filled with the Spirit, Elizabeth displays knowledge of Mary and Jesus that she otherwise had no opportunity to learn (vv. 41-45). But there, Luke clearly indicates the source of Elizabeth's knowledge. Here, a simpler explanation for how the gap is to be filled commends itself: Elizabeth and Zechariah have discussed it as most would expect of a married couple. Wouldn't readers assume that Zechariah must have explained to his wife through gestures and a writing tablet why he lost his voice, and also filled her in on the details concerning their son? Finally, and most decisively, the narrative leading up to the crowd's inquiry and Zechariah's response has emphasized the conflict surrounding the name to be given to the child, hence Elizabeth's adamant "Not so!" and the crowd's consternation. At issue in that conflict dominating the narrative is the propriety of a name that does not reflect the child's family of origin. In short, the immediate context points to the *countercultural oddity* of the naming as the focus of the people's amazement, not the supposedly coincidental manner in which it is bestowed.

But more is at stake than simply a name, as the convergence of important literary and cultural trends in this passage help us to see. Similar to annunciations, birth accounts in historical and biographical works often served to express something fundamental about the child who was born, as is clear from both Greco-Roman and Old Testament precedents recounting the births of key figures.[8] The pairing of John's birth with Zechariah's canticle further elaborating the significance of his son, as well as the clear connections between the birth account and the annunciation of John's birth, confirm that the birth story is meant to fulfill this role. In addition, kinship was the most fundamental category of one's identity in antiquity, often determining one's basic social unit, status, and vocation. Relatedly, the act of naming was the primary means by which a child was claimed by parents and symbolically grafted into a household.[9] Altogether the conventional character of birth accounts and the allusions here to cultural norms governing personal identity and kinship lead us to recognize that the essential issue at hand in the naming of John is, *Who shall define the identity and mission of this child?* The reader knows—it is God. Elizabeth and Zechariah know this as well: he is to be named John as Gabriel has commanded. The crowd, however, does not know John's true identity and mission, at least not yet, and so they insist on a name that reflects his parentage or at least his kin.

By noting how these literary and cultural trends amplify and enrich the controversy surrounding John's naming, we find an additional reason to conclude that the crowd's amazement is directed at Elizabeth's and Zechariah's eschewal of social convention in the naming of their son, rather than the not-so-astounding coincidence that parents awaiting the birth of a child would agree on a name.[10] In essence, what Elizabeth and Zechariah are doing is granting their newborn son an identity that is not to be seen primarily in terms of his parentage or kin. They are disassociating John, their miracle child and source of great rejoicing, from themselves, and honoring the revelation that his significance transcends the blessing his birth has brought to them. The name given to the child constitutes such an irregular act (at least as Luke portrays it) that it is regarded by the crowd as another extraordinary event surrounding the birth of the child, even though they have yet to discern its full significance.

The return of Zechariah's voice serves as yet another confirmation of Gabriel's word (see v. 20). Fittingly, Zechariah's first words are that of praise—belated indeed, but better late than never, and once again Luke presents the pattern of prophecy → fulfillment → praise. All together, the unfolding of these extraordinary events strikes the gathered as nothing less than the work of God in their midst. They are filled with "holy fear," and word quickly spreads throughout the hill country of Judea. The reception of "all these things" is eloquently narrated by Luke:

> All who heard them pondered them and said, "What then will this child become?" For, indeed, the hand of the Lord was with him. (v. 66)

The people's reaction and question regarding John sets the stage for Zechariah's psalm of praise. It is uncertain whether or not Luke intends us to see the canticle as the praise reported in verse 64 or as a subsequent instance. Still, the canticle functions as a fitting response to the people's question, "What then will this child be?" suggesting a time frame that places it after the praise reported in verse 64. Zechariah is reintroduced as the father of John. Like his wife before him, he is filled with the Spirit, and utters his remarkable prophecy of praise.

What is immediately noteworthy about Zechariah's prophecy is that even though it addresses the people's wonderment concerning his son, John, it is for the most part about another figure who will usher in the saving reign of God. John isn't even mentioned until verse 76, ten verses into the song! The implication is clear. John's significance and mission is to be seen wholly in relationship to and as preparatory for God's wider plan of salvation accomplished by the awaited Messiah. Joel Green offers a fine summary of the relationship of the canticle to the rest of the infancy narrative:

> Zechariah's Song recapitulates major emphases of the birth narrative as a whole. (1) It stresses the import of John as forerunner to and preparer for the coming of the Lord (cf. 1:16-17, 76) and as prophet (1:15-17, 76). (2) It subordinates John to Jesus, especially in its reference to John as "prophet of the Most High" (1:76; cf. 1:32: "Son of the Most High"). (3) It weaves the stories of John and Jesus into one tapestry of God's purpose. (4) As with the other hymns in the Lukan birth narrative, Zechariah's Song completes a three-part pattern, in this case: promise of a son → birth of a son → praise response. (5) It highlights key motifs that pervade Luke 1–2—for example, the covenant making God, the continuity with Abraham and fulfillment of eschatological expectations associated with David, the socio-political

context in which the narrative is set and from which God will deliver his people, and the decisive coming of the epoch of salvation.[11]

I would tweak Green's summary by again proposing that the comparison of John with Jesus has not so much to do with John's subordination as it has to do with the convergence of mission and person between Jesus and God. As we have seen, the preceding episodes suggest this dimension by implying that Jesus is the one for whom John prepares, when it has been directly said of John that he prepares the way for Yahweh. This implication continues and is pointedly expressed in the contrast between the content of the canticle and its narrative context. The setting of the song (vv. 57-67, 80) is clearly focused on the significance of John. Moreover, the hymn follows the peoples' question, "What then will this child become?" (v. 66). Yet the Benedictus, with the exception of verses 76-77, centers on the redemption to be won by the messianic "horn of salvation" (v. 69).[12] The obvious tension between the setting of the canticle and its actual contents indicates that the person and significance of John is to be wholly understood with respect to the accomplishment of God's promised deliverance *in the person of the Messiah*. Although John himself will give knowledge of salvation for the forgiveness of sins (v. 77), such granting of knowledge is explicitly cast as *preparatory* (v. 76) for the salvation that comes in the visitation of the messianic "dawn from on high" (vv. 78-79).[13] Thus, once again—and with greater directness than before—Luke indicates that John prepares the way not simply for the Lord God (1:15-17), but also for the Lord Jesus. Or better said, John prepares the way of the Lord God, and in doing so, he prepares the way of the Lord Jesus. This says a lot about John and the importance of his ministry. But Luke also intends it to say a lot, perhaps even more, about Jesus.

Other features of the canticle also contribute to the convergence of mission and person between Jesus and God. That Jesus' messianic mission is to be seen as synonymous with Yahweh's awaited arrival is clearly implied in Zechariah's words of praise. At the very start of the hymn, the visitation of God (v. 68b) is made equivalent to the raising up of the Davidic Messiah (v. 69), who in the context of the infancy narratives can only be Jesus (1:32-35). Furthermore, at the conclusion of the hymn, the event that embodies the salvation stemming from the tender mercy of God is the advent of the messianic dawn from on high (v. 78). Thus, as further indicated by a key terminological parallel bracketing Zechariah's praise and prophecy, the visitation (ἐπισκέπτομαι [v. 68]) of God, as already suggested by verse 69, is fully encompassed by the visitation (ἐπισκέπτομαι [v. 78]) of the Messiah.

The close relation between Jesus and God is further suggested when John is proclaimed as one who will prepare the way of "the Lord" (v. 76). That κύριος should here be taken as referring to Yahweh is suggested by the fact that in the previous description of John's mission (1:15-17, esp. v. 16), it was clearly God for whom John was to prepare. Also, the expression τῷ λαῷ αὐτοῦ ("his people') in verse 77 would likewise seem to indicate that Yahweh is in view. On the other hand, the narrative up to this point has identified Jesus as the one who has come to establish God's salvation (1:32-35). Moreover, the step-parallelism at work between the two annunciations of birth followed by the leaping of John in the womb strongly implies that it is Jesus for whom John is to prepare the way. Finally, the present canticle, as we have seen, relates John's role and significance as one who prepares the way of the Lord to the deliverance accomplished by *the visitation of God's Messiah*, who can be none other than Jesus. All of this suggests that Jesus is the one for whom John prepares, and thus it is Jesus who is here in view as the "Lord" whose way John makes ready. That Luke would intend to move his audience in this direction is further supported by the use of κύριος for Jesus already in 1:43 and again in the very next episode (2:11). Accordingly, many see the use of "Lord" in verse 76 as a direct reference to Jesus.[14] Yet perhaps John Nolland is closest to the mark when he refers to the occurrence of κύριος here as a "happy ambiguity."[15] If so, the ambiguous appearance of the title in the present episode also invites consideration of the relationship between Jesus and Yahweh. Luke has set all of the pieces in place for us to make the connection that Jesus is the one who comes after John—*in fulfillment of God's coming*. The ambiguity of verse 76 further leads Luke's audience to see that somehow both Jesus and Yahweh are the "Lord" whose way John readies.

Another feature of the hymn that stands out is its emphasis on deliverance from "our enemies" (vv. 71, 74) and from "the hand of those who hate us" (v. 71). Zechariah goes on to characterize God's deliverance as both forgiveness and "light to those who sit in darkness and in the shadow of death, to guide our feet into the way of peace" (vv. 77, 79). These statements draw out the conflicted and desperate situation in which God's people find themselves, needing deliverance from both substantial external threat as well as their own waywardness.[16] The seeking or celebration of both God's forgiving mercy and salvation from enemies is not unique to Luke; these two blessings are occasionally juxtaposed in psalms of lament and thanksgiving (Psalms 25, 34, 38, 139) as well as in the prophetic oracles of salvation (Isa 40:1-11; Ezek 36:16-38; Jer 31:33-37) to which Luke refers in verse 70. The "oath that he [God] swore to our ancestor Abraham" that Zechariah cites (v. 73) likely alludes back to the covenant God made with Abram, promising him the blessing of protection from all that might do him and his descendants harm (see Gen 12:1-3). Luke also likely intends an allusion to the exodus story here, pairing the deliverance of enemies with "that we . . . might serve him without fear, in holiness and righteousness before him all our days" (vv. 74-75), a common motif in the exodus and wilderness traditions (Exod 12; 15:1-21; 19:1-6; Deut 4:1-40). Mary's preceding announcement of impending reversal suggests conflict between the lowly and proud, but here Zechariah more explicitly draws out the reality that many will contest God's will for God's people. God's reign, as it has been in the past, will once again be opposed by the forces of this world.

Affective-Rhetorical Analysis

Essential relevance, sequencing, sympathy, admiration, reversal, paradox, nostalgia, and conflict continue to be employed by Luke as a means of affectively engaging his readers. Our analysis of the preceding passages has addressed Luke's paradoxical portrait of Jesus and how the evangelist has used sympathy and admiration as a means of leading readers to bear with and even entertain the extraordinary claims being made about Jesus and God. This rhetorical strategy continues in this passage as Zechariah emerges as another sympathetic and admirable character promoting this paradox. Here, however, I want to zero in on two other features of the passage whose rhetorical function can be further illuminated by considering their emotive impact on Luke's readers.

The first is the controversy over the naming of John. At first glance, the controversy may simply seem to function as a means of emphasizing Elizabeth's and Zechariah's faithfulness in following God's will, for Gabriel had instructed Zechariah that "you will name him John" (1:13). Zechariah's compliance with the divine will also signals his restoration, for he writes the words "His name is John" and "immediately his mouth was opened and his tongue freed, and he began to speak, praising God" (v. 64). Thus, on one level, the controversy underscores Zechariah's return to faith. Readers are thus invited to be relieved at the resolution to Zechariah's doubt, and also happy for Zechariah as he now reclaims his voice and offers his belated praise to God, elevating him once again to a place of honor in the remembrance of the Gospel story. But the controversy is operative on another level as well, functioning as a means by which Luke once again weaves the theme of reversal into his narrative. Not only shall the older serve and make way for the younger, not only shall the proud be brought low and the lowly exalted, the extraordinary in-breaking of God's reign is marked by yet another eschewal of the social order. As stated well by Nolland, "Only a name outside the range of all expectation can do justice to the decisive discontinuity in human affairs marked by John's coming."[17] The newness, uniqueness, and import of John (as well as Jesus) require not that his naming be in accord with human custom, but with *God's* will for John and the rest of humanity. The controversy surrounding the naming of John and its deviation from social convention helps the reader to appreciate that what is important to God and the future of God's people transcends human custom and expectation. Here again, Zechariah serves as an effective object lesson, but this time as a positive one who acts in accord with God's designs. Via sympathy, conflict, and reversal, readers are put into a position where Luke is once again challenging them to set aside the norms of the world in order that they may be open to the kind of world willed by God.

Yet the reversal and affective edge of this passage cuts deeper than what I just described. As we discussed earlier, the traditional and cultural trends converging in this passage help us to see that the essential issue in the naming of John is, Who or what will define John's identity? Human custom surrounding naming and kinship, or God's naming of John, including his call to serve as the prophet who will go before the Lord? Or, to put it another way, the essential issue is, *To whom does John belong?* Elizabeth and Zechariah answer that question, and the poignancy of their answer affectively charges this scene. The elderly, barren couple whose unceasing prayer for a child was miraculously answered, identify their beloved son, source of great joy, rejoicing, and vindication, not in relationship to themselves or their family as would be expected, but in relationship to God's purpose and plan. The crowd's protest and amazement help readers appreciate what is at stake. "What do you mean he's not to be named Zechariah? What? John? Who the heck is John? Surely that can't be right. Where's Zechariah? He'll set his wife straight!" But like Hannah and Elkanah who left their toddler son, Samuel, behind in the house of the Lord, Elizabeth and Zechariah accept God's will that their beloved son is called to a mission that will ultimately take him beyond their household, and from them. When Samuel was weaned, Hannah gathered up the child for whom she had desperately yearned and traveled back to Shiloh. "She left him there for the Lord" (1 Sam 1:28). Here, Zechariah and Elizabeth do the same, and the nostalgic allusion to the Samuel story deepens the pathos emanating from their decision. Their naming of John was not a mindless recitation of Gabriel's command. The defiant tone of Elizabeth's "Not so!" and Zechariah's scrawl tell us that they realized well what was at stake. And yet readers who have sympathized with Elizabeth and Zechariah and rejoiced in their blessing of a son are also led to recognize and participate in the sense of loss that also pervades this scene, to hear the sorrow mixed in with Elizabeth's and Zechariah's righteous resolve. Luke reveals through this affectively laden moment that the restoration of Israel will be accompanied by great personal sacrifice. This is the first of several indications throughout the infancy narrative that the coming of God's kingdom will come at a cost, not only for the proud and Israel's enemies, but for the faithful as well. Zechariah and Elizabeth prove up to the challenge, even if it means that they have to leave their beloved son, John, for the Lord. The reader is led to ponder, "Would I do the same?

Another feature of the passage that is likely intended by Luke to engage his readers emotively is his emphasis on God's deliverance from enemies. As we have seen, Zechariah's proclamation of God's salvation holds in view the prophetic promises of restoration (v. 70-71), God's covenant with Abraham and his descendants (vv. 72-73), and the paradigmatic, saving event of the exodus (vv. 74-75), in which God frees Abraham's offspring in order that they may serve Yahweh. With these manifold allusions, nostalgia once again abounds and affectively colors the births of John and Jesus as the culmination of God's promises to Israel and central to the salvation long yearned by God's people. I wonder, however, how Luke intended Zechariah's emphasis on enemies to strike his readers. What would Theophilus and others like him have in view when encountering these lines? We saw with Mary's song that Luke took the familiar and emotionally charged hopes of Jewish folk and recast them in ways that challenge his readers to expand their understanding of God and faith. Might Luke be up to a similar reorientation here on who is to be considered the enemies of God?

One way Theophilus and others might view the references to Israel's historic enemies is to spiritualize them and to understand them as metaphors for the spiritual enemies facing all of humanity, such as sin and the demonic. Zechariah's mention of forgiveness and God's mercy here (along with Luke's emphasis upon these concepts throughout his two-volume work) is taken by some as indicating Luke's attempt to encourage such spiritualization of traditional, Second Temple Judaic hopes already at this point in his Gospel.[18] In other words, human sin is "the enemy" that God now vanquishes among the faithful, and whose defeat ensures the blessing of God's people into eternity. However, just as commentators find that there is good reason to avoid an overly spiritualized understanding of Luke's emphasis on the poor and eschewal of social convention, many also think there is also good reason to resist the temptation to spirit away his reference to enemies. To be sure, the category of enemies is undergoing some transformation.[19] The defeat of enemies that Luke envisions is not along the same lines as that hoped for and expected by many Jews in the years leading up to Jesus. But these enemies are still found within the sociopolitical structure of that day. They are among the proud and powerful Mary identifies in her song. They hold the office of the emperor, as will become apparent in the very next episode. They are the ones that are destined to fall, as Simeon will prophecy. And as will become evident in Jesus' own ministry and in the ministry of the early church, there are those within the current world order who will oppose the faithful, but who will ultimately fail in their attempt to thwart the in-breaking of God's reign.[20]

Just how much of this would begin to dawn on Luke's readers at this point in the narrative is hard to know. But the repeated references to enemies in Zechariah's Song cry out for the reader's attention, and the reader will at least begin to wonder how these references to enemies are to be understood within the world Luke is fashioning. And the more attentive would, I think, sense a connection between these enemies and the proud and powerful in Mary's Song. For them, Luke's references to enemies will again likely elicit cognitive and affective dissonance as he leads Theophilus and others to consider who, specifically, are those that oppose the salvation Zechariah proclaims. More poignant still, perhaps his readers may be led to wonder if those who are truly the enemies of God's new kingdom are also their enemies, or their associates, friends, or family members. It may lead readers to wonder to whom they are more closely aligned and with whom they more closely identify: Are the proud and powerful their foes or friends, and if the latter, then why? If the latter, then who are the readers themselves? Would Zechariah consider them friend or foe? The reader is thus potentially placed in the emotionally untenable position of being identified as an enemy of God's reign.

Summary

As we have seen, Luke continues to hammer home the paradoxical intersection of Jesus' and God's mission and person by claiming that in preparing the way for the Lord God, John is also preparing the way for the Lord Jesus. But our affective analysis of John's birth and Zechariah's canticle has focused on the controversial and countercultural character of John's naming and the emphasis on enemies in Zechariah's prophecy. To be sure, several exegetical considerations play a decisive role in how we understand the controversy and whether the crowd's wonderment focuses on the coincidental or the countercultural character of the name choice. However, affective analysis provides another resource for discerning Luke's intent in the passage. In other words, which of the competing readings yields an affective response that better advances Luke's rhetorical aims? The affective and rhetorical payoff of Luke presenting the crowd as amazed over the miraculously coincidental agreement among John's parents on what their child should be named seems rather meager when compared to the alternative promoted here. The reader already knows that the child is to be named John and that the hand of the Lord is upon him. The reader has already been told that those gathered have sensed God's intervention in

Elizabeth's pregnancy. Indeed, this information affirms what has already been proclaimed, and in that there is some rhetorical import. However, it pales in comparison to the affective and rhetorical charge yielded by a reading that instead focuses on the countercultural and sacrificial character of Elizabeth's and Zechariah's insistence that their son's name represent not their household but God's purpose for his life. The reader's appreciation for what Elizabeth and Zechariah must hand over to the Lord is likely meant by Luke to lead them to consider what they themselves are willing to sacrifice in order that they too may be part of promoting rather than hindering God's purposes for them and all of humanity. In tandem with the emphasis on enemies to follow in Zechariah's Song, it may lead Theophilus and others to reconsider their own treasured associations and to realize what is at stake in their day-to-day decisions of whose interests, and which Lord, they really serve.

The Birth of Jesus (2:1-20)

[1] In those days a decree went out from Emperor Augustus that all the world should be registered. [2] This was the first registration and was taken while Quirinius was governor of Syria. [3] All went to their own towns to be registered. [4] Joseph also went from the town of Nazareth in Galilee to Judea, to the city of David called Bethlehem, because he was descended from the house and family of David. [5] He went to be registered with Mary, to whom he was engaged and who was expecting a child. [6] While they were there, the time came for her to deliver her child. [7] And she gave birth to her firstborn son and wrapped him in bands of cloth, and laid him in a manger, because there was no place for them in the inn.

[8] In that region there were shepherds living in the fields, keeping watch over their flock by night. [9] Then an angel of the Lord stood before them, and the glory of the Lord shone around them, and they were terrified. [10] But the angel said to them, "Do not be afraid; for see—I am bringing you good news of great joy for all the people: [11] to you is born this day in the city of David a Savior, who is the Messiah, the Lord. [12] This will be a sign for you: you will find a child wrapped in bands of cloth and lying in a manger." [13] And suddenly there was with the angel a multitude of the heavenly host, praising God and saying,

[14] "Glory to God in the highest heaven,
     and on earth peace among those whom he favors!"

[15] When the angels had left them and gone into heaven, the shepherds said to one another, "Let us go now to Bethlehem and see this thing that has taken place, which the Lord has made known to us." [16] So they went with haste

and found Mary and Joseph, and the child lying in the manger. [17] When they saw this, they made known what had been told them about this child; [18] and all who heard it were amazed at what the shepherds told them. [19] But Mary treasured all these words and pondered them in her heart. [20] The shepherds returned, glorifying and praising God for all they had heard and seen, as it had been told them.

Overview

Throughout the preceding episodes, Luke has employed reversal and paradox to help his readers appreciate that the kingdom inaugurated in the conceptions and births of John and Jesus is one that will turn the tables on the current world order. Later in Acts, believers will be dragged in front of the Thessalonian authorities and accused of "turning the world upside down" (Acts 17:6). The crescendo in Luke's portrayal of this "upside-down" world in the infancy narrative takes place here in the story of Jesus' birth. With a concentration of dramatic artistry that is remarkable even for Luke, the evangelist smoothly but not so subtly invites readers to discern who is truly Lord and to join those who praise and bear witness to the world's one true Savior.

Yet as the passage opens, it is the one known to the Mediterranean world and beyond as Lord who speaks and moves "all the world" to action (2:1). Caesar Augustus, the Roman emperor and father of the empire, orders a census to be taken, and his underlings, such as Quirinius, governor of Syria, make it happen. Caesar wants to take stock of his subjects and possessions, the objects of his rule. His word is spoken, and the world has no choice but to comply: "All went to their own towns to be registered" (v. 3).[21] The father of Jesus is no exception: "Joseph also went from the town of Nazareth in Galilee to Judea, to the city of David called Bethlehem" (v. 4). Caesar's command rules the cosmos, or so it seems.

Scholars have long noted and debated a serious problem with Luke's chronology here. As many point out, reliable historical sources place the reign of Quirinius and the census undertaken while he was governor several years later in 6 C.E.[22] We will not engage this debate here, but note that is common for scholars to view the census as a device employed by the evangelist to get Mary and Joseph to Bethlehem. In their view, Luke may be fudging a bit with the dating, or may simply be mistaken, but he needs to place Jesus' birth in Bethlehem in order to cohere with early Christian tradition and fulfill Micah 5:2-4, which identifies this little Judean village as the birthplace of the Messiah (see Matt 2:1-6 and Matthew's citation of Mic 5:2-4 [5:1-4 in the Hebrew Bible]). Luke's interest in Bethlehem for these reasons seems likely, but the census serves another function as well. If Luke, along with Matthew, understands Jesus' birth in Bethlehem as the divinely ordained fulfillment of Micah's prophecy, then notice how the mighty rule of Caesar is already being undercut in the opening verses of Luke's account. Ironically and unknowingly, Caesar Augustus, the world's venerated sovereign, puts into motion events that lead to the fulfillment of *God's* will for Israel and all the world.[23] For as the reader's attention is shifted from Caesar to Joseph, Mary, and the child they will bear, the mention of the city, house, and lineage of David reminds the reader of Jesus' messianic identity and once again grounds him in the soil of Judaism (v. 4). Also likely in view and energizing Luke's description here is the long-standing enmity between pious Jews and Roman rule. Caesar rules the world, including Palestine, but the Jewish Messiah who will deliver Israel from its enemies is about to be born (cf. 1:71, 74). And Caesar helps to bring it all to pass, unknowingly pushing the unborn Messiah to Bethlehem, that he might be born just as God "spoke through the mouth of his holy prophets from of old" (1:70).

In her song of praise, Mary claimed that the coming of her child would result in the bringing down of the powerful from their thrones and the lifting up of the lowly (1:52). But even this warning leaves the reader unprepared for Luke's description of Jesus' birth and humble state of his first resting place. In simple, unadorned prose, we are told that Jesus is born, wrapped in bands of cloth, and laid in a feedbox "because there was no place for them in the inn" (2:7). It can't get much lowlier than this.[24] The κατάλυμα, the hostel-like shelter or room set aside for travelers adjoining a house, is full.[25] None move aside so that the very pregnant and eventually laboring Mary can give birth in the security of even these very sparse quarters.[26] So the young couple nestle in among the sheep, goats, and chickens, deliver their child, and employ a manger for a crib. A stable (or cave) full of animals and a feedbox greet Jesus' advent. One can only hope that Joseph cleaned the feeder out and put in some fresh straw before so enthroning his son, and that the goats and chickens left Jesus alone! It may sound romantically rustic to us, but Luke's readers are confronted with an image of the Jewish Messiah that could not be more incongruous with the pomp and might of Emperor Augustus on his throne, commanding the world at will. The repeated references to the bands of cloth and manger as the "sign" that identifies Jesus (2:12, 16-17) keep these lowly elements in view even as he is exalted by the heavenly host and found by the shepherds.[27]

As the scene shifts from stable to darkened field, we once again encounter a setting far removed from Caesar's seat in Rome: shepherds tending their flocks by night. This is another element of the story that modern readers have long romanticized. But the lowliness of the shepherds and the locale of their labor would have held social and political overtones for Luke's readers. Recall my description of Roman society and economy back in the beginning of chapter 3. Shepherds, as well as all agricultural workers, were among the large peasant class whose servitude fueled the economy of empire and hegemony of Roman rule. Their economic exploitation was maintained by their lack of social and political standing. As Green explains:

> Shepherds in an agrarian society may have small landholdings, but these would be inadequate to meet the demands of their own families, the needs of their own agricultural pursuits, and the burden of taxation. As a result, they may hire themselves out to work for wages. There were, then, peasants, located toward the bottom of the scale of power and privilege. That they are here cast in this dress is unmistakable, for the same contrast introduced in Mary's Song—the enthroned versus the lowly (1:52)—is represented here: Augustus the Emperor and Quirinius on the one hand (2:1-2), the shepherds on the other.[28]

To claim that the birth of this Jewish child in a setting so far removed from the center of Roman rule poses any sort of meaningful challenge to Caesar would by nearly all sane accounts of the time be simply laughable. But this is just the announcement that explodes into the darkened night as an angelic host appears and the very glory of God engulfs the shepherds.[29] That Luke intended his readers to hear this birth announcement as an implied but quite clear repudiation of Caesar's sovereignty is indicated by the fact that many of the very same things celebrated about Caesar and his birth are now attributed to this infant lying in a feedbox. In their decision to honor Augustus by beginning the new year on his birthday, the Roman provincial assembly announced:

> Whereas the providence which divinely ordered our lives created with zeal and munificence the most perfect good for our lives by producing Augustus . . . for the *benefaction of mankind*, sending us a *savior* who put an end to war . . . and whereas the *birthday* of the god marked *for the world* the beginning of *good tidings* through his coming.[30]

The parallels to the angel's announcement in 2:10-11 are apparent:

> Do not be afraid; for see—I am bringing you *good news* of great joy for *all the people*: to you is *born this day* in the city of David a *Savior*, who is the Messiah Lord [my translation].[31]

112

Luke has the angels present the ludicrous claim that Jesus, not Caesar, is Lord and Savior. They announce that it is the birth of this infant, resting in a feed-box, which is truly εὐαγγέλιον ("good news") for "all the people." He, not the emperor, will be the one to bring peace to those on whom God's favor rests.

The infant Jesus, whose advent and station are described in the lowliest terms, is now exalted by the heavenly host in the grandest fashion. In a manner similar to what we find in the previous episodes, the angelic announcement points to Jesus' advent as the fulfillment of Yahweh's awaited visitation. Once again, step-parallelism and an exalted description of Jesus' person and significance emerging from that step-parallelism serve to express this dimension. While John's birth is portrayed in the preceding episode as a manifestation of God's intervention, with the birth of Jesus that manifestation takes the much more obtrusive form of a theophanous announcement and a proclamation by the heavenly host. Also, whereas John was designated by Zechariah as "prophet of the Most High," Jesus is hailed by the angelic messenger as σωτὴρ ὅς ἐσ τιν Χριστὸς κύριος ("a Savior, who is Messiah Lord").[32] As in the preceding narrative, however, the primary function of this parallelism is not simply to portray the greatness of Jesus with respect to John, but to portray the two of them in a fashion that indicates that Jesus is the one for whom John prepares, even though John (also) readies the way for Yahweh.

The designation of Jesus as σωτὴρ ὅς ἐστιν Χριστὸς κύριος ("Savior, who is Messiah Lord") develops the implicit claim of the step-parallelism in two ways. First, in conjunction with the preceding episode (to which the present stands in parallel), the designation of Jesus as Χριστὸς κύριος clearly recalls John's role as one who prepares for Jesus. As we saw, John's ministry of preparation was presented in context celebrating the coming of God's salvation in the person of the Messiah, leading to the clear implication that it is the Messiah, and hence Jesus, for whom John prepares. In addition, Zechariah announced that John was to "prepare the way of the Lord," which in the context of the infancy narrative was likely best seen as a highly ambiguous use of κύριος suggestively referring at the same time to both Yahweh and Jesus. Thus, the angel's proclamation of Jesus as "Messiah" and "Lord" (v. 11)—in light of the parallelism between the two episodes—not only reveals Jesus as the greater of the two, but it once again sets him squarely in view as the one for whom John prepares.

Second, Luke's use of the titles σωτήρ and χριστὸς κύριος for Jesus again suggests the convergence of mission and person between Jesus and Yahweh that has been implied throughout the birth narrative. Mark Strauss argues that there are at least four different ways to understand the expression Χριστὸς κύριος: (1) χριστός may serve as an adjective modifying κύριος, thus "anointed Lord"; (2) χριστός may be used as a personal name and κύριος as a title ("Christ, the Lord"); (3) both terms may function as titles, with κύριος being either appositional or epexegetical; or (4) both terms may reflect a single compound title "and should be translated something like 'Messiah-Yahweh' with implications of an epiphany."[33] Strauss disregards the last possibility, claiming that "there is little in the context to suggest such a meaning, and it is unlikely that a Greek reader would immediately take it as such."[34] However, there is ample precedent of the use of compound titles for Greek leaders. Robert R. Hann has argued in his defense of χριστός κύριος as the genuine reading in *Psalms of Solomon* 17:32—the only other known place where the expression occurs—that the designation is a messianic title that developed in response to the Hellenistic practice of using compound titles for royal figures.[35] Moreover, the present passage, in which the lordship of Caesar is being challenged by the lordship of Jesus, certainly provides a context in which such a compound title would be fittingly attributed to Jesus: Jesus, not Caesar, is anointed King and Lord over all.

At the same time, the royal connotations of χριστός κύριος do not exhaust the full implications of the title for Luke.[36] The compound title as well as σωτήρ must also be viewed in connection with their use in the preceding narrative. Σωτήρ is predicated of God in 1:47 (its only other occurrence in Luke-Acts). Here it is Jesus who is called "Savior." In addition, by referring to Jesus as κύριος, Luke once again brings forth the ambiguity that has surrounded his use of the term throughout the infancy account. These connections indicate that Luke is again deliberately portraying Jesus in very close relation to Yahweh, both in terms of his mission and person. Both are "Savior." In Jesus' birth, both visit God's people with God's awaited salvation. Both are "Lord."

In sum, Luke once again joins reversal with paradox, but with an intensity of contrast that transcends what has come before. Luke's claim dramatically relayed is this: the Jewish infant lying in a feedbox among sheep, goats, cattle, and fowl drastically marginalizes the significance of Caesar and Rome itself, as he manifests the presence and power of God! For *his* birth day, not Caesar's, is truly good news for all of humankind. He, not Caesar, is Lord and Savior of the world. His reign, not Caesar's, will lead the heavens to erupt in praise of God (not the gods) and the celebration of enduring peace: "Glory to God in the highest heaven, and on earth peace to those whom he favors!" (vv. 13-14). This, Luke shows, is how God's plan for the redemption of Israel, and even all of humanity, unfolds.[37] In this peasant infant, God does nothing less than come into the world and turn it upside down.

Not only are the shepherds recipients of this good news, they become its heralds as well. Immediately, the shepherds accept the angel's message as that which "the Lord has made known to us" (v. 15) and, as did Mary after receiving the sign from Gabriel, set off in haste (σπεύδω) to behold the sign they had been given (v. 16). At this point in the infancy narrative, we are in the position to look back and perceive that each act of revelation "from the Lord" is followed by a corresponding act of celebration, which itself witnesses to God's saving deeds. The annunciation to Zechariah led to his (albeit belated) canticle in 1:68-79; the Spirit-led leaping of John in the womb resulted in Elizabeth's greeting to Mary (1:41-45); and the annunciation to Mary and Elizabeth's greeting were answered by Mary's Song in 1:46-55. In each of these instances of character speech offered by those who were recipients of God's revelation, praise took the form of *testimony* that witnessed to what God had and would yet accomplish in John and Jesus. In Luke's portrayal of the shepherds as "making known" (γνωρίζω [v. 17]) and "telling" (λαλέω [v. 18]) what the Lord had "made known" (γνωρίζω [15]) and "told" (λαλέω [v. 17]) to them, he now presents in more direct fashion the notion implicit in the preceding episodes: a faithful response of believing and rejoicing also includes witnessing to the salvation that God has revealed and would achieve in Jesus.[38] But in this we find reversal as well. Those who could be regarded as the "first evangelists" of this "good news of great joy for all the people" are those who in the world's eyes would have little of importance to say.[39] Wiser folks—Mary and Joseph, and those overhearing the shepherd's words—know to listen. Once again the crowd marvels, and "Mary treasured all these words and pondered them in her heart" (v. 19).

Affective-Rhetorical Analysis

As I mentioned at the start of the overview, Luke 2:1-20 strikes me as the crescendo of the infancy narrative. In 2:1, the setting suddenly widens. We hear of an emperor and governor, a census, and an entire empire on the move. A world stage hosts the long-awaited moment of the Messiah's advent, and yet the quarters welcoming the newborn King are of a most lowly kind. But heaven is not deterred from celebrating his birth. The glory of God bursts into the night as a heavenly choir proclaims good news to shepherds, celebrating the one in mean estate as Savior of all. The shepherds rush to find the child and encounter this incredible scene, just as the angels had said: a babe, the Messiah Lord, in a stable, nestled in a feedbox. Then they make known to others what the Lord had made known to them, and Mary treasures all these words in her heart. This is just plain good storytelling, drama that engages nearly all our senses. The story is also meant to engage the reader's heart. Here we find Luke's narrative intensely laden with affective triggers as the significance of this newly born child is more fully unveiled.

In the passages leading up to this climactic pericope, we have seen Luke employ a variety of means to affectively engage his audience as he portrays the most relevant good news of Jesus' advent. The main rhetorical ends Luke's use of pathos thus far appears to serve are fourfold. He aims to encourage Theophilus and others to:

1. respond to the most relevant and amazing good news of God's salvation in Jesus with devotion, praise, and witness;
2. be assured that God's act of salvation in Jesus emerges from God's long-standing relationship with and covenantal commitment to God's people, Israel;
3. embrace the paradoxical reality of Jesus' mission and person as one who walks among us but is uniquely related to and uniquely manifests God as the Spirit-conceived Divine Son, Savior, Messiah, and Lord; and
4. recognize that the in-breaking of God's reign in John and Jesus subverts humanly contrived systems of power and status and turns the world "upside down."

That these same rhetorical ends dominate 2:1-20 is apparent as each receives a decisive hammer stroke in Luke's shaping of the account. Also apparent is Luke's use of pathos to serve these rhetorical ends. The following affective analysis will focus on Luke's employment of emotion through by-now familiar means: essential relevance, reversal, paradox, and characterization inviting reader identification and admiration.

Essential Relevance

Clearly, it is rather obvious throughout Luke's infancy narrative that the evangelist casts the events he portrays as of paramount significance. His is a narrative of the "matters fulfilled among us" (1:1), and his account of John's and Jesus' advent has repeatedly proclaimed the importance of these figures for God's historic people, Israel: the long-awaited moment of God's deliverance is now at hand. However, here in this climactic scene the reader receives word that Jesus' significance and the salvation he inaugurates is not only to be seen against the backdrop of Jewish history and hope but also against the backdrop of "all the world" (2:1), for this is "good news of great joy for all the people" (2:10). Thus, what begins as a story deeply rooted in the hopes, life, and traditions of Judaism, now becomes a story inclusive of and relevant for "all." For Gentile readers of this narrative, including—presumably—Theophilus, this scene reaffirms their own inclusion in this story, lest the strongly Jewish flavor of the tale thus far has led them to feel like "outsiders looking in." Simeon will reaffirm this welcome in the following scene. But here Luke broaches the issue, reminding Gentile readers that this is their story too. He calls them to remember that the Jewish babe lying in a feedbox, surrounded by the sights and smells of a stable, is also *their* Lord and Savior, for he is Lord and Savior of *all*.

Reversal

Luke's shaping of this account is marked by an artistry that feigns subtlety, and yet hardly any informed reader of Luke's day could miss its penetrating edginess. Luke confronts his readers with the extraordinary claim that the one whom the world celebrates as the venerated sovereign, the lord and savior of all, is really an imposter. The birth that is really good news, the one who is really Lord and Savior of humankind, is this Jewish infant stabled in a feed trough. Implicit in this world-reversing claim is a call for Luke's readers to make a decision: Jesus or Caesar? Luke doesn't try to hide the fact that on the face of it all, to choose this Jewish infant is simply silly. It is almost as if he is daring his readers not to believe. After all, this same babe is destined for the humiliation of the cross.[40] This is lowliness to the extreme. But Luke still issues a challenge to his readers: Jesus or Caesar, whom will you embrace as Lord and Savior? The Jewish child who becomes a crucified criminal or the Roman emperor? Whose good news will be good news to you, the proclamation of the Roman Provincial Assembly or the proclamation of the heavenly host only made known through the rambling of shepherds? (Everyone knows how shepherds like their wine on cold nights.)

To be sure, there may have been some zealous Jewish peasants among Luke's readers who would have identified strongly with Jesus and found very attractive and readily believable the claim that one from "among them" would pose such a challenge to Roman rule. Most of Luke's readers, however, whether they be Jewish peasants or Gentiles attracted to Christianity, would recognize the outrageous, world-subverting nature of what Luke is now claiming of Jesus. This story would confront them with the profession that what God is accomplishing in the birth of this peasant child problematizes all human claims to control and power. And so, for Theophilus and others, a decision needs to be made. I imagine that as Luke's original readers encountered this tale, many of them were led to an emotionally liminal moment in which they heard Joshua's exhortation echoing through the ages and dancing among these verses, "Choose this day whom you will serve" (Josh 24:15).

Paradox

Once again, paradox joins reversal in leading Luke's readers to cognitive and affective dissonance, challenging them to revise their understanding of power and lordship, and expand their conceptions of how God may be intimately present with humanity. Luke remains uncompromising in his exaltation of Jesus as one who manifests the will, work, and, to some undefined and unexplained degree, the person of Yahweh in his own person and ministry. But here in 2:1-20, the paradoxical character of this claim is pushed to even greater extremes. The proclamation of Jesus as Savior and Messiah Lord whose birth ushers in God's awaited salvation not only for Israel but for "all people" once again assigns attributes to Jesus' mission and person that are normally reserved for God in Jewish tradition. And yet these attributes are juxtaposed to the startlingly lowly and marginalized portrait of Jesus at his birth. The claim that one who would be God's Messiah is also somehow a holy, great, divinely conceived "Son of God," "Lord," and "Savior" who reigns forever was likely hard enough for many to swallow. Now these divine-like attributes are drawn of an infant lying in a feedbox. Thus, not only is the presumptuous pomp and claim to power of Caesar contrasted with (and contested by) these humble origins, but Luke suggests the even more extraordinary claim that such lowliness is consistent with the workings and very character of God.

Therefore, Luke's use of paradox further accentuates the reality-reversing character of this good news and the tremendous significance of what is at stake. For what is at stake here is not simply a choice between Caesar and this Jewish infant destined to become a crucified criminal, but between Caesar and the manifestation of *God's* very mission and person in this Jewish infant destined to become a crucified criminal. It is not just about Caesar and this infant lying in a feedbox. It is about choosing between the Lord Caesar whose power and person are defined by economic, political, and military might, and the Lord God whose power and person are defined in Jesus, helpless infant now, crucified and resurrected Messiah later.

Admiration and Identification

As Luke has done throughout his infancy account, he gives his readers examples of admirable characters to reflect upon even as they wrestle with the world-reversing, paradoxical claims Luke promotes. Once again, we find the prophecy → fulfillment → proclamation pattern at work in the combination of angelic proclamation and the shepherds' response, and the attention Luke draws to the shepherds faithfully making known what the Lord had made known to them

118

elevates their paradigmatic role (2:15, 17). We also encounter Mary treasuring these words and pondering them in her heart (2:19). As before, these para-digms of faithfulness invite readers to respond to the amazing good news Luke portrays with similar devotion and thoughtfulness. However, Mary and the shepherds are likely meant by Luke to function as more than simply paradigms of faithfulness, worthy of readers' admiration. Luke also invites readers to iden-tify with these characters, perhaps even against their normal inclinations.

Two features of Luke's portrayal suggest that he is calling his audience to "join ranks" with the shepherds in their embrace and celebration of the good news. One is another dimension of the reversal Luke weaves into the passage. Not only does the evangelist draw a contrast between Caesar and Jesus (and God) and issue an implicit call to embrace the world being fashioned by God's reign, but Luke also challenges long-standing conceptions of status, or honor. In the ancient world, status was in large measure determined by one's social identity, which in turn was determined by one's social proximity to those in power, or one's "location on the social ladder," as Bruce Malina puts it.[41] By calling readers to entrust themselves to a Lord and Savior boxed in a manger, Luke also calls them to reorient radically their understanding of desirable social location. Or, to put it better, Luke calls them to set aside established norms of social location and adopt a wholly new way of both conceiving of one's self in relationship to others, and of presenting one's self to the rest of the world. Sta-tus, in other words, at least the status that really matters, is redefined by Luke not as one's proximity to family, social class, and (ultimately) to Caesar, but as one's proximity to Jesus and those who embrace God's reign in his person.[42] Moreover, by also presenting the shepherds as those who faithfully embrace the angelic message and the Savior they proclaim, Luke challenges his readers to become like those whom the world holds in little regard, in order that they may be among those "whom God favors" (2:14).

A second feature of the narrative that calls readers to join the shepherds is the use of the second-person plural pronoun (ὑμεῖς) in the direct discourse of 2:10-12. On the one hand, the direct address implied by the pronouns underscores that the shepherds themselves are beneficiaries of the good news the angel announces:

> But the angel said to them, "Do not be afraid; for see—I am bringing you good news of great joy for all the people: *to you* is born this day in the city of David a Savior, who is the Messiah, the Lord. This will be a sign *for you*: you will find a child wrapped in bands of cloth and lying in a manger."

Darrell Bock notes that "the personal nature of the address to them is sig-nificant, since it individualizes the message" and indicates that "what is for all the people (2:10) is also for the shepherds." On the other hand, he astutely points out that the pronouns also call the reader "to identify with the shepherds as they hear this good news" to see themselves as among the "y'all" the angels address.[43] Just as readers were earlier led to wonder to what extent the announcements of a son and his wider significance were good news, not only for Zechariah and Elizabeth, Mary and Joseph, but for them as well, so here, too, are readers meant to stand alongside the shepherds and receive this good news as though this child were born "to them" as well.

Finally, Mary again emerges as one with whom readers are likely to identify as she "ponders" the shepherd's news "in her heart" (2:19). Her wonderment, as did her puzzlement in a previous scene (1:26-38), serves to assure readers that what is being proclaimed here really is a radical departure from how the world is normally conceived. Reflection and further consideration—pondering—is thus an appropriate response, even for one who also "treasured all these words." Mary thus continues to serve as a "bridge character" of sorts for readers, as one whose tremendous faith is matched with an understandable puzzlement and wonderment. Via her character, Luke admits to readers that in light of the extraordinary good news she receives from a rather extraordinary array of messengers (from angels to shepherds), she—and the readers themselves—have good reason to scratch their heads a bit. But in the end, Luke's hope for readers is that they will also respond with Mary's, Elizabeth's, Zechariah's, and the shepherd's faithfulness, and rejoice in the Savior that has been born and made known to them as well.

Summary

The four rhetorical aims Luke pursues throughout his infancy narrative dominate his casting of this climactic scene, and pathos continues to play an important role in promoting them. Here we encounter reversal and paradox in the extreme, as Luke presents to his readers the infant Jesus lying in a feed trough and draws comparisons to the lord Caesar, on the one hand, and the Lord God on the other. The one comparison is energized by the stark contrast that exists between Jesus and Caesar, and the incredible, if not ludicrous, claim that Jesus, not Caesar, is the Lord and Savior whose birth is a source of good news and salvation. The other is energized by the implicit, yet equally incredible claim that this helpless infant of lowly estate somehow mirrors the Lord and Savior known to Israel as Yahweh, the very God who called the worlds into being and sustains all things. As Luke turns the world upside down on his readers, he brings characters to the fore to show Theophilus and others what to do with this amazing news. Join the shepherds, Luke urges. Become those who glorify and praise God for all they have heard and seen, just as it has been told to them. Join Mary, ponder these words and treasure them, even when it all seems too strange, and too good, to be true.

The Circumcision, Naming, and Presentation of Jesus (2:21-40)

[21] After eight days had passed, it was time to circumcise the child; and he was called Jesus, the name given by the angel before he was conceived in the womb.
[22] When the time came for their purification according to the law of Moses, they brought him up to Jerusalem to present him to the Lord [23] (as it is written in the law of the Lord, "Every firstborn male shall be designated as holy to the Lord"), [24] and they offered a sacrifice according to what is stated in the law of the Lord, "a pair of turtledoves or two young pigeons."
[25] Now there was a man in Jerusalem whose name was Simeon; this man was righteous and devout, looking forward to the consolation of Israel, and the Holy Spirit rested on him. [26] It had been revealed to him by the Holy Spirit that he would not see death before he had seen the Lord's Messiah. [27] Guided by the Spirit, Simeon came into the temple; and when the parents brought in the child Jesus, to do for him what was customary under the law, [28] Simeon took him in his arms and praised God, saying,

[29] "Master, now you are dismissing your servant in peace,
    according to your word;
[30] for my eyes have seen your salvation,
    [31] which you have prepared in the presence of all peoples,
[32] a light for revelation to the Gentiles
    and for glory to your people Israel."

[33] And the child's father and mother were amazed at what was being said about him. [34] Then Simeon blessed them and said to his mother Mary, "This child is destined for the falling and the rising of many in Israel, and to be a sign that will be opposed [35] so that the inner thoughts of many will be revealed—and a sword will pierce your own soul too."
[36] There was also a prophet, Anna the daughter of Phanuel, of the tribe of Asher. She was of a great age, having lived with her husband seven years after her marriage, [37] then as a widow to the age of eighty-four. She never left the temple but worshiped there with fasting and prayer night and day. [38] At that moment she came, and began to praise God and to speak about the child to all who were looking for the redemption of Jerusalem.
[39] When they had finished everything required by the law of the Lord, they returned to Galilee, to their own town of Nazareth. [40] The child grew and became strong, filled with wisdom; and the favor of God was upon him.

Overview

The account of Jesus' circumcision, naming, and presentation in the temple is often viewed as standing in parallel relationship to the circumcision and naming of John back in Luke 1. Moreover, several factors suggest that Simeon's and Anna's rejoicing upon seeing the infant Jesus is to be viewed as a counterpart to Zechariah's hymn. First, both sets of responses follow an account of the birth, naming, and circumcision of the child. Second, both display a similar structure in their movement from praise to prophecy or witness. Finally, each concludes with a summary statement concerning the child's growth (1:80; 2:40). Despite these correspondences, however, the intervening episode reporting the angelic proclamation and the shepherds' response disrupts the neat parallelism between these two scenes. In addition, Simeon's and Anna's acts of praise are not placed in the narrative context of Jesus' birth, naming, and circumcision but are set in the temple during the rites of purification and dedication. Furthermore, it is also uncertain to what extent Simeon's and Anna's praise is meant to recall what has been said in the Benedictus regarding the character of John, for there are virtually no parallels between the character speech of the two episodes. Perhaps the most helpful way to view the relation of this episode to its surrounding context is to recognize that while the structuring of the infancy narrative may still maintain a loose parallelism, Luke's account has now turned to focusing nearly exclusively on the significance of Jesus—a transition begun already in Zechariah's prophecy.

Deeply Rooted in Jewish Faith, Hope, and Witness

By means of summary, Luke 2:21-40 revolves around three primary impulses. First, Luke is concerned to reassert that the advent of God's salvation is deeply rooted in the life and faith of Judaism. He achieves this by several means. Luke portrays the characters in this episode as among the most faithful of Israel. No less than four times does Luke inform us that Mary's purification and Jesus' presentation took place "according to the law," including references that envelope the account (vv. 22, 24, 27, 39).[44] The resulting picture of Mary and Joseph is that of a pious couple faithfully devoted to God's torah. Luke's casting of Simeon and Anna is no less complimentary and is intended to display their unmatched piety and their persistent hope in God's deliverance. Simeon is described as righteous and devout, earnestly looking for the consolation of Israel, and one upon whom God's Spirit perpetually rests (v. 25). Luke tells us that Anna tirelessly devoted herself to God. Never leaving the temple, she worshiped there with fasting and prayer night and day (v. 37).[45] Jesus is proclaimed as God's awaited redemption by those representing the "best of expectant Israel."[46]

Still another feature of the setting that establishes its ties to Israelite tradition is the common observation that the scene is patterned after the Samuel story. As summarized by Brown:

> We remember that after the God-given conception and birth of her child, Hannah (or Anna—note the name), brought the child Samuel to the sanctuary at Shiloh and offered him to the service of the Lord (1 Sam 1:24-28). There she and her husband encountered the aged priest Eli, even as Mary and Joseph encountered the aged Simeon. We are told that Eli blessed Elkanah and Hannah (1 Sam 2:20), even as Simeon blessed Joseph and Mary (Luke 2:34). The Samuel story mentions women who were ministering at the door of the sanctuary (1 Sam 2:22), even as Luke describes Anna who "never left the Temple courts; day and night she worshipped God, fasting and praying" (2:37). The conclusion in Luke 2:40, describing how "the child grew up and became strong, filled with wisdom and favored by God," echoes 1 Sam 2:21, 26: "The young child grew in the presence of the Lord . . . Samuel continued to grow both in stature and in favor with the Lord and men."[47]

A third prominent element of the passage displaying the interconnectedness between the events in view and Jewish tradition is the content of Simeon's hymn and prophecy. In conjunction with the narrative setting, which tells us that Simeon was looking for the consolation of Israel (v. 25) and had been informed by the Spirit that he would not die before the advent of God's Messiah (v. 26), Simeon's praise following his reception of the infant Jesus into his arms names this child as the fulfillment of Israel's messianic hopes for deliverance (vv. 29-30).[48] The remainder of Simeon's Song adds further depth to this dimension, as it celebrates Jesus' advent while echoing the visions of restored Israel announced in the latter chapters of Isaiah.[49]

Salvation witnessed by all people	(vv. 30-31)	Isa 40:5 (LXX); 49:6; 52:10
Israel as a light to the Gentiles	(v. 32)	Isa 42:6; 49:6
Revelation to the Gentiles	(v. 32)	Isa 52:10
Glory given to Israel	(v. 32)	Isa 46:13
Light and glory as synonymous terms for God's salvation	(v. 32)	Isa 60:1

The salvation Simeon witnesses is not only that which he himself has long sought (προσδέχομαι [v. 25]), but that which has been eagerly awaited by "all who were looking for [προσδέχομαι] the redemption of Jerusalem" (v. 38). Green identifies the manifold significance of these allusions:

> The echoes function at a number of levels: (1) they root Simeon's message firmly in the purpose of God, manifest in the Scriptures; (2) they root Simeon's message more particularly in the Isaianic vision of divine restoration and healing; (3) they emphasize the universalistic reach of God's redemption; and (4) they point to the image of the Isaianic Servant of Yahweh as a fundamental scriptural metaphor for interpreting the mission of Jesus as a whole.[50]

Finally, both Simeon and Anna fittingly embrace the revelation of Jesus as God's awaited salvation and respond with praise and witness. Like that of Zechariah, Simeon's Song ends with a prophetic pronouncement concerning the future significance of the child. The evangelist reports that Anna "began to praise God and to speak [λαλέω] about the child to all who were looking for the redemption of Jerusalem" (v. 38). Thus, the reader is reminded that those who first bear witness to this good news of redemption are among the most faithful of Israel.

Luke's portrayal of Jesus' parents and Simeon and Anna as among the most faithful of Israel, his use of a well-known Old Testament narrative to guide his account, allusions to Isaiah, and the placement of the episode at the center of Judaism (in the temple) recall the very similar features in his presentation of Elizabeth and Zechariah at the start of the birth narrative. With the final episode proclaiming God's coming salvation in the infancy narrative, Luke returns to an idyllic scene of Jewish piety and faith. Enveloping the infancy narrative with announcements of God's coming salvation in the setting of the temple and among "the best of expectant Israel," Luke again underscores that the coming of Jesus is rooted in Israel's history and hope as God's own people. Moreover, in providing this setting, Luke also shows that the inauguration of God's salvation in Jesus—and its proclamation—took place among those who most ideally represented Israel's faith. Thus, Luke grounds elements that may not have conformed to typical Jewish expectation, such as (for some) the inclusion of the Gentiles in God's plan of salvation and (for nearly all) the Messiah's rejection by many in Israel, in the prophetic announcement of Israelites who, as righteous, devout, and filled with the Holy Spirit (vv. 25, 26, 27), are well qualified to profess the shape and significance of the Messiah's mission.

Salvation for Israel and for All the World

A second major impulse of the passage is to indicate more directly than before that the salvation inaugurated in Jesus is for both Jews and Gentiles. Through

124

Simeon's words of praise, Luke announces that God's awaited salvation manifest in Jesus has implications that include but also transcend the people of
Israel. Whereas in the previous episode a contrast was drawn between Caesar
and Jesus that invited Luke's audience to see a universalistic coloring in the
expression "all the people" (v. 10) and "those of God's favor" (v. 14), here Simeon explicitly refers to "all peoples" (πάντων τῶν λαῶν), both Gentiles and
Israel, as recipients of God's salvation (vv. 31-32):

> for my eyes have seen your salvation,
> ὅτι εἶδον οἱ ὀφθαλμοί μου τὸ σωτήριόν σου,
> which you have prepared in the presence of all peoples,
> ὃ ἡτοίμασας κατὰ πρόσωπον πάντων τῶν λαῶν,
> a light for revelation to the Gentiles and for glory to your people Israel.
> φῶς εἰς ἀποκάλυψιν ἐθνῶν καὶ δόξαν λαοῦ σου Ἰσραήλ.

The parallelism of the brief canticle places φῶς ("light") in apposition to
σωτήριον ("salvation"), with "for revelation to the Gentiles and for glory to
your people Israel" as the manifestation of φῶς, that is, God's saving work.[51]
Moreover, the listing of both Gentiles and Jews in verse 32 serves as a description of the πάντων τῶν λαῶν of verse 31. The resulting meaning of the verses
can thus be paraphrased as follows: "for I have seen your salvation which you
have prepared for all peoples, namely, a light which brings saving revelation
to the Gentiles and the awaited glory of restoration to your people, Israel."
Exactly what is meant by the expression "a light for revelation to the Gentiles"
is unclear. Taking into account the Isaian parallels, especially Isaiah 49:6, the
phrase suggests that with the enactment of God's consolation of Israel a way has
now been established for the Gentiles to recognize and thus also to embrace
the sovereignty and saving power of Israel's God.[52] With regard to the phrase
"Glory for your people Israel," John J. Kilgallen has shown that Deutero- and
Trito-Isaiah commonly speak of God's glory coming upon Israel as a manifestation of their awaited deliverance (Isa 44:22-23; 45:22-25; 46:13; 58:8;
60:1-2; 61:1).[53] For the prophet, glory and salvation were treated as nearly
synonymous, as glory would be bestowed upon and characterize redeemed
Israel. Similar expressions occur in Baruch 5:1-4; Daniel 7:14; Ezekiel 39:21,
28-29; 2 Maccabees 5:17-20; and Psalm 84:10 (LXX).[54]

A Costly Calling

The praise and jubilation dominating the preceding episodes has, at times,
been punctuated by hints that the coming of God's saving reign in Jesus will

entail sacrifice and struggle among the faithful. Elizabeth and Zechariah honor Gabriel's command and refuse to name their son after one of their own household, implying their recognition that John's significance and ministry will transcend the claims of his kin. Then Zechariah speaks of enemies that still need to be overcome, indicating that there will be opposition to the new world God is fashioning among God's people. Here in this episode, the notion that the newborn child belongs to the Lord more so than to his parents is also in view. We are told that "he was called Jesus, *the name given by the angel before he was conceived in the womb*" (2:21), likewise indicating that it is God who defines Jesus' identity and life calling, rather than his familial ties. In the episode recounting John's naming, I suggested that the story of Samuel's birth and dedication to God may be in view. As we have seen, there are even clearer allusions to that story in this pericope, further lending credit to the view that in so depicting the naming and presentation of Jesus, Luke once again wanted to show both the momentous importance of this child and the fact that his life as *God's* Son is to be set apart in service of God and all of God's people.

Then Simeon offers a postscript to his praise that further manifests and develops these themes of service, sacrifice, and opposition. Simeon pronounces that Jesus is set for the "falling and rising of many in Israel" (v. 34). Similar to Mary's statements of reversal in her song of praise (cf. 1:52-53), Simeon announces that Jesus' ministry will lead to the fall of some and the exaltation of others.[55] Here, however, the reversing effect of God's awaited deliverance is closely connected to the rejection that Jesus himself will experience, for Jesus is also destined (κεῖμαι) to be a "sign spoken against" (σημεῖον ἀντιλεγόμενον [v. 34]).[56] Thus, as in the previous episode, we encounter a reversal associated with Jesus' own person—and a reversal similarly expressed through a jarring juxtaposition of ideas concerning Jesus (cf. 2:11-12).[57] Simeon's proclamation of Jesus as "God's salvation" who will be "a light for revelation to the Gentiles and glory to Israel" (v. 32) quickly gives way to his description of Jesus as a "sign" many will reject.

In discussing the reversal associated with Jesus' person in the previous episode, I proposed that the reader would likely draw a connection between Jesus' lowly entrance into the world and the humiliation of the cross. Here, Luke takes a step further in connecting the condescension associated with Jesus' person to the negative response Jesus will evoke from others, and it is again hard to believe that Luke's readers would not make an immediate connection between this rejection and Jesus' passion.[58] That this would be Luke's intent seems further indicated by Simeon's parenthetical yet emphatic remark to Mary in verse 35a: "and the soul of you yourself will also be pierced by a sword" (my translation).[59] According to I. Howard Marshall, "the thought is of the anguish that Mary would share at the general rejection of her Son, culminating in the

passion."[60] Brown, however, laments the continuing attractiveness of this interpretation for many, complaining that "it is disheartening to see that the tendency
to interpret Luke by John [John 19:25-27] continues in terms of understanding
this as her suffering at the cross."[61] Instead, Brown argues that the closest Old
Testament parallel to the expression "sword passing through" (Ezek 14:17 and
its reproduction in the Sibylline Oracles [3.316]) refers to the sword as God's
discriminating judgment.[62] In the context of Luke's Gospel, Brown argues, the
"special anguish" caused Mary by God's discriminating judgment through Jesus
"will consist in recognizing that the claims of Jesus' heavenly family outrank any
human attachments between him and his mother, a lesson that she will begin to
learn already in the next scene (2:48-50)."[63]

The naming of Jesus (2:21) has already suggested Luke's interest in pointing out that Jesus' identity and calling for Jesus will ultimately transcend his
familial bonds, and thus Brown's reading of the phrase would fit well in this
context. However, Brown's interpretation does not seem to account fully for
the intense pathos implied by the statement "and the soul of you yourself will
also be pierced by a sword." Perhaps Mary's struggle to "let go" of her son
accounts for part of the pain Simeon speaks of here, but other, more painful
events are likely in view. In fact, as Brown himself argues, Mary is later characterized as one who does not let her family connections to Jesus get in the way
of her obedience to God's word (8:21; 11:28).[64] This makes it unlikely that
Luke would here describe Mary's faithful discipleship in such extraordinarily
painful terms—we just don't see such struggle affecting Mary's character or
discipleship in the remainder of the Gospel. Moreover, the placement of the
parenthetical remark immediately following the reference to Jesus as "a sign
spoken against" indicates that Mary's future experience of suffering is to be
understood primarily in relation to Jesus' rejection and suffering.[65]

> This child is destined for the falling and the rising of many in Israel, and
> to be a sign that will be opposed (and the soul of you yourself will also be
> pierced by a sword) so that the wayward thoughts of many will be exposed
> [my translation].

> Ἰδοὺ οὗτος κεῖται εἰς πτῶσιν καὶ ἀνάστασιν πολλῶν ἐν τῷ Ἰσραὴλ
> καὶ εἰς σημεῖον ἀντιλεγόμενον (καὶ σοῦ [δὲ] αὐτῆς τὴν ψυχὴν
> διελεύσεται ῥομφαία,), ὅπως ἂν ἀποκαλυφθῶσιν ἐκ πολλῶν καρδιῶν
> διαλογισμοί.

Simeon says in effect, "Jesus will be rejected (and, as a result, you yourself will
deeply suffer), in order that the wayward hearts of many shall be exposed."

How would an allusion to Jesus' death here serve Luke's rhetorical interests? By placing the foreshadowing of Jesus' death at the start of the narrative in the mouth of Simeon, a faithful Israelite filled by the Holy Spirit, Luke reveals here what he will also repeat throughout the Gospel and especially in the passion predictions: namely, Jesus' death was no accident. Rather, it was from the beginning part of God's plan to redeem God's people. Thus, here in the small confines of this episode, the wondrous news of God's saving embrace of all nations collides with the tragic truth that many of those whom God has called God's own will turn their backs on the one begotten as their Savior and Lord. The reverberations from this collision are guiding impulses for the rest of Luke's story.

Affective-Rhetorical Analysis

Perhaps it is fitting as Luke begins to round out his proclamation of Jesus and his significance in the infancy narrative proper that he should employ a host of affective devices. A final parting shot, if you will, at the hearts of Theophilus and others before transitioning to the body of the Gospel. In this passage alone we encounter the solicitation of reader admiration and sympathy, nostalgia, paradox, reversal, conflict, and the striking contrast of the beautiful and ugly, the hopeful and desperate.[67]

As we've seen, Luke goes to great pains to paint the setting and events surrounding Jesus' circumcision, naming, and presentation as a most idyllic scene. The actors couldn't be depicted in more glowing terms, and the significance of Jesus—accentuated by nostalgic allusion to the Isaian vision of salvation—couldn't be cast in a more hope-filled manner. The obtrusively repetitive references to the piety of Jesus' parents, and the extended introductions for both Simeon and Anna, including Luke's celebration of their faithfulness, persistence, and long-standing trust in God's promises for deliverance even into old age, are surely aimed to cultivate admiration in Luke's readers, as well as the sympathetic satisfaction of seeing ones such as these receive and celebrate the tidings of great joy they have long awaited. This is a most just reward for those who have set their hearts on serving the Lord. In leading Theophilus and others to admire and sympathize with these characters, Luke once again invites them to embrace the good news these characters proclaim as good news for themselves, and to join in the celebration.

Yet there is an undercurrent that sweeps into view with Simeon's final, unexpected words that threatens to undermine the joy of this scene. Readers have been granted glimpses of this undercurrent before: Mary's announcement of reversal, Zechariah's references to enemies, the radical claim that

Jesus, not Caesar, is the one true Lord and Savior of all, the lowliness of Jesus' birth, the fact that John and Jesus' identity and vocation will set them apart from their own families. These hints have reminded readers that the blessing God is working among them will be opposed by many and come at a cost. Here, Luke undercuts his readers' participation in the jubilant character of this moment with Simeon's ominous afterword: "This child, God's very own salvation, is set for the fall and rising of many among God's own people. He will be a sign of God's favor that is protested and rejected. And Mary, it will be as though a sword is piercing your very own soul." Once again the reader encounters paradox, reversal, and conflict, born from yet another startling juxtaposition of images relating to Jesus' person and mission: his advent will lead to the rise and fall of many; the embodiment of God's salvation, the cornerstone, will be rejected; conflict will characterize his reign among us; lines of allegiance will be drawn. But the pathos cuts deeper still. Here the reader is also confronted with what is so right and also what is so wrong with humanity. The beatific vision of enduring trust in God and joyous celebration of God's promise fulfilled in Jesus is set in jarring opposition to an ugly nightmare. Many who consider themselves Yahweh's own will reject God's Messiah. The one who is to deliver Israel from its enemies will be handed over by many of Israel to its enemies. Some will trust, rejoice, and mourn while others castigate and crucify!

Summary

By so affectively casting this final scene in the infancy narrative proper, I believe Luke was after several rhetorical aims. First, Luke wanted to emphasize what he has suggested throughout the infancy narrative, that the in-breaking of God's reign will come at a cost, not only for the proud that are cast down and the many who will fall, but for the righteous as well, even those as blessed as Elizabeth, Zechariah, John, Jesus, and Mary. Jesus will further inform readers what it means for them to "take up their cross daily and follow me" (9:23) in the pages to follow, but already in the infancy narrative Luke challenges them to consider their place in the conflict that will inevitably result between those who entrust themselves to the "sign" God provides and those who reject it. Second, Luke continues to show that even though Jesus may have been rejected by many of his own people, his inauguration of God's salvation couldn't be more deeply rooted in Jewish hope and tradition, including the prophetic promises speaking of God's awaited redemption. The best of expectant Israel readily recognized the significance of this child and what God would accomplish in his person.[68] Third, through nostalgia and the startling contrast between what is most beautiful and ugly about humanity, Luke encourages Theophilus and other readers to appreciate more deeply the significance of what is at stake, as well as the tragedy that many Israel have rejected God's own Son. Luke's Gospel is, in many ways, a tragic tale.[69] Simeon's prophecy of the fall and rising of many paired with Anna's reference to the "redemption of Jerusalem" (2:38) certainly would have struck a painful note for many of Luke's readers. The Messiah's coming was, in the hopes of many Second Temple Jews, to redeem Jerusalem, but Jerusalem and the temple—at the writing of this Gospel—lay in ruins because (as Jesus will later explain) "you did not recognize the time of your visitation from God" (Luke 19:44). Finally, even though Luke wants readers to appreciate the tragedy of what will transpire in Jesus' rejection and passion, and Jerusalem's ruin, Luke also wants them to know that it is *expected* as part of the collision between the reign of God and the desperate ways of this world (see also Luke 21:22). Even more, the tragedy of Jesus' rejection, while painful (cf. Luke 19:41-44), does not ultimately undermine or overcome the joyful proclamation of the salvation God will accomplish in Jesus. It is added to Simeon's hymn as a painful countermelody, a reminder of what was and is tragically lost, but one that in the end cannot keep up with the dominant currents of the song. And so, Simeon's own proclamation stands as testimony that both triumph and tragedy are part of the story of God's salvation. What is lost will not be forgotten, and the heartache it causes Luke is apparent in the shaping of this story line here in this passage and throughout his two-volume work (see also Luke 20:9-18; 21:20-24; 23:34; Acts 26:24-28; 28:23-28). But tragedy is not the end of the story Luke tells. Indeed, many have rejected God's Messiah and the temple is now gone. But God's redemption is still drawing near (Luke 21:28), and forgiveness is offered even from the cross (23:34).

Conclusion

From Scripture's Heart to Ours

The preceding two chapters have explored Luke's use of pathos in his infancy narrative to draw readers into his story and lead them to consider the world to which he bears witness. The purpose of this investigation was to test further and illustrate the guiding premise of the work: *affective appeal in varying forms is the means by which narratives, including biblical narratives, compel us to enter their storied world and entertain the version of reality they present.* If this premise is indeed true, then our affective-rhetorical analysis should have in at least some instances enriched our understanding of the intended function of individual passages. Moreover, it should also offer at least a tentative indication of the particular concerns of Luke-Acts as a whole. In what follows, I will summarize our findings from the previous two chapters and propose what our analysis suggests about the rhetorical aims of Luke's two-volume work. In addition, I will also offer some suggestions on how this mode of reading biblical narrative can serve as a resource for pastors and Christian communities.

Exegetical Insights

In chapter 3, I stated that one of the potential benefits of affective analysis is that when used alongside historical- and literary-critical methods, it can provide additional data for making judgments about the intended meaning and function of individual passages. There are several occasions in our investigation of Luke 1–2 where we found this to be true. By focusing on how Luke encouraged reader admiration, sympathy, and nostalgia in the annunciation of John's birth (1:5-25), we were led to note the disappointment that likely would have resulted for most readers when reading of Zechariah's failure to believe the joyous news of John's birth as announced by Gabriel. We further discerned that the passage ends without resolution, thus magnifying the dissatisfaction Luke intended for the reader. This suggested to us an assessment of the passage that significantly differs from that of most commentators, yet one that other elements of the passage and surrounding context affirm. Rather than seeing Zechariah's failure as a peripheral element of the passage, and even as fortuitous development since it delays Zechariah's song of praise until John's birth, I argued that it is instead central to the story's rhetorical function: it confronts readers with an emotively charged depiction of the importance of believing and bearing witness to the good news. Several additional features of the passage and immediate context participate in and affirm the reading suggested by our affective-rhetorical analysis: the vehemence of Gabriel's rebuke, the imbalanced structure of the passage (resulting from Zechariah's absence in the final chiastic element), and the examples of faithful witness by Elizabeth and (later on) Mary that further highlight Zechariah's failure to believe and praise.

My analysis of the annunciation of Jesus' birth (1:26-38) also led to a plausible explanation for the much-debated narrative gap created by Mary's perplexing question in verse 34. I argued that the gap is best explained as serving not only Luke's interest to say more about Jesus, but also his desire to cultivate a connection between Mary and his readers via sympathy and even reader identity. Mary's question is meant to sound rather silly because it is one more way Luke portrays the understandable difficulty she is having in comprehending Gabriel's announcement concerning herself and the child she will somehow bear. In so casting Mary, Luke encourages readers who may be similarly taken aback by Gabriel's revelation concerning Jesus as the Spirit-conceived Divine Son to identify with Mary and her confusion. With this connection forged between Mary and Luke's readers, readers are then also encouraged to join Mary in responding with faith in response to Gabriel's proclamation, "For with God nothing will be impossible," despite the reservations and uncertainties that may remain. Because we examined this passage looking for ways Luke might be utilizing reader sympathy and identity as an affective device, we were led to consider this alternative and plausible explanation for how the gap created by Mary's question could be resolved.

Another example of how the investigation of Luke's use of pathos can contribute to an exegetical assessment of a passage was presented in the discussion of the crowd's amazement directed at Zechariah's naming of John (1:63). Here affective-rhetorical analysis offered guidance in determining which of the competing interpretations of this element would foster greater emotive impact among Luke's readers and also more effectively promote Luke's rhetorical aims. I argued that it was the countercultural, not the coincidental, character of Zechariah's naming of his son that better serves Luke's affective and rhetorical interests, and that also makes better sense within the immediate context of the pericope. Once again, attention to the affective dimensions of the passage led to a reincorporation of all of the relevant data and our reconsideration of the dominant view among interpreters.

There is still another way in which affective-rhetorical analysis has guided our exegesis of Luke 1–2. By considering the affective impact certain ways of framing material likely has on readers, we have also been led to identify motifs that stand out as particularly important to Luke in his infancy narrative. As already noted, the disappointment cultivated by Zechariah's lack of faith in 1:5-25 and its contrast to the admiration solicited by Luke's portrayals of characters faithfully embracing disclosures of God's salvation suggested Luke's emphasis on faithful response. In addition, by understanding that paradoxical and world-reversing portrayals often unnerve readers and compel them to reexamine their own worldviews, we have also been led to see the importance Luke places on challenging his readers to embrace the exalted complexity of Jesus' identity as well as the reversal of social order portended by the in-breaking of God's kingdom. Moreover, we found that one of the characteristic ways Luke casts his characters as admirable is by presenting them as the "best of expectant Israel." This, along with his frequent use of nostalgic allusion, indicates Luke's interest in leading the reader to appreciate the essential rootedness of the good news in Jewish hope and tradition. It also plays a key role in setting up Jesus' eventual rejection by many of his fellow Jews as a tragic element of the Gospel story.

Rhetorical Insights: Understanding the Purpose of Luke–Acts

This leads us to a second important benefit offered by an affective-rhetorical analysis of Luke's infancy narrative: the input it provides for helping us determine the rhetorical interests of Luke-Acts as a whole. Of course, due to the limited scope of the work that has been presented, we can only offer some very tentative suggestions here on how Luke's account engages the ideological context of his time. Although the infancy narrative plays a key role in introducing the primary motifs and interests of Luke-Acts as a whole, we would have to investigate much more of Luke's two volumes to affirm the findings presented here. That said, here is what our exegesis of Luke 1–2, supplemented by affective-rhetorical analysis, suggests about Luke's motives.

In chapter 4, I listed four rhetorical ends Luke's use of pathos appears to serve, to which I now add one more. These five correspond to the dominant themes of the infancy narrative I just mentioned. In review, Luke aims to encourage Theophilus and others to:

1. respond to the most relevant and amazing good news of God's salvation in Jesus with devotion, praise, and witness;
2. be assured that God's act of salvation in Jesus emerges from God's long-standing relationship with and covenantal commitment to God's people, Israel;
3. embrace the paradoxical reality of Jesus' mission and person as one who walks among us but is uniquely related to and uniquely manifests God as the Spirit-conceived Divine Son, Savior, Messiah, and Lord;
4. recognize that the in-breaking of God's reign in John and Jesus subverts humanly contrived systems of power and status and turns the world "upside down";
5. appreciate the tragic nature of many Jews' refusal to embrace Jesus as the messianic Son of God.

At the beginning of chapter 3, I offered a survey of Luke's ideological landscape, the primary perspectives in play among Luke's potential readers. If we take the rhetorical character of Luke's narrative seriously, then we must account for how Luke's retelling of the story of Jesus and the early church is meant to confront and challenge claims he viewed as incompatible with the gospel. Allow me to offer a brief assessment of how Luke's rhetorical interests counteract those competing perspectives of his day by speculating on the questions, "Who is Theophilus?" and "How does Luke seek to affirm for him and other readers the truth of the gospel?"

The reader implied by Luke's infancy narrative is either a Hellenized Jew or a Gentile intimately familiar with and favorably disposed toward Jewish tradition, possibly a "God-fearer." He is also favorably disposed toward Christianity, and may even consider himself a Christian, but is troubled by the reality that so many of Jesus' fellow Jews, including many of the Jewish religious authorities, have not believed in Jesus. In response to those concerns, Luke emphasizes that the arrival of God's salvation in Jesus emerges from the age-old relationship between God and God's people, and fulfills the long-standing prophetic promises that God would restore Israel. He also shows this good news emerging among and embraced by the most faithful of Israel, including folks as varied as a priestly couple, a young virgin and her betrothed, a group of shepherds, and an elderly prophet and prophetess, all of whom are led to recognize and celebrate the arrival of God's salvation in Jesus. By presenting these characters as admirable, some with whom Theophilus and others might identify, Luke invites Theophilus and others to join these characters in their embrace of both Jewish tradition and their celebration of Jesus as God's long-awaited Messiah. Far from ignoring the concern that so many Jews have rejected Jesus, Luke has it foretold by the eminently faithful Simeon and thereby incorporates it as a tragic part of the Gospel story. In doing so, Luke addresses this concern, readily admitting its significance, but contextualizes it as tragedy that nevertheless does not overwhelm the joy-filled response of the faithful to the in-breaking of God's saving reign in Jesus.

Given his attraction or commitment to mainstream Jewish tradition, Theophilus also struggles with the notion prominent among many (if not most) Christians that Jesus—to some notable degree—participates in God's divinity. Rather than steering away from the mind-bending dissonance this claim creates, Luke daringly exploits it as a means of challenging his readers to consider that what God does in and through Jesus is so extraordinary that long-standing categories of human and divine need to be redrawn—at least in this particular case—in order to grasp Jesus' character and calling as the Divine Son of God. Luke is not interested in explaining *how* it could be so that the boundaries between human and divine have become so permeable in Jesus' person (the attempts of Nicea and Chalcedon are still a long ways away). Rather, he repeatedly confronts readers with this claim, a confrontation energized by their own cognitive and affective dissonance, through several prominent features of his paradoxical portrayal: in preparing the way for God, John also prepares the way for Jesus; Jesus is conceived not through normal human union but by God's very Spirit; Jesus, holy and great, will reign on Jacob's throne forever; Jesus and God are both to be known as Lord and Savior. This is indeed perplexing stuff, but Gabriel assures Theophilus and others, that "with God, nothing is impossible" and thus Luke invites readers to follow the lead of Mary. She, understandably, ponders this incredible news yet ultimately entrusts herself to it.

Theophilus also appears to be a member of the social elite. This is suggested not only by his ability to commission Luke's work as a patron, but by the affectively laden proclamation of social, political and economic reversal that dominates Luke's infancy narrative. Theophilus is, I think, one of those I described at the start of chapter 3 struggling to live out the claim that Jesus, not Caesar, is Lord. He struggles to align himself with those who are among the faithful stewards of the gospel but members of a much lower social and economic status. He is trying to live as a member of two kingdoms, that of

Jesus and that of Caesar. Through the portrayal of startling reversal, Luke seeks to help him appreciate the fact that he must choose one realm or the other, for the values and commitments of one are not compatible with the other. Those who opt for Caesar are the enemies of God's saving reign, the proud and wealthy who will be brought down from their thrones. The ones who opt for Jesus and the kingdom of God are the lowly who will be exalted. To be sure, on the face of it, it seems ridiculous to throw in one's lot with the babe squirming in the feedbox and embrace the outrageous claim that he will turn the world upside down. But heaven knows the true Lord and Savior of all, the one whose birth leads to true peace for the faithful.

Readers who are familiar with discussions of Luke's purpose for writing Luke-Acts will readily notice some points of contact and departure between this summary and leading theories.[1] For instance, several commentators have argued that Luke at least in part intends to offer a theodicy, a defense of God's faithfulness to Israel, given that so many of God's people have not believed. In the words of Luke Timothy Johnson:

> Luke sets himself to write the continuation of the biblical story, not alone to defend the Christian movement, but above all to defend God's ways in the world. By showing that the story of Jesus was rooted in that of Israel, and by demonstrating how God kept his promise by restoring Israel, Luke assured his Gentile readers that they could have confidence in "the things in which they were instructed" (Luke 1:4). Luke's purposes are not determined by a momentary crisis or by doctrinal deviance, but by the very existence of a messianic sect in the Gentile world.[2]

Similarly, Robert Tannehill has emphasized that the tragic refusal of many Jews to believe in Jesus is also an integral element of Luke's two-volume work. In discussing what Christian communities may learn from Luke-Acts, he argues that

> Luke-Acts does more than share a grand vision. It tells the story from which we are able to learn. It can help us precisely because the mission it narrates was not as successful as early Christians hoped. The vision of God's purpose, to be realized through the mission, had to encounter hard reality, especially in the form of Jewish resistance to the new movement. Rejections and resistance are major factors in the unfolding story, and rejection by Jews is most keenly felt. . . . Jewish rejection is emphasized in Paul's final remarks to the Roman Jews, the last major scene in Acts (28:23-28). This and related scenes indicate that the mission to bring salvation to the Jewish people through the message of Jesus Messiah has fallen short if its goal. . . .

> The grand vision of salvation for Jews and Gentiles through Jesus in Luke
> 2:30-32 and 3:6 appears to lead to tragic disappointment.[3]

Far less commonly proposed as integral to Luke's purpose are the social, political, and christological emphases we found in the infancy narrative. While interpreters have long pointed out Luke's interest in the poor and marginalized, as is evident throughout the Gospel, only recently have some concluded that this was part of his essential purpose for writing the Gospel and that he was interested in advocating a reversal of the current world order.[4] Still more common is the view that Luke wrote his work to show the Roman authorities that Christianity is a legitimate extension of Judaism and politically and socially benign.[5]

Likewise, commentators have long noted Luke's emphasis on the exalted character of Jesus in the infancy narrative and throughout Luke-Acts. Yet discussions of Lukan Christology are typically devoid of any analysis of the *rhetorical* purpose of Luke's portrait of Jesus other than the more general assertion that it was to provide "assurance" for Luke's readers. One exception has been the claim that Luke's use of step-parallelism in the infancy narrative is part of the evangelist's polemic against those claiming that John was the Messiah. However, my own reading argues that Luke's interest was not so much to present John as inferior to Jesus, but to emphasize the exalted character of both, with the focus coming to rest on the extraordinary character of Jesus as the Divine Son. So consistently and affectively is this claim made of Jesus throughout the infancy account, via sharply drawn paradox, it commends the view that Luke is trying to help Theophilus move to an understanding of Jesus that blurs the lines of distinction between Jesus and God, and that this is one of Luke's primary aims.

Larry Hurtado, in his impressive work on early Christian devotion, *Lord Jesus Christ*, argues that a binitarian devotion focused on both God and God's unique, divine agent, Jesus, developed very early in Christian circles. Accordingly, such devotion would have been commonly practiced among Christians when Luke when was writing his Gospel.[6] At the same time, early Christian devotion to Jesus and claims about Jesus' divinity was met with vigorous resistance from non-Christian Jews.[7] It stands to reason that there were likely Christians or prospective Christians caught in the middle of this debate (as Mark's use of the adoptionist model for portraying Jesus' divine sonship suggests). They were attracted to most dimensions of the Christian message but hesitant to accept claims regarding Jesus' divinity and the devotional practices that presuppose it. Luke's rhetorically charged portrait of Jesus suggests that Theophilus shares these very concerns. Again, to argue this is not to claim that Luke was presenting a systematic treatise on Jesus' nature as the Spirit-conceived Son of God. But it is evident to me that he is clearly pushing beyond the adoptionist notions of divine sonship formerly attributed to the Jewish king and likely applied by some Christians to Jesus. This is an element of his Gospel he wished to emphasize in order to encourage Theophilus and others to join other Christians in exalting and worshiping Jesus, the Messiah Lord and Son of God.

Reading with Heart: Benefits for Clergy and Christian Communities

In the introduction, I proposed that the pursuit of affective-rhetorical analysis among trained interpreters could lead to a form of biblical scholarship that pays significant dividends for pastors and Christian communities. Thus far, I've presented this method as it might be employed by biblical scholars, as one that could supplement an eclectic mix of historical, social-scientific, and literary approaches designed to discern the intended meaning and function of a biblical narrative. Before I conclude the work, I would like to say a word about how this approach may be of some benefit to pastors, and how attention to affect in biblical narrative might also foster new opportunities for spiritual discernment among believing communities.

1. Provides more useful exegetical resources for clergy and laity.
This is perhaps too obvious to need mentioning, but the advances in exegesis resulting from scholarly focus on affect in biblical narrative will also serve clergy and members of Christian communities as they draw on these resources for preaching, Bible studies, and personal reflection. Moreover, and perhaps less obvious, scholarly resources that engage the manifold dimensions of biblical narrative will likely be more attractive to clergy and laity, for the very reason that they provide clergy and laity more opportunities to make connections between the scholarly results offered and their own purposes or interests (as I will discuss below). I assume this is why commentaries offering literary and theological analysis, alongside historical and social-scientific investigation, dominate the market focusing on a clergy and lay audience. With affective analysis, we can take the usefulness of scholarly commentary one step further by exploring yet another dimension of biblical narrative that is both integral to understanding the function of these texts and a mode of analysis that clergy and lay folk can readily integrate into their own interpretive endeavors.

2. Invites a richer engagement of biblical narrative that naturally leads believers to consider how texts might speak to us in our time and place.

Understanding the role of pathos in biblical narrative enables us to appreciate more fully its narrative and rhetorical artistry. It leads to, in others words, a heightened sense of its aesthetic quality that many clergy and laity will appreciate. But even more importantly, and rewarding, this mode of studying biblical narrative invites a more thoroughgoing engagement with the rhetorical force of the text than is typical of other approaches. It calls us as modern readers to put ourselves in the place of Scripture's first readers and imagine what was going on not only in their heads, but also in their hearts. This intensely situational, affective, and rhetorical mode of engaging biblical narrative can help us better appreciate and imagine the situations and struggles of the believers to which these stories are originally addressed. It can lead us to discern what fears, hopes, doubts, and joys they experienced and how the stories woven by biblical authors provided them with assurance or called them to greater faithfulness.

By so thoroughly engaging these texts and the audiences for whom they were written, we are already intently focused on the role of these texts as proclamation that is both rhetorically charged and situationally relevant. In other words, we are already engaged in a mode of inquiry that readily transitions into the pursuit of discerning how these texts might speak to the heads and hearts of believers today. We have also gained an enriched pool of insights from which to draw to help us not only reconstruct what dynamics occasioned the casting of the biblical narrative, but also to discern its connections to our lives of faith in the present. For example, in discovering that the story of Jesus' birth was cast in part to challenge Theophilus and similar readers to reflect on what was problematic about their own social standing and commitments, readers of today may likewise reflect on how that story may similarly speak to and challenge themselves and others to rethink their own social and political priorities, to question who and what it is that they truly serve. Or, to see the sacrifice implicit in Elizabeth's and Zechariah's naming of their son, and consider the way in which Luke meant that story to engage Theophilus, may lead us to consider how we, too, have been called to sacrifice those things society tells us we deserve to have as we seek to serve God and the good news. In short, deeper insight into the affective and rhetorical force of biblical narrative provides a valuable resource for considering how the text can similarly engage believing communities in our time and place.

Accordingly, by paying attention to how biblical authors utilize pathos as a means of engaging their readers, pastors can gain additional direction for shaping their sermons. For instance, preachers guided by literary readings of the text often find it helpful to allow the structure of the story to guide or influence the arrangement and delivery of their sermon. In a sense, and in varying degrees, they are "retelling the story" in their preaching, and the narrative flow of the story serves as an outline of sorts for guiding their own proclamation of the passage. In doing so, they are assisted in re-presenting the story in ways that make connections with the lives of congregants while still remaining faithful to the overall movement and witness of the passage. In similar fashion, the affective and rhetorical dimensions of a passage could also assist preachers, providing them with additional guidance for shaping their retelling of a biblical story in ways that similarly engage the hearts of congregants. Exploring how a biblical author employed pathos as a means of influencing his readers in the shaping of the story may helpfully suggest to a pastor how he or she could go about the same task today, so that the pastor's rhetoric may be informed by the biblical author's use of pathos. This is something that some pastors already do intuitively. But how many have preached on Jesus' annunciation and drew on Mary's confusion as means of connecting with congregants who might have similar troubles with the claim of Jesus' virgin birth and divine sonship? How many have focused on the disappointing denouement and lack of closure to John's birth announcement as a means of calling congregants to more faithful lives of witness, or looked at the story of John's birth as a story of sacrifice, or not only celebrated Simeon's prophecy for its joyful zeal but also ruminated on its recognition of tragedy as part of the gospel story? Of course, preachers must know their congregants, and it may be that the setting and struggles of their congregation are not similar enough to that of Luke's readers that they would want to employ the same affective-rhetorical strategy in the telling of a particular passage. And I am not advocating that they necessarily should. But I do think that knowing how biblical authors employ emotions for rhetorical ends can be very useful for preachers. It not only better enables them to discern the function of the passage, but also gives them the opportunity to draw from—in ways that are appropriate to their own time and place—the biblical authors' use of pathos as a resource for their own faithful proclamation of the text.

3. Enriches our engagement of texts apart from their original historical settings.
Our study of Luke 1–2 has been greatly assisted by the fact that Luke states the purpose for writing his two-volume work in the prologue (Luke 1:1-4) and we know some things about Greco-Roman culture and early church history. This has enabled us to offer a plausible account of the situations and concerns that might have occasioned Luke's shaping of his narrative, to match his use of pathos with particular circumstances encountering his readers. But in

many cases when we examine biblical narrative we lack this degree of background information and cannot reliably reconstruct the situation occasioning the author's or final redactor's casting of the material he presents, or can only do so in a very generalized fashion (for example, the shaping of Old Testament narrative as a response to the destruction of Jerusalem and exile).

Yet even in cases where we are not able to draw reliably on knowledge of a text's historical situation, we can still recognize the narrative artistry evident in the text and also discern ways in which pathos is likely employed to foster a particular kind of response. For instance, back in chapter 2 we turned to the story of the golden calf affair to illustrate how the use of astonishing inversion was to lead readers to appreciate both the breathtakingly egregious nature of Israel's betrayal of Yahweh as well as the remarkable force of God's steadfast love and grace. We also found in the story of Jacob the author's shaping of a threshold moment of intense expectation in order to highlight not only the importance of this impending moment for Jacob, but also one that defines Israel as a people who will struggle with God and humans and prevail, provided they cling to *God's* blessing above all else. With stories such as these, our discernment of the author's use of pathos can guide reflection and preaching in the very same manner discussed above: that is, it can not only guide our sense of the passage's intended function, but also serve as a resource for how we might discern and proclaim its meaning for our lives and the lives of fellow believers. It's just that our exploration of the passage and search for analogues in our own lives is focused solely on the situation depicted within the narrative (and in relationship to its literary and canonical context), rather than also including the situation we imagine that passage speaking to in the lives of its original readers. In other words, the mode of engagement is basically the same. We simply center our discernment squarely on the activity depicted by the narrative, attentive to how the author / final redactor was likely employing pathos among other things to shape readers' response to the passage.

4. *Leads to opportunities for reflection on and transformation of our own affective response to biblical stories.*
Over the last several months as I have pursued this mode of reading Scripture, I have become more aware of my own emotional reaction to biblical narrative. In fact, I have used it as a resource for this study as I imagined how authors were attempting to utilize pathos as a means of influencing readers, while also trying to be mindful of the function of the text in its literary and historical setting. Even so, there have also been times when my emotional response to the text has not matched up all that well with what I sense the author is encouraging.

It strikes me that reading biblical narrative attentive to our own emotional response could be an exceptionally fruitful form of spiritual reflection, especially when we compare our own response to that which seems to be called forth from the biblical author. This could become, in other words, another way in which our dialogue with a biblical passage leads us to greater faithfulness in our own walks of faith. Allow me to share an example.

For years now I have been aware of the strong note of reversal dominating Luke's infancy account. It has long been one of the features of these stories that I most admire: the infant Jesus, lying in a feedbox, dethroning Caesar with all his pomp and pretense. The very glory of God illuminating not the emperor's palace or even the temple courts, but shepherds in their fields. The rich being cast down from their thrones, and the lowly exalted. What great stories these are—God's embrace of the underdog, the casting down of all that oppresses and keeps others from participating in the blessings God intends for all of humanity. You go, Mary! Rock on, shepherds! Turn those tables, baby Jesus!

Then I had the opportunity to spend a week teaching these same texts to a group of Haitian students as part of a course on the Synoptic Gospels at a seminary in Port au Prince. Many of the seminarians walked or rode "tap taps" (dangerously dilapidated pick-up trucks serving as taxis) miles each day to attend the classes, some through literal war zones. I had seen enough of Haiti to guess the state of their housing, mere shacks compared to the house I live in, cobbled combinations of cement, plywood, and corrugated steel with sewage draining out of pipes into tiny yards or the edge of roads. Much of my energy during that week was spent fussing over my own safety and health, while for them the precariousness of life was a daily reality. The celebration they threw to honor me and other instructors at the end of the week seemed to them a great feast, but for me a not-so-attractive meal. The treats I handed out to Haitian children were cherished as gifts of great worth, while my children expect them as a matter of right. And so when it was time to talk about Luke's Gospel and we came to these very same passages in the infancy narrative announcing God's reversal, I was not surprised to see them become even more alert, their bodies energized and eyes gleaming, the very tip of the righteous indignation welling up in their souls. And for a moment, I shared their celebration and hope-filled expectation. Yes, that's right! The powerful and proud, the wealthy and well fed will be brought down from their thrones! The lowly will be exalted, the hungry filled with good things! But only for a moment did I share it with them. For just then, I suddenly remembered that Luke meant these words not just for the lowly and downtrodden, but also, even first and foremost, for the proud and powerful. I realized that I was a heck of a lot more like Theophilus than like my Haitian friends, and that Luke might wonder why

I was so quick to join in their celebration, given that I have done so little to ease their plight. I realized that all along I had been reading these passages in a way that was at odds with the affective and rhetorical edge Luke intended for Theophilus, and would likely intend for me and other privileged Americans if he were writing it today.

Most instances of "misappropriating" the affective and rhetorical edge of a passage will not (I hope!) be so painfully humbling. But by noting our own affective responses to a passage and comparing them with what the author seems to intend for particular members of his audience—or the audience in general if no specific historical setting is in view—can serve as another helpful means of assessing our own response to these stories and how they are challenging us to embrace God's will and ways. Am I responding to this story in a manner consistent with the author's intentions? If not, why? Is it because I don't fit the "reader profile" assumed by the author? Am I sure? How then should I respond in a way that still honors its rhetorical intent and yet fits who I am?

This type of reflection could also be productively done with a larger segment of narrative. For instance, one could explore what sorts of dispositions the biblical author is seeking to cultivate in his readers throughout an entire book or section of the narrative. Here, for example, is a list one might scribe for Luke 1–2.

a. admiration/sympathy for faithful characters
b. disappointment with faithlessness
c. trust in God's ability to fulfill promises, no matter how amazing they might seem
d. affective and cognitive dissonance that challenges readers to see Jesus, God, and the world through new eyes
e. willingness to sacrifice in order that God's purposes for humanity might be fulfilled
f. rejoicing in the salvation God is inaugurating among us
g. saddened by the tragedy that not all will believe

Once again, a process of discernment that could be helpful to individual readers and Bible study groups would be to determine which of these dispositions they see applying to themselves and which do not, and then reflect on why this is the case for them. Of course, some elements of a biblical narrative will speak more readily to certain readers than others. The point here is not that the response of readers should always conform to that of others or to that invited by the text. Indeed not, for a variety of reasons: different reader profiles, readers at different places in their faith journeys, readers with different sets of experiences they bring to the text, and so forth. The point is not to demand conformity, but to invite *conversation* that explores the differences between a reader's affective response and that invited by the text, as well as different responses among readers. Such times of reflection can lead to the blessing of learning from one another as we share our reactions to the text and take stock of the inclinations of our own hearts.

5. *Compels our recognition of Scripture's diversity.*

There is still another reason that it might be appropriate for a reader's affective response to a biblical story or passage to be at odds with that invited by the author. It may be that the affective response sought by the text is deemed by the reader to be at odds with a disposition cultivated by the biblical story as a whole. These instances, in my view, are likely not common, but I would guess that they have occurred at one time or another for many biblical readers. Imagine, for instance, the affective response invited by the author of Joshua 11:16-20, which is part of a larger narrative describing Israel's conquest of Canaan, the promised land, under the leadership of Joshua:

> So Joshua took all that land: the hill country and all the Negeb and all the land of Goshen and the lowland and the Arabah and the hill country of Israel and its lowland, from Mount Halak, which rises toward Seir, as far as Baalgad in the valley of Lebanon below Mount Hermon. He took all their kings, struck them down, and put them to death. Joshua made war a long time with all those kings. There was not a town that made peace with the Israelites, except the Hivites, the inhabitants of Gibeon; all were taken in battle. For it was the LORD's doing to harden their hearts so that they would come against Israel in battle, in order that they might be utterly destroyed, and might receive no mercy, but be exterminated, just as the LORD had commanded Moses.

In the narrative that immediately precedes these verses we hear an unceasing refrain that the extermination willed by God was not restricted to able-bodied Canaanite males who posed a threat to the fulfillment of God's promise to Israel, but included "utterly every person" and "all that breathed" (Josh 10:28, 30, 32, 33, 34, 37, 39, 40; 11:12, 14). All were to be put to the sword, from frail widow to infant child (see also 1 Sam 15:1-33). It seems to me a rousing, "Give 'em hell, Joshua, servant of Yahweh, Warrior God!" is likely close to the affective response intended by the author of these verses.

Or, we could turn to Ezra 9–10 and read the story of Israelite men sending away their foreign wives and their own children in order to be faithful to God's torah, which commands the Israelites to remain separate from the peoples of the land (Exod 34:11-16; Deut 7:1-6). "What an honorable, noble thing to do!" is how the writer of this story likely intends us to respond, since he glowingly describes Ezra as "a scribe skilled in the law of Moses that the LORD God of Israel had given" and says "the hand of the LORD his God was upon him" (Ezra 7:6). Or, we could look to 1 Timothy 2:8-15, which requires that women have no authority over men and not even speak a word in the presence of the gathered community of believers. Instead, bearing in mind that a woman brought the cursing of sin upon humankind, female believers are to seek their salvation "through childbearing, provided they continue in faith and love and holiness, with modesty" (1 Tim 2:15). What emotional response is the author seeking here? Perhaps relief mixed with pious indignation: "It's about time somebody put those women back in their place!"

It seems to me that when we take honest stock of the affective and rhetorical aims of passages such as these, it is more difficult for us to ignore the fact that they express sentiments that for many are at odds with the dominant tendencies of the biblical witness. If we are dealing with them simply on the *cognitive* level, then it is easier for us to ignore their emotive force and seek to harmonize them with the rest of the scriptural testimony to God and what it means to walk in God's ways. For instance, with the Joshua passage, we might euphemistically argue—with a hint of remorse in our voice—that (sadly) warfare was a common feature of life in that day and age, and in order for God to establish Israel in the promised land and protect them from the temptation of idolatry, other peoples, unfortunately, needed to be "displaced" in this manner. On the cognitive level, this may serve for some as a satisfactory explanation of the passage within the larger context of the biblical story, but it certainly reads against the grain of the text's emotive and rhetorical intent. Or, with this and other "problem texts," we seek to salvage an underlying, affectively sterile, principle. So, as is commonly argued with respect to 1 Timothy 2:8-15, the important point we are to take from this passage is that worship is to be orderly and respectful, conducted in a way that builds up and does not threaten the community of believers. Often serving as the justification for this explanation is the speculation of a setting in which female enthusiasts were disrupting worship with their wild displays of prophecy and tongue speaking. There is no evidence to support such a scenario, but it helps us deal with this text without engaging its affective and rhetorical force, or its seemingly absolute and universal intent: "I permit no woman . . ."

145

Attending to the affective character of the biblical texts certainly complicates matters, for it makes it more difficult for us to see and claim Scripture as a unitary, or "monological" witness to the ways and will of God.[8] Instead, it points us to the reality that Scripture is comprised of a diversity of voices, some of which call us to an emotional response that contrasts with those dispositions we have come to associate with faithful service in the example of Jesus.

A Concluding Word

As with any other approach to Scripture, this one will have its own set of shortcomings and pose its own set of challenges. My hope is that the benefits as summarized in this chapter and illustrated throughout the book will convince many that this way of engaging biblical narrative is worth the effort. I also hope that it will lead other scholars to explore and further develop affective analysis in ways that improve upon the work offered here. For when set alongside other interpretive methods aiming to discern how the text was meant to engage its readers, I believe this approach provides yet another opportunity for biblical scholarship to contribute to the needs of believing communities and help believers delve more deeply into the heart of Scripture's witness.

Notes

INTRODUCTION: The Bible's Neglected Heart

1. Many studies that address the role of emotion in biblical narrative offer psychologizing readings on the emotional response of characters within the narrative and are not focused on how the narrative is designed to engage the emotions of its readers. See, for example, Paul A. Kruger, "On Emotions and the Expression of Emotions in the Old Testament: A Few Introductory Remarks," *Biblische Zeitschrift* 48 (2004): 213–28; and the works Kruger reviews in n.1. To my knowledge, there are only a small handful of book-length discussions addressing the affective impact of biblical narrative on readers. Douglas Geyer (*Fear, Anomaly, and Uncertainty in the Gospel of Mark* [ATLA 47; Lanham, Md.: Scarecrow, 2002]) explores a wealth of comparative material contemporary to the Gospels expressing what he calls "the anomalous frightful," and identifies elements commonly indentified in this literature as causing fear and terror (superstitions). He finds many of these same cultural triggers of fear in Mark's narrative, leading him to read Mark as a literary work designed to elicit fear and discomfort among its readers. Thea Vogt (*Angst und Identität im Markusevangelium: Ein textpsychologisher und sozialgeschichtlicher Beitrag* [NTOA 26; Freiburg: Vandenhoeck & Ruprecht, 1993)] similarly focuses on the presentation of fear in Mark's narrative. Applying several different psychological theories of emotion to the text, she seeks to show that through the evangelist's portrayal of characters experiencing anxiety and suffering but also God's restoring power, the readers' own emotions are engaged and they learn to confront and manage their own fear. Robert Alter (*The Art of Biblical Narrative* [New York: Basic, 1981], 46) stresses that biblical literature, like other forms of literature, manifests "the most serious playfulness, endlessly discovering how the permutations of narrative conventions, linguistic properties, and imaginatively constructed personages and circumstances can crystallize subtle and abiding truths of experience in amusing or arresting or gratifying ways," but only occasionally notes how the literary shaping of a particular passage may affectively engage a reader. David Rhoads, Joanna Dewey, and Donald Michie (*Mark as Story: An Introduction to the Narrative of a Gospel* [Minneapolis: Fortress Press, 1999], 127–29, 153) briefly address the role

of emotion when discussing how Mark's narrative leads readers to respond to the disciples. The authors also invite readers to consider their own affective response to episodes in Mark's Gospel as one means of analyzing the Gospel's rhetoric, but do not pursue this reading strategy in their own discussion of Mark's narrative. Only a few articles tackle the subject, with most of these offering a brief, introductory salvo into the form of affective analysis they promote. Drawing on the work of art philosopher Susan Langer, Ronald Allen ("Feeling and Form in Biblical Interpretation," *Encounter* 43 [1982]: 99–107) argues that biblical narrative, as an art form, embodies and awakens human feeling and claims that "by being sensitive to the first century echoes we can let feelings analogous to those of the early hearers be awakened in us" (107). Robert O. Baker ("Pentecostal Bible Reading: Toward a Model of Reading for the Formation of Christian Affections," *Journal of Pentecostal Theology* 7 [1995]: 34–48) proposes that "it is not unreasonable to assume that the Bible contains texts designed to evoke not just proper understanding (orthodoxy) or just proper actions (orthopraxy) but also proper feeling (orthopathy or orthokardia)" (39) and goes on to explore how John has structured his Gospel in order to inculcate the Christian affections of love and fear in readers. Walter Reinsdorf ("How Is the Gospel True?" *Scottish Journal of Theology* 56 [2003]: 328–44) seeks to show how several features of John's portrayal are intended to lead readers to identify emotionally with Jesus. Cornelia Cross Crocker ("Emotions as Loopholes for Answerability in the Unfinalized Gospel According to Mark," *Perspectives in Religious Studies* 32 [2005]: 281–94) offers one of the more detailed treatments of the role of affect in Gospel narrative as she examines the prominent role emotions play throughout Mark's story. Drawing from concepts introduced by the twentieth-century philosopher and literary critic Mikhail Bakhtin, she goes on to argue that Mark's exemplary characters repeatedly display emotions of longing and hope that enable them to overcome situations of fear or shame. This patterning throughout Mark's narrative is thus meant to prepare readers to respond with longing and hope when encountering the unsatisfactory, even shameful ending of the Gospel, thus propelling them to "finish the story."

2. Patrick Colm Hogan, *The Mind and Its Stories: Narrative Universals and Human Emotion* (Studies in Emotion and Social Interaction; New York: Cambridge University Press, 2003). Hogan argues that romantic union and the quest for political power are the two predominant prototypes for eliciting conditions of happiness (see 94–101), and then goes on to identify and discuss the following "paradigm stories" (see 101–238): romantic tragic-comedy, heroic tragic-comedy, sacrificial tragic-comedy, and the epilogue of suffering.

3. Ibid., 5.

4. David S. Miall, "Anticipation and Feeling in Literary Response: A Neuropsychological Perspective," *Poetics* 23 (1995): 275–98; David S. Miall and Don Kuiken, "A Feeling for Fiction: Becoming What We Behold," *Poetics* 30 (2002): 221–41.

5. Rojer J. Kreuz and Mary Sue MacNealy, eds., *Empirical Approaches to Literature and Aesthetics* (Advances in Discourse Processes 52; Norwood, Mass.: Ablex, 1996). See especially the essays in part 5, pp. 221–74. See also Linda J. Levine and Stewart L. Burgess, "Beyond General Arousal: Effect of Specific Emotions on Memory," *Social Cognition* 15 (1997): 157–81; James Barton, "Interpreting Character Emotions for Literature Comprehension," *Journal of Adolescent & Adult Literacy* 40 (1996): 22–33; J. Many, "The Effect of Reader Stance on Students' Personal Understanding of Literature," in R. Ruddell, M. R. Ruddell, and H. Singer, eds., *Theoretical Models and Processes of Reading* (4th ed.; Newark: International Reading Association, 1994), 653–67.

6. Keith Oatley, "Why Fiction May Be Twice as True as Fact: Fiction as Cognitive and Emotional Simulation," *Review of General Psychology* 3 (1999): 101–17.

7. For example, Robert C. Solomon, "Literacy and the Education of the Emotions," in *Literacy, Society and Schooling: A Reader* (New York: Cambridge University Press, 1986), 38–57; Carol S. Witherall, Hoan Tan Tran, and John Othus, "Narrative Landscapes and the Moral Imagination: Taking the Story to Heart," in Suzanne De Castell, Allan Luke, and Kieran Egan, eds., *Literacy, Society and Schooling: A Reader* (New York: Cambridge University Press, 1995), 39–49; K. Egan, *Teaching as Storytelling* (Chicago: University of Chicago Press, 1986); M. Greene, *Stories Lives Tell: Narrative and Dialogue in Education* (New York: Teachers College Press, 1991); Jenefer Robinson, *Deeper Than Reason: Emotion and Its Role in Music, Literature and Art* (Oxford: Clarendon, 2005), esp. chap. 6, "A Sentimental Education," 154–94; Cornelia Hoogland, "Educational Uses of Story: Reclaiming Story as Art," *Canadian Journal of Education* 23 (1998): 79–91; Solomon Schimmel, "Some Educational Uses of Classical Jewish Texts in Exploring Emotion, Conflict and Character," *Religious Education* 92 (1997): 24–37.

8. See Trent S. Parker and Karen S. Wampler, "Changing Emotion: The Use of Therapeutic Storytelling," *Journal of Marital and Family Therapy* 32 (2006): 155–65; Melanie C. Green, "Narratives and Cancer Communication," *Journal of Communication* 56 (2006): 163; Jack Coulehan, "Empathy and Narrativity: A Commentary on 'Origins of Healing: An Evolutionary Perspective of the Healing Process,'" *Families, Systems and Health* 23 (2005): 261; Scot E. Caplan, Beth J. Haslett, and Brant R. Burleson, "Telling It Like It Is: The Adaptive Function of Narratives in Coping with Loss in Later Life," *Health Communication* 17 (2005): 233; Jessica McDermott Sales and Robyn Fivush, "Social and Emotional Functions of Mother-Child Reminiscing about Stressful Events," *Social Cognition* 23 (2005): 70–90; Dan P. McAdams, Nana Akua Anyidoho, Chelsea Brown, and Yi Ting Huang, "Traits and Stories: Links between Dispositional and Narrative Features of Personality," *Journal of Personality* 72 (2004): 761; Jennifer Travis and Milette Shamir, "Boys Don't Cry? Rethinking Narratives of Masculinity and Emotion in the U.S.," *American Studies International* 42 (2004): 267–68.

9. The narrative construction of life events is a common subject of psychological research. See Jody Koenig Kellas and Valerie Manusov, "What's in a Story: The Relationship between Narrative Completeness and Adjustment to Relationship Dissolution" *Journal of Social and Psychological Research* 20 (2003): 285; Valerie Gray Hardcastle, "Emotions and Narrative Selves," *Philosophy, Psychiatry and Psychology* 10 (2003): 353–55; Joakim Ohlen, "Evocation of Meaning through Poetic Condensation of Narratives in Empirical Phenomenological Inquiry into Human Suffering," *Qualitative Health Research* 13 (2003): 557–66; Rita Charon and Martha Montello, eds., *Stories Matter: The Role of Narrative in Medical Ethics* (New York: Routledge, 2002); Jeffrey P. Bishop, "Residents and Patients: Telling Stories to Cope with Stress," *JAMA* 280 (1998): 1960.

10. For a psychological investigation on the ability of narrative to alter our views of the world and ourselves with supporting clinical evidence, see Miall and Kuiken, "A Feeling for Fiction," 221–41. See also Keith Oatley, "A Taxonomy of the Emotions of Literary Response and a Theory of Identification in Fictional Narrative," *Poetics* 23 (1994): 53–74; Solomon, "Literacy," 49–55.

11. For this reason, there has also been increasing interest in the role of narrative in moral formation. In addition to *Upheavals of Thought* (see n.13, below), see also Nussbaum's *Love's*

Knowledge: Essays on Philosophy and Literature (New York: Oxford University Press, 1990) and *Poetic Justice: The Literary Imagination and Public Life* (Boston: Beacon, 1995); Witherall et al., "Narrative Landscapes," 39–49; Cornelia Hoogland, "Educational Uses of Story," 83; T. Alexander, "The Moral Imagination and the Aesthetics of Human Existence," in *Moral Education and the Liberal Arts* (Westport, Conn.: Greenwood, 1992), 93–111; R. Coles, *The Call of Stories: Teaching and the Moral Imagination* (Boston: Houghton Mifflin, 1989).

12. Witherall et al., "Narrative Landscapes," 40.

13. Martha Nussbaum, *Upheavals of Thought: The Intelligence of Emotions* (New York: Cambridge University Press, 2001), 243.

14. Joel B. Green, "The (Re-)Turn to Narrative," in *Narrative Reading, Narrative Preaching: Reuniting New Testament Interpretation and Proclamation*, ed. Joel B. Green and Michael Pasquarello III (Grand Rapids: Baker, 2005), 17. Gilman ("Reenfranchising the Heart," 234) likewise states, "Biblical narratives become meaningful, in other words, for those who choose to mold their own life to the pattern of life plotted in those narratives."

15. Gilman, "Reenfranchising the Heart," 237. Jonathan Edwards would concur. In his "A Treatise Concerning Religious Affections" (in *The Works of Jonathan Edwards*, vol. 1 [Edinburgh: Banner of Truth Trust, 1990], 238), he argues that "holy affections not only necessarily belong to true religion, but are a very great part of such religion." For "he that has doctrinal knowledge and speculation without affections, never is *engaged* in the business of religion." My thanks to Rev. Dr. Mark Yurs for directing me to these citations.

16. Mark Allan Powell, *Chasing the Eastern Star: Adventures in Reader Response Criticism* (Louisville: Westminster John Knox, 2001).

17. Ibid., 54.

18. Ibid., 55.

19. Cornelia Hoogland ("Educational Uses of Story," 86) finds a similar disparity between the responses of the young students she teaches and the learned reflections of literary critics when it comes to fairy tales: "I am impressed by the difference between children's discussion I hear in my classroom work and scholars' criticism of the tales. The children want to talk about the fairy tale in terms of the feelings it evokes. What does it feel like to enter the bears' house? To wake up to huge figures looming over the bed? The literary critic, on the other hand, asks about the symbolism of entering a stranger's house, and of those ursine characters over the bed."

20. Powell speaks to this as well (*Chasing the Eastern Star*, 53): "Most seminaries train their clergy to interpret texts in light of their historical context and in light of the apparent intentions of the author. This seems to be working. Most, if not all, of the clergy demonstrate a certain commitment to doing this. But when I have shown the results to groups of laity, they have invariable shaken their heads in dismay. Whatever benefits clergy may derive from their studies, they moan, something has gone terribly wrong when pastors need special prompting to regard scripture as applicable to themselves."

21. For a helpful discussion of ancient rhetorical theory and the role of pathos as a primary means of persuasion, see Thomas H. Olbricht, "*Pathos* as Proof in Greco-Roman Rhetoric" in *Paul and Pathos*, ed. Thomas H. Olbricht and Jerry L. Sumney (SBL Symposium Series 16; Atlanta: Society of Biblical Literature, 2001), 8–22. See also Mario M. DiCicco, *Paul's Use of Ethos, Pathos and Logos in 2 Corinthians 10–13* (Mellen Biblical Press Series 31; Lewiston, N.Y.: Mellen, 1995), 16–28.

22. See Olbricht and Sumney, *Paul and Pathos*, 39–202; DiCicco, *Paul's Use*. Steven J. Kraftchick (Πάθη in Paul: The Emotional Logic of 'Original Argument,'" in *Paul and Pathos*, 53–55) points out that in the writings of the later Roman rhetoricians of Cicero and Quintilian, *ethos* and *pathos* came to be regarded as degrees of emotional response that could sway the objections of a jury or audience. *Ethos* came to refer to milder forms of emotional appeal, including but not limited to the character of the speaker, and *pathos* to fervent emotions.

23. We will further explore Aristotle's discussion of how certain elements of tragedy elicit emotional response in chap. 2.

24. Quintilian, *Institutes*, 4.2.111, cited in James W. Thompson, "Paul's Argument from *Pathos* in 2 Corinthians," in *Paul and Pathos*, 127.

25. Quintilian, *Institutes*, 6.2.26, cited in DiCicco, *Paul's Use*, 129.

26. DiCicco, *Paul's Use*, 130, citing Quintilian, *Institutes*, 6.2.29–32.

CHAPTER 1: On the Emotions

1. Martha Nussbaum, *Love's Knowledge: Essays on Philosophy and Literature* (New York: Oxford University Press, 1990), 40.

2. William James, *The Works of William James*, ed. Frederick H. Burkhardt, 3 vols. (Cambridge: Harvard University Press, 1981), 1065. Because James's published comments on emotion coincided with the similar statements of Danish physician Carl George Lange, who independently and similarly concluded that emotion was primarily the experience of physiological alterations, this view is often referred to as the "James/Lange theory" of emotion.

3. Antonio R. Damasio, *Descartes' Error: Emotion, Reason, and the Human Brain* (New York: Grosset/Putnam, 1994), 128.

4. Several scholars remark that James's comments on emotion are rather obtuse and open to varying interpretations. Andrew Ortony, Gerald L. Clore, and Allan Collins (*The Cognitive Structure of Emotions* [New York: Cambridge University Press, 1988], 5) report that James also "acknowledged that there can be more complex emotion-inducing perceptions, ones which, in modern terms, would have to be described as involving a relatively high degree of cognition." Jenefer Robinson (*Deeper Than Reason: Emotion and Its Role in Music, Literature and Art* [Oxford: Clarendon, 2005], 28) argues that James's view has actually been misunderstood by most: what James was really claiming is that the sensation of bodily changes is a *necessary condition* of emotion, *not* that emotions are nothing more than bodily changes. Nevertheless, the perception that emotion is wholly or primarily a physiological reaction, which is widely attributed to the James/Lange theory, became the dominant view for many years to follow.

5. See Martha Nussbaum, *Upheavals of Thought: The Intelligence of Emotions* (Cambridge: Cambridge University Press, 2001), especially chap. 2, and the fine overview provided by Jenefer Robinson, *Deeper Than Reason*, 1–99. My own review is in many ways informed by their work.

6. Robert C. Solomon, *The Passions* (Notre Dame, Ind.: University of Notre Dame Press, 1976), 251, cited in James E. Gilman's helpful essay, "Reenfranchising the Heart: Narrative Emotions and Contemporary Theology," *The Journal of Religion* 74 (1994): 218–39.

7. Robert C. Solomon, "Literacy and the Education of Emotions," in *Literacy, Society and Schooling: A Reader* (Cambridge: Cambridge University Press, 1986), 44. Solomon's comments were anticipated a decade before in the writings of psychologist Nathaniel Brandon (*The*

Psychology of Self-Esteem: A New Concept of Man's Psychological Nature [Los Angeles: Nash, 1969], 64), who similarly concluded, in reaction to current thinking, that "an emotion is the psychosomatic form in which man experiences his estimate of the beneficial or harmful relationship of some aspect of reality to himself." Brandon's work was brought to my attention by my Lakeland College colleague, Karl Elder, Fessler Professor of Creative Writing.

8. William E. Lyons, *Emotion* (Cambridge Studies in Philosophy; Cambridge: Cambridge University Press, 1980), 58.

9. Ibid., 59.

10. For a helpful review of contributors, see Nussbaum, *Upheavals of Thought*, 100–12.

11. Richard S. Lazarus, "Thoughts on the Relation between Emotion and Cognition," *American Psychologist* 37 (1982): 1019–24.

12. Ortony et al., *The Cognitive Structure of Emotions.*

13. Ibid., 13.

14. Nussbaum has published numerous works on emotion and is commonly regarded as one of the more important and erudite voices on the matter given her ability to integrate numerous fields in her discussion. Her most complete work on emotion is *Upheavals of Thought.*

15. Nussbaum, *Upheavals of Thought*, 24–33.

16. Ibid., 32. See also Richard Wollheim, *On the Emotions* (New Haven: Yale University Press, 1999), for a philosophical (though less integrative) discussion that similarly views emotion in connection with worldview. Wollheim addresses this connection in his discussion of desire, which he views as a cognitive precursor to emotion.

17. See John Corrigan, ed., *Religion and Emotion: Approaches and Interpretation* (Oxford: Oxford University Press, 2004), 10–13.

18. Ibid., 11.

19. Nussbaum, *Upheavals of Thought*, 142.

20. There is some ambiguity created by the use of the terms *cognitive/cognition* in reference to what are regarded as automatic, unconscious "affective appraisals." Some reserve the terms for higher thought process that neuroscientists locate in the neo-cortex, while others use it to refer to any brain-centered activity. On this point, see Robinson, *Deeper Than Reason*, 45.

21. Joseph LeDoux, *The Emotional Brain: The Mysterious Underpinnings of Emotional Life* (New York: Simon & Schuster, 1996).

22. Ibid., 126.

23. Ibid., 299.

24. Robinson, *Deeper Than Reason*, 38. See pp. 37–41 of Robinson's work for a survey of these studies.

25. Robert Zajonc, "Feeling and Thinking: Preferences Need No Inferences," *American Psychologist* 35 (1980): 151–75; W. R. Kunst-Wilson and R. B. Zajonc, "Affective Dscrimination of Stimuli That Cannot Be Recognized," *Science* 207 (1980): 557–58; Robert Zajonc, "On the Primace of Affect," *American Psychologist* 39 (1984): 117–23; S. T. Murphy and R. B. Zajonc, "Affect, Cognition and Awareness: Affective Priming with Suboptimal and Optimal Stimulus," *Journal of Personality and Social Psychology* 64 (1993): 723–39; Robert Zajonc, "Evidence for Nonconscious Emotions," in *The Nature of Emotions: Fundamental Questions*, ed. Paul Eckman and Richard J. Davidson (New York: Oxford University Press, 1994), 293–97. Robinson, *Deeper Than Reason*, 39–41, provides a helpful summary of these experiments.

26. Brandon, *Psychology of Self-Esteem*, 64–65.

27. Damasio, *Descartes' Error*, xv (emphasis mine).

28. Nussbaum, *Upheavals of Thought*, 117.

29. Damasio, *Descartes' Error*, 130.

30. Nussbaum, *Upheavals of Thought*, 231–32.

31. Ibid., 234.

32. Robinson, *Deeper Than Reason*, 59.

33. Richard S. Lazarus, *Emotion and Adaptation* (New York: Oxford University Press, 1991), 153.

34. For a helpful overview and contribution to the discussion, see Nussbaum, *Upheavals of Thought*, 139–73.

35. Ortony et al, *Cognitive Structure*, 3.

36. This is a common critique raised against the view that specific emotions can be consistently correlated with certain behaviors or mannerisms, such as facial expression. See, for example, Nussbaum, *Upheavals of Thought*, 158–59, and Ortony et al., *Cognitive Structure*, 27–28.

37. Ortony et al, *Cognitive Structure*, 3.

38. This principle even applies when confronted with cultures that typically manifest in response to certain circumstances affective responses that are very different from our own. The only way we are able to discern how their responses differ from ours is because we share enough of an emotional repertoire that we are able to recognize what emotions, in fact, they are displaying in response to a particular circumstance.

39. For a sample of this discussion, see David G. Suits, "Really Believing in Fiction," *Pacific Philosophical Quarterly* 87 (2006): 369–86; Amy Coplan, "Empathic Engagement with Narrative Fictions," *The Journal of Aesthetics and Art Criticism* 62 (2004): 141–52; Robert J. Yanal, *Paradoxes of Emotion and Fiction* (University Park: Pennsylvania State University Press, 1999); E. M. Dadlez, *What's Hecuba to Him? Fictional Events and Actual Emotions* (University Park: Pennsylvania State University Press, 1997); Oswald Hanfling, "Fact, Fiction and Feeling," *British Journal of Aesthetics* 36 (1996): 356–66; Alex Neill, "Fiction and the Emotions," *American Philosophical Quarterly* 30 (1993): 1–12; Walton Kendall, *Mimesis as Make-Believe* (Cambridge: Harvard University Press, 1990); Radford Colin, "How Can We Be Moved By the Fate of Anna Karenina?" *Proceedings of the Aristotelian Society Supplement* 49 (1975): 67–80.

40. Solomon, "Literacy and the Education of Emotions," 51–52.

41. See, for example, Jerzy Trzebinski, "Narratives and Understanding Other People," *Research in Drama Education* 10 (2005): 15, which reports that "presenting a story of an ill person, in comparison to a description of an illness, as well as activating a narrative approach to this person increased the probability in subjects of helping behaviour—in this case the promise of donations of bone marrow for leukemia patients." The study goes on to conclude that "the narrative mode results in greater attention to the [ill] person's motivation and emotions, better empathic understanding of this person as well as higher emotional involvement in this person's problems."

CHAPTER 2: The Cardiography of Biblical Narrative

1. Martha C. Nussbaum, *Poetic Justice: The Literary Imagination and Public Life* (Boston: Beacon, 1995), 53.

2. Aristotle, *Poetics*, 4.1. This and the following translations are from Aristotle, *Poetics*, trans. Malcom Heath (New York: Penguin, 1996). The precise meaning of *katharsis* here is hotly debated among scholars, and Heath ("Introduction," *Poetics*, lxix, n.15) reports that no consensus on the term has emerged. I used the ambiguous "more complete understanding" above to capture the lowest common denominator of what most scholars addressing the issue would affirm.

3. The remaining four elements of tragedy listed by Aristotle serve to dramatize the plot and its characters: diction (the shaping of language spoken by the characters), reasoning (the speech agents use to argue a case or explain their action), spectacle (the dramatization of the story by actors), and lyric poetry (the formal medium of expression).

4. Heath, "Introduction," *Poetics*, xlv.

5. Martha Nussbaum, *Upheavals of Thought: The Intelligence of Emotions* (Cambridge: Cambridge University Press, 2001), 242.

6. See Martha Nussbaum, *Love's Knowledge: Essays on Philosophy and Literature* (New York: Oxford University Press, 1990), 297–353; Susan L. Feagin, *Reading with Feeling: the Aesthetics of Appreciation* (New York: Cornell University Press, 1996) 1–144; Jenefer Robinson, *Deeper Than Reason: Emotion and Its Role in Music, Literature and Art* (Oxford: Clarendon, 2005), 105–35; Richard J. Gerrig, *Experiencing Narrative Worlds: On the Psychological Activities of Reading* (New Haven: Yale University Press, 1993); Keith Oatley, "Why Fiction May Be Twice as True as Fact: Fiction as Cognitive and Emotional Simulation," *Review of General Psychology* 3 (1999): 101–17; Lester H. Hunt, "Sentiment and Sympathy," *Journal of Aesthetics and Art Criticism* 62 (2004): 339–54; Amy Coplan, "Empathic Engagement with Narrative Fictions," *Journal of Aesthetics and Art Criticism* 62 (2004): 141–52; Diana Fritz Cates, "Ethics, Literature, and the Emotional Dimension of Moral Understanding," *Journal of Religious Ethics* 26 (1998): 409–31.

7. Ronald J. Allen, "Feeling and Form in Biblical Interpretation," *Encounter* 43 (1982): 103, 104.

8. Robert O. Baker, "Pentecostal Bible Reading: Toward a Model of Reading for the Formation of Christian Affections," *Journal of Pentecostal Theology* 7 (1995): 43, 45.

9. Cornelia Cross Crocker, "Emotions as Loopholes for Answerability in the Unfinalized Gospel according to Mark," *Perspectives in Religious Studies* 32 (2005): 282.

10. See Robinson's analysis in chaps. 4, 6, and 7 of *Deeper Than Reason*.

11. Baker, "Pentecostal Bible Reading," 46.

12. Walter Reinsdorf, "How Is the Gospel True?" *Scottish Journal of Theology* 56 (2003): 337. Crocker's analysis in "Emotions as Loopholes" is a bit more sophisticated as it identifies a *patterning* Mark weaves in the depiction of multiple characters responding to situations of threat with longing and hope, and argues that this patterning is meant to evoke a similar emotional response in Mark's audience when they encounter the Gospel's disappointing ending.

13. On this feature of Luke 24, see John Dillon, *From Eyewitness to Ministers of the Word* (AB 82; Rome: Biblical Institute, 1978), and Karl A. Kuhn, "Beginning the Witness: The αὐτόπται καὶ ὑπηρέται of Luke's Infancy Narrative" *NTS* 49 (2003): 237–55.

14. The disciples' misunderstanding is clearly and ironically implied by the fact that they are relaying to Jesus the essential elements of the *kerygma* without realizing what they are really saying!

15. Aristotle, *Poetics*, 5:1.

16. And nearly all agree that none of the endings included and indicated as secondary in most critical translations are original to the Markan text.

17. See, for example, T. E. Boomershine, "Mark 16:8 and the Apostolic Commission," *JBL* 100 (1981): 225–39; Andrew T. Lincoln, "The Promise and the Failure: Mark 16:7, 8" *JBL* 108 (1989): 283–300; Donald H. Juel, *A Master of Surprise: Mark Interpreted* (Minneapolis: Fortress Press, 1994), 107–21; J. David Hester, "Dramatic Inconclusion: Irony and the Narrative Rhetoric of the Ending of Mark's Gospel," *JSNT* 57 (1995): 61–86; David Rhoads, Joanna Dewey, and Donald Michie, *Mark as Story*, rev. ed. (Minneapolis: Fortress Press, 1999), 127–29; Joel F. Williams, "Literary Approaches to the End of Mark's Gospel," *JETS* 42 (1999): 21–35; Joan L. Mitchell, *Beyond Fear and Silence: A Feminist-Literary Reading of Mark* (New York: Continuum, 2001); Marvin Meyer, "Taking Up the Cross and Following Jesus: Discipleship in the Gospel of Mark," *CTJ* 37 (2002): 230–38; Raymond Pickett, "Following Jesus in Galilee: Resurrection as Empowerment in the Gospel of Mark," *CurTM* 32 (2005): 434–44; Cornelia Cross Crocker, "Emotions as Loopholes," 281–94; Morna D. Hooker, "Believe and Follow: The Challenge of Mark's Ending," in *Preaching Mark's Unsettling Messiah*, ed. Dave Bland and David Fleer (St. Louis: Chalice, 2006), 45–58.

18. Mary Ann Tolbert, *Sowing the Gospel: Mark's World in Literary-Historical Perspective* (Minneapolis: Fortress Press, 1989), 298–99.

19. Rhoads et al., *Mark as Story*, 128–29.

20. See Daniel Marguerat, "The End of Acts (26:16-31) and the Rhetoric of Silence," in *Rhetoric and the New Testament: Essays from the 1992 Heidelberg Conference*, ed. Stanley E. Porter and Thomas H. Olbricht (JSNTSup 90; Sheffield: Sheffield University Press, 1993), 74–89; William S. Kurz, "The Open-Ended Nature of Luke and Acts as Inviting Canonical Actualisation," *Neotestamentica* 31 (1997): 289–308.

21. Heath, "Introduction," xxx. See *Poetics*, 6.3, for Aristotle's discussion on reversal.

22. Scholars differ over whether or not the Israelites in Exodus 32 were intending to replace Yahweh with a different god or simply attempting to force Yahweh or Yahweh's messenger to be present among them through the creation of an idol. Yet so consistently is the creation of idols linked with the worship of other deities throughout the Old Testament that I think the most natural way to understand the action is as an attempt to replace devotion to Yahweh with the worship of other gods (see, for example, Exod 20:2-5). This is also suggested by the author's use of *elohim* in this context (lit. "gods") to refer to the object of the people's worship in contrast to the nearly singular use of *YHWH* (translated "Lord") for Yahweh in 32:1-14. Although *elohim* is often used for Yahweh, it is also frequently employed to designate gods other than Yahweh. Finally, Ps 106:19-20 clearly refers back to this event and understands what took place as an idolatrous act of *replacing* Yahweh with the worship of another god: "They made a calf at Horeb and worship a cast image. They exchanged the glory of God for the image of an ox that eats grass. They forgot God, their Savior, who had done great things in Egypt, wondrous works in the land of Ham, and awesome deeds by the Red Sea." Nevertheless, in either case, the end result is nearly the same: the people are setting the terms for their relationship with G(g)od, and their ritual indicates that what they now worship is a far cry from the God revealed to Abraham's descendants and through the exodus.

23. I realize that my attempt to discern the intentions of the real, flesh-and-blood author, Luke, may be disappointing to those who consider the quest for "authorial intent" at best problematic and

at worst hermeneutically fallacious. I, however, still stubbornly cling to authorial intent as a good and proper, and even marginally attainable, goal of exegesis. (For a helpful defense of pursuing "authorial intent" as a chief aim of biblical interpretation, see Stephen E. Fowl, "The Role of Authorial Interpretation in the Theological Interpretation of Scripture," in *Between Two Horizons: Spanning New Testament Studies and Systematic Theology*, ed. Joel B. Green and Max Turner [Grand Rapids: Eerdmans, 2000], 71–87). For readers who are troubled by my quest for the real author's intent yet still want to read on, may I suggest a compromise? Every time I refer to the author of a biblical text, simply insert the phrase "implied author" (and you may also want to insert "implied reader" when I refer to Luke's reader or audience). That way, I can go on talking about the real author, Luke, and you can just take what I am saying as applying to the author *implied* by my particular (idiosyncratic and contextually driven) reading of the narrative. Perhaps the merit of my work can be judged on the benefits of its approach, and we can disagree on the specific outcome of its analysis: better understanding of (real) Luke's authorial intent vs. better appreciation for another dimension of the text's potentiality of meaning.

24. Robinson, *Deeper Than Reason*, 120.

CHAPTER 3: Passionate Conceptions (Luke 1:5-56)

1. The analysis to follow will cover 1:5—2:40 and not include the story of Jesus slipping away from his parents to spend some time in his "father's house" (2:41-52). Two reasons commend this limitation: (1) this story, with its account of Jesus not as an infant but a youth of twelve years, serves the purpose of transitioning the reader from the infancy narrative to the body of the Gospel, and does not belong to the infancy narrative proper; this is further indicated by its lack of Semitic stylizing and the fact that the story does not present the rich array of themes common to other units of the infancy narrative; (2) the material we encounter in the infancy narrative proper, 1:5—2:40, will be more than sufficient to illustrate the affective analysis advocated here.

2. As Raymond Brown (*The Birth of the Messiah: A Commentary on the Infancy Narratives in Matthew and Luke*, rev ed. [New York: Doubleday, 1993], 242) argues, "The infancy narrative should be seen as a true introduction to some of the main themes of the Gospel proper, and no analysis of Lucan theology should neglect it." Similarly, Charles H. Talbert (*Reading Luke: A Literary and Theological Commentary on the Third Gospel* [New York: Crossroad, 1982], 17) remarks, "the reader should expect to find introduced in the section many themes that will be developed later in Luke-Acts." See also I. Howard Marshall, "Luke and His 'Gospel,'" in *Das Evangelium und die Evangelien*, ed. P. Stuhlmacher (WUANT 28; Tübingen: J.C.B. Mohr, 1983), 289–308; J. Bradley Chance, *Jerusalem, the Temple, and the New Age in Luke-Acts* (Macon, Ga.: Mercer University Press, 1988), 47–56. Robert Tannehill, *The Narrative Unity of Luke-Acts: A Literary Interpretation*, 2 vols. (Philadelphia: Fortress Press, 1986, 1994), 1:15–44; Mark Coleridge, *The Birth of the Lukan Narrative: Narrative as Christology in Luke 1–2* (JSNTSup 88; Sheffield: JSOT, 1993).

3. Luke's use of direct discourse in Acts has received much scholarly attention. See Marion Soards, *The Speeches in Acts: Their Content, Context, and Concerns* (Louisville: Westminster John Knox, 1994), for a review of this discussion and Soards's own helpful treatment of the topic. In my doctoral dissertation (Karl Allen Kuhn, "In Their Own Words: Character Speech in the Gospel of Luke (Ph.D. diss.; Marquette University, 1999), 58–220), I argue that Luke's use of character

speech in his infancy narrative and Luke 24 serves much the same function Soards and others identify for the speeches in Acts: to draw attention to and interpret the significance of key events in the narrative, and in so doing present Luke's understanding of the "matters fulfilled among us" (1:1).

4. John A. Darr, *On Character Building: The Reader and the Rhetoric of Characterization in Luke-Acts* (Literary Currents in Biblical Interpretation; Louisville: Westminster John Knox, 1992), 29.

5. On the relationship of God-fearers to Judaism and Christianity, see Everett Ferguson, *Backgrounds of Early Christianity* 2nd ed. (Grand Rapids: Eerdmans, 1993), 515–17.

6. See Joseph A. Fitzmyer, *The Gospel According to Luke (I–IX): Introduction, Translation, and Notes* (AB 28; Garden City, N.Y.: Doubleday, 1981), 8–11; Fred B. Craddock, *Luke* (Interpretation; Louisville: John Knox, 1990), 19; Luke Timothy Johnson, *The Gospel of Luke* (Sacra Pagina 3; Collegeville, Minn.: Liturgical, 1991), 10; Darrell L. Bock, *Luke 1:1—9:50* (Baker Exegetical Commentary on the New Testament 3a; Grand Rapids: Baker, 1994), 15; Joel B. Green, *The Gospel of Luke* (NICNT; Grand Rapids: Eerdmans, 1997), 22–23.

7. John Nolland (*Luke 1:1—9:20* [WBC 35a; Dallas: Word, 1989], xxxii), among others, proposes that Theophilus was such a God-fearer, as his name (possibly a pseudonym) implies: "lover of God."

8. Green, *Luke*, 21–22.

9. I recognize that the use of "readers" to refer to Luke's audience is somewhat inaccurate and anachronistic, given the fact that the vast majority of those encountering his Gospel in antiquity could not read and would have heard it read by others. Here and in what follows I use the term interchangeably with "audience" and intend it to express in a looser, general sense those who participate, in some fashion, in the reading and hearing of Luke's text.

10. Green, *Luke*, 65–66.

11. As stated by Brown (*Birth*, 269): "While there are several examples of barren women who are made capable of childbearing through divine intervention, in only one other instance in the Bible are both parents incapacitated by age as well."

12. Brown, *Birth*, 259; Nolland, *Luke 1:1—9:20*, 27. Note also that the casting of lots was viewed as a means of discerning God's will.

13. Nolland (*Luke 1:1—9:20*, 32) reports that Gabriel's Old Testament role is that of a revealer of the eschatological mysteries (Daniel 8–12), and in later Jewish angelology he is one of the four (*1 Enoch* 9:1; 4:2) or seven (*1 Enoch* 20; *t. Levi* 8; Tob 12:15; Rev 8:2, 6) angels who stand in God's presence.

14. Green, *Luke*, 67.

15. As Green (*Luke*, 65) notes: "Given the preceding affirmations, v. 7 is startling."

16. Brown (*Birth*, 279) argues that in having Zechariah object, Luke is following an established annunciation form carrying over from the Old Testament traditions, which includes an objection or request for a sign. However, of the Old Testament annunciations Brown lists as precedents (see p. 156: he reviews the annunciations of Ishmael [Gen 16:7-12], Isaac [Gen 17:1-8; 18:1-15], and Samson [Judg 13:1-23]), only the annunciations of Isaac's birth contain this element. Such a request or objection is not present in Ishmael's annunciation, and what we find in Judges with the annunciation of Samson's birth (Judg 13:1-23) are neither requests for a sign nor an objection (as Brown indicates), but simply requests for more information (Judg 13:8, 17). Instead of labeling this element as "an objection or request for a sign," it would be better to indentify it more generally as "a response from the recipient."

17. Green, *Luke*, 79.

18. See Karl A. Kuhn, "Beginning the Witness: The αὐτόπται καὶ ὑπηρέται of Luke's Infancy Narrative" *NTS* 49 (2003): 237–55. We will further explore this motif in the discussion to follow.

19. Green's commentary (*Luke*, 63) is an exception to this tendency. At the start of his treatment of the passage, he provides the following overview:

> Though the spotlight seems to be on Zechariah in this section, it shines brightest on Elizabeth. Their introduction stresses their mutual righteousness and old age. In going on to mention Elizabeth's barrenness, the narrative raises a need (1:5-7) subsequently addressed by means of an angelic announcement (1:8-17) followed by individual responses from Zechariah (1:18-23) and Elizabeth (1:24-25). The dramatic crescendo turns the tables on Zechariah, chosen priest, in favor of Elizabeth. Hence, descriptions of her conditions frame 1:5-25—barren and disgraced at the outset, pregnant and restored to a position of honor at the close.

Green's overview, in my mind, captures much that is integral to Luke's shaping of the passage. Later, Green (*Luke*, 81) also helpfully notes that the implicit comparison between Zechariah and Elizabeth that Luke draws through his plotting "poses the question for the reader: Will we believe, acknowledging the gracious hand of God?" However, Green does not address the imbalance created by the framing of 1:5-7 and 1:24-25, and he also deemphasizes the seriousness of Zechariah's lack of faith in his commentary on v. 18. It seems to me that by focusing on the affective dimensions of the text, we can identify elements of the passage that further support his astute observations.

20. I. Howard Marshall, *The Gospel of Luke: A Commentary on the Greek Text* (NIGTC 3; Grand Rapids: Eerdmans, 1978), 61; Bock, *Luke 1:1—9:50*, 93; Fitzmyer, *Luke*, 328; Green, *Luke*, 79–80.

21. For a helpful presentation of these verbal parallels, see Green, *Luke*, 83.

22. Fitzmyer (*Luke*, 343) observes: "Nazareth is not mentioned in the OT, Josephus, or rabbinical writings."

23. Joel B. Green, "The Social Status of Mary in Luke 1,5-2,52: A Plea for Methodological Integration" *Bib* 73 (1992): 465; so also Bock, *Luke 1:1—9:20*, 107.

24. In light of the context of this episode in which God's favor upon Mary and her role in the unfolding of God's plan is emphasized, ὁ κύριος μετὰ σου is here best rendered in a declarative sense as in Judg 6:12, rather than as a wish, "May the Lord be with you."

25. Exceptions consist of Judg 2:18, where it is predicated of all the judges in general; 2 Chron 19:11, generally of "the good"; 1 Esdras 8:52, generally of those who seek God; and Isa 41:10; 43:2, 5; and Jer 46:28, of Israel. My search included all verses from the LXX that contained μετά and all forms of κυρίος, and all those verses containing εἰμι (in the first-person singular, present, and future active indicative) and σου.

26. Johnson, *Luke*, 37.

27. The instances of step-parallelism created by these correspondences are commonly considered to consist of the following (from Brown, *Birth*, 300):

1. John the Baptist is great before the Lord (1:15a), but Jesus is "great" without qualification (1:32).
2. John the Baptist is filled with the Holy Spirit even from his mother's womb (1:15c), but the very conception of Jesus involves a creative act of God through the Holy Spirit (1:35b).
3. John the Baptist will make ready for the Lord a prepared people (1:17e), but Jesus will actually rule over the house of Jacob/Israel and possess a kingdom without end (1:33).

In addition to these, Nolland (*Luke 1:1—9:20*, 40–41) adds:

4. John is consecrated to Nazarite abstinence, but Jesus' holiness as the Divine Son extends to the very basis of his existence.

28. For example, Fitzmyer, *Luke*, 335–36; Marshall, *Luke*, 62; Nolland, *Luke 1:1—9:20*, 40–41, 57; C. F. Evans, *Saint Luke* (London: SCM, 1990) 154; Bock, *Luke 1:1—9:20*, 124, 27; Green, *Luke*, 84.

29. Brown, *Birth*, 283–84. Although Brown rejects the proposal that Luke drew from an underlying Baptist source in his shaping of the two annunciations, the claim of an existing, rival community comprised of followers of John the Baptist is often tied to the additional proposal that much of the material concerning John in Luke 1–2, including the Magnificat, has been adapted from a Baptist source. For a discussion and critique of this position, see Pierre Benoit, "L'Enfance de Jean-Baptiste Selon Luc I," *NTS* 3 (1956): 169–94, and Walter Wink, *John the Baptist in the Gospel Tradition* (SNTSMS 7; Cambridge: Cambridge University Press, 1968), 60–72. An alternate version of the theory represented by Brown has been proposed by René Laurentin (*Structure et théologie de Luc I-II* [Paris: J. Gabalda, 1957], 111–16), who argues that John and Jesus were originally conceived by some Christians as co-redeemers, corresponding to the "two messiahs" concept found in some of the writings of Qumran. In this view, the step-parallelism of Luke 1–2 suppresses this understanding of the relationship between Jesus and John by making no mention of John's messiahship and emphasizing the superiority of Jesus.

30. Hans Conzelmann, *The Theology of Luke* (New York: Harper & Row, 1961). So also H. H. Oliver, "The Lucan Birth Stories and the Purpose of Luke-Acts," *NTS* 10 (1963–64): 202–26; John Drury, *Tradition and Design in Luke's Gospel: A Study in Early Christian Historiography* (Atlanta: John Knox, 1976), 63–64; Mark L. Strauss, *The Davidic Messiah in Luke-Acts: The Promise and Fulfillment in Lukan Christoology* (JSNTSup 110; Sheffield: Sheffield Academic Press, 1995), 83–84; contra Wink, *John the Baptist*, 49–57.

31. For a fuller articulation of this argument, please see Karl A. Kuhn, "The Point of the Step-Parallelism in Luke 1–2," *NTS* 47 (2001): 38–49.

32. Athalya Brenner, "Female Social Behavior: Two Descriptive Patterns within the 'Birth of the Hero' Paradigm," *VT* 36 (1986): 258–59.

33. As Brenner (ibid., 269–70) states: "[Mary and Elizabeth] could well have been presented as rivals, for a number of features point to their being a contrasted pair. They differ from—and complement—each other on counts such as age, social standing, and probably beauty. They are kinswomen (Luke i 36), which may be another potential reason for contention between mothers-to-be and future sons alike. Once more, as in the Naomi/Ruth story, one is an older woman and one a younger one; and the generation conflict is resolved without competition. This time, however, the elder and superior member of the pair acknowledges the

superiority of the younger: Elizabeth readily admits that Mary's son will be greater than hers (i 39-45). . . . This is a new development, a sublimation of older themes and motifs. Faith, as it should, triumphs over personal ambition and ensures not only the peaceful survival of a divinely ordained human condition but also, through the birth of two heroes (John and Jesus), the evolution of a new socio-religious era."

34. Augustin George, *Études sur l'oeurve de Luc* (Paris: Gabalda, 1978), 64. See also Wink, *John the Baptist*, 58.

35. Luke continues to imply that John prepares the way for Jesus throughout the following narrative. In the very next episode, in which the story lines of Jesus and John converge, the unborn John leaps upon the arrival of Mary (1:41), and in so doing appears to hail the advent of the recently conceived Jesus. Later Zechariah proclaims the significance of his son in a canticle that is largely devoted to celebrating the arrival of God's promised salvation in the person of the Messiah (1:67-79). Finally, in 3:16, John answers those who were wondering if he was the Messiah, stating, "I baptize you with water, but one who is more powerful than I is coming; I am not worthy to untie the throng of his sandals. He will baptize you with the Holy Spirit and fire" (cf. Mark 1:7-8). Not only does this culminating episode again present Jesus as the one who is to come, it also continues Luke's emphasis on the exalted character of Jesus' person.

36. Laurentin (*Luc I-II*, 360–67, 122) points out that absolute greatness is a trait reserved for Yahweh in the Jewish Scriptures (Pss 48:2; 86:10; 135:5; 145:3), noting that where the description is used of humans (2 Sam 19:33; Lev 19:15; Sir 48:22), it is always qualified in some sense ("great before God," or "great before humans"). So also Fitzmyer, *Luke*, 325.

37. The grammatical function of ἅγιον is difficult to determine (predicate or substantive), but, as suggested by the use of ἅγιος as a title for Jesus in Luke 4:34 (see also Acts 3:14; 4:27, 30), it is most likely a predicate of the verb κληθήσεται ("He will be called holy, Son of God"). Laurentin (*Luc I-II*, 122) notes that this term is also typically predicated of God in the Jewish Scriptures. Although there are numerous instances in which it is predicated of others (see also Luke 2:24), it is not so used in the titular, absolute sense that appears here.

38. Brown, *Birth*, 312. Similarly, Strauss (*Davidic Messiah*, 93) concludes:

> Luke's *primary* interest in v. 35 is in the grounding of Jesus' *divine sonship* in the creative power of God. . . . While the Jewish conception considered the Davidic king to be Son of God by virtue of his *role* as God's representative, Luke grounds this sonship not in Jesus' role but in his *origin*. Luke seems to be consciously opposing the view that Jesus' sonship is merely "functional"—a special relationship with God by virtue of his role as king. He is rather the Son of God from the point of conception, before he has taken on any of functions of kingship.

So also George, *Études*, 236, 270; Fitzmyer, *Luke*, 340; Green, *Luke*, 90–91; François Bovon, *Das Evangelium Nach Lukas: 1 Teilband, Lk. 1,1–9,50* (EKKNT; Zürich: Neukirchen-Vluyn: Benziger Verlag, Neukirchener Verlag, 1989), 47; Culpepper, *Luke*, 53. In contrast, Bock (*Proclamation from Prophecy and Pattern* [JSNTSup 12; Sheffield: JSOT, 1987], 64–69) argues that the title in 1:35 serves as "*another aspect* of Luke's *regal messianic* declaration." While an "ontological statement may be implied here . . . it is not what Luke *emphasizes* in using and describing the title." The description of the virgin birth, therefore, is not a "clear and conscious metaphysical

declaration of Jesus' divinity," but rather simply a way of expressing the "'supernatural' character of his birth into the role of the Davidic redeemer." Bock adds, "It is the lack of any explicit
development of a metaphysical sonship in Luke through his other uses of the term 'Son of God'
that produces our non-ontological view of this text." Several points speak against Bock's argument. First, while it is certain that Luke draws a close connection between Jesus' messiahship
and divine sonship here and elsewhere in the Gospel, this does not entail that the significance
of the title "Son of God," is to be seen solely or even primarily in terms of traditional notions
of Davidic messiahship. Instead, by his use of the title, which he here directly relates to Jesus'
conception by the Spirit, Luke is likely following and further developing another stream of
Jewish tradition (as preserved in the Qumran fragment, 4Q246, and the *Similitudes*) that linked
Davidic traditions with expectations of a coming, transcendent, and divine-like redeemer. On
this point, see also Karl A. Kuhn, "The 'One like a Son of Man' Becomes 'The Son of God,'" *CBQ*
69 (2007): 22–42. Even Strauss, who argues that Davidic messiahship is the primary christological category Luke presents in the infancy narrative (see *Davidic Messiah*, 123–24), recognizes
the significant reshaping of that concept in the evangelist's portrayal of Jesus' divine sonship, as
he indicates in the above citation. Second, in determining the meaning of "Son of God," Bock
does not take into consideration other references to Jesus' divine sonship throughout the Gospel
that do not specifically contain the title (2:41-52; 10:21-22; 24:49). Consequently, Bock treats
Luke's use of the title apart from the broader notion of divine sonship that is well represented
throughout Luke and Acts in Jesus' designation as "son" and God's designation as "Father." Such
references in 2:41-52 and 24:49 further emphasize the close relation between Jesus and Yahweh
with respect to their shared mission of salvation and person, and are not adequately explained
solely in terms of traditional Davidic categories. Third, Bock argues that his "non-ontological
view" of the text is required by the lack of "an explicit development of metaphysical sonship" in
the passage and throughout Luke-Acts. I'm not sure what such an explicit development could
entail beyond what Luke already says, given the constraints of the passage and Luke's milieu.
However, any perceived lack of explicitness on Luke's part does not preclude the possibility that
Luke was intentionally suggesting or pointing to *something like* what we would call an ontological
or metaphysical understanding of Jesus' person or nature. Rather, what seems apparent from
Luke's portrayal is his interest in collapsing together the mission and person of Jesus and God
to the extent that the lines of distinction between them become rather fuzzy. Following the
lead of others, I argue that in drawing a direct connection between Jesus' designation as "Son
of God" and his conception by the Holy Spirit, Luke deliberately portrays the very close relation between Jesus and his Father in both mission *and* person, and does so in a manner that far
transcends the adoptionist sonship attributed to the Davidic king.

39. A helpful question to ask at this point, I think, is: What categories besides the ones
included here (divine sonship, eternal reign, conception by the Holy Spirit, unqualified greatness, and holiness) could Luke have used to more directly portray Jesus' divine and transcendent
character, and the close relation between Jesus and God?

40. Luke commonly utilizes ἰδού throughout Luke-Acts to attract attention to an event
and/or to indicate that what is to be said next is of special importance. Its use in the direct
discourse of his characters leading up to Mary's response in 1:38 draws attention to an event or
reality as a manifestation of God's power or will to redeem God's people (see 1:20, 31, 36). It
serves, in other words, to mark the following statement as one that announces a revelation from

God and/or reveals how God's plan is to unfold. Of the five instances of the word in the infancy narrative following 1:38, four appear to have this same function (1:44, 48; 2:10, 34), the exception being Luke 2:48 when Mary exclaims to the child, Jesus, "Behold, your father and I have been earnestly searching for you!" Even more importantly, the word is used twice by Gabriel in this same episode, first to announce the conception and birth of Jesus (v. 31) and secondly to report the conception of John (v. 36). Thus, in also beginning Mary's response to Gabriel with ἰδού, it appears that Luke intends us to see Mary here as wholeheartedly accepting her role in the unfolding of God's salvation.

41. Bock, *Luke 1:1—9:50*, 119–20.

42. See Brown, *Birth*, 307–9; Fitzmyer, *Luke*, 350; Green, *Luke*, 90.

43. While some segments of Judaism before Jesus' time looked for the coming of a divine-like redeemer figure, or divine agent, there is no evidence to suggest that this was ever paired with the notion of virgin birth or conception by the Holy Spirit. Moreover, there are strong indications that early Christian devotion to Jesus was an ongoing source of friction between Jewish Christians and non-Christian Jews. On this matter, see Larry Hurtado, *Lord Jesus Christ: Devotion to Jesus in Earliest Christianity* (Grand Rapids: Eerdmans, 2003), 349–407. Scholars differ in their assessment of the possible influence of Greco-Roman and Egyptian traditions (which included stories of gods copulating with human women to produce divinely gifted offspring) on the virgin birth tradition. However, many conclude that the influence of these traditions was negligible, if not explicitly countered by the Gospel writers, given the fact that Luke and Matthew present the scene in thickly Jewish coloring and—unlike these pagan traditions—do not refer to any sexual activity on the part of the deity and human mother. Still, it is likely that the aversion of most Jewish folk, and many Gentiles attracted to Jewish tradition, to such Greco-Roman and Egyptian legends would have resulted in their unease with the early Christian claim promoted by Matthew and Luke (and others before them) concerning the manner of Jesus' conception. In addition, Mark's lack of the virgin birth tradition and his commissioning scene (1:9-11) of Jesus at his baptism in which the heavenly voice cites the enthronement psalm, Psalm 2, suggest that some Christians adapted the "adoptionist sonship" concept commonly applied to Jewish kings as a means of understanding Jesus' divine sonship, rather than the "divinely begotten" model promoted by Luke, Matthew, and John (see John 3:16). By this I do not mean to say, as some have, that Mark's Gospel reflects a "low" Christology. In my view, it clearly does not. But I do think it likely that Matthew and Luke are claiming a tradition here that they perceive as going a step further in emphasizing Jesus' divine and transcendent character.

44. Strauss, *Davidic Messiah*, 93.

45. Nolland (*Luke 1:1—9:50*, 57) also argues that Luke was interested in portraying the development of Mary's response "from the troubled state of v 29 to the questioning of v 34 to this final unreserved readiness for God's purpose." In fact, this same pattern characterizes the response of many throughout Luke-Acts when confronted with the salvation God is inaugurating among them (for example, Luke 24). On this point, see Kuhn, "Beginning the Witness," 252–55.

46. Harold K. Moulton, *The Analytical Greek Lexicon Revised 1978 Edition* (Grand Rapids: Zondervan, 1978), 96, offers "to throw into a state of perturbation, to move or trouble greatly" as the meaning of the term in Luke 1:29.

47. This is also pointed out by Bock, *Luke 1:1—9:50*, 118, and Johnson, *Luke*, 39.

48. This is also suggested, perhaps, by the repeated notices throughout the infancy narrative that Mary continued to ponder the significance of the child she would bear: 2:19, 51.

49. For similar use of the expression "with haste," see Mark 6:25; Exod 12:11; Wis 19:2; 3 Macc 5:24, 27; Josephus *Ag. Ap.* 2.4.

50. Marshall, *Luke*, 77.

51. σκιρτάω is also the verb used in the LXX in Gen 25:22 in reference to the struggle between Esau and Jacob in the womb. As Nolland (*Luke 1:1—9:50*, 66) points out, the idea that unborn children may take part in events of the world and anticipate prenatally their later positions in life is not unknown in Jewish tradition (e.g., *Tg. Ket.*; Ps 68:27).

52. Brown, *Birth*, 341. So also Fitzmyer, *Luke*, 358; Marshall, *Luke*, 77, 80; Green, *Luke*, 95; René Laurentin, *The Truth of Christmas: Beyond the Myths* (Petersham, Mass.: St. Bede's Publications, 1986), 155.

53. In a manner consistent with the way Luke portrays the Spirit throughout his two-volume work, Luke reveals the role of the Spirit to help the faithful understand the significance of the events taking place around them and to inaugurate the proclamation of the good news of God's coming salvation. On this, see Kuhn, "Beginning the Witness," 244–46.

54. Robert P. Menzies (*Empowered for Witness: The Spirit in Luke-Acts* [Sheffield: Sheffield Academic Press, 1994], 71–102) surveys a number of intertestamental and rabbinic texts that connect the emergence of the Spirit with the end times. Peter's citation of Joel 3:1-5 at Pentecost (Acts 2:16-21) directly expresses this motif. See also Isa 32:15; Ezek 11:19; 36:26; Zech 12:10; PsSol 18:7.

55. Brown, *Birth*, 333; Fitzmyer, *Luke*, 364; Marshall, *Luke*, 81.

56. Brown, *Birth*, 344; Marshall, *Luke*, 81; Strauss, *Davidic Messiah*, 96.

57. Fitzmyer, *Luke*, 365. Similarly, Green (*Luke*, 96) states, "Mary is the mother of 'my Lord'—a designation by which Elizabeth articulates her own submission to this unborn baby and which anticipates the identification of Jesus as 'Lord' on the basis of his exaltation (cf. Ps 110:1; Acts 2:34-36)."

58. Fitzmyer, *Luke*, 202–3. Larry W. Hurtado, *One God, One Lord: Early Christian Devotion and Ancient Jewish Monotheism* (Philadelphia: Fortress Press, 1988), 108–9.

59. René Laurentin (*Luc I-II*, 129, and George (*Études*, 255) offer similar understandings of the appearance of κύριος here in v. 43.

60. Brown, *Birth*, 333.

61. Green, *Luke*, 94.

62. Allusions to the Jewish Scriptures abound in every line of the hymn, so much so that many have characterized the Magnificat as a pastiche of scriptural allusions and quotations. For a listing of the more obvious allusions contained in the Magnificat, see the helpful chart provided by Brown, *Birth*, 358–60. It has been common for scholars to see Hannah's Song (1 Sam 2:1-10), which similarly celebrates God's deliverance of herself and Israel as the primary model for the Magnificat. Yet others point out that while Hannah's Song may provide a paradigm for the general shape of the hymn, nearly every allusion to the Jewish Scriptures, with the exception of v. 48a, finds a closer parallel elsewhere. See, for example, Stephen Farris, *The Hymns of Luke's Infancy Narratives: Their Origin, Meaning and Significance* (JSNTSup 9; Sheffield: JSOT, 1985), 116; Paul Bemile, *The Magnificat within the Context and Framework of Lukan Theology: An Exegetical Theological Study of Lk 1:46-55* (New York: Lang, 1986), 79; Douglas R. Jones, "Background and Character of the Lukan Psalms," *JTS* 19 (1968): 19–50, here 25–26; Fitzmyer, *Luke*, 359.

63. As Jones ("Lukan Psalms," 28) helpfully states: "Here the psalmist looks back upon the whole history of God's people and sees the unspecified 'great things' as the realization of

the hitherto unfulfilled promises to the fathers. This can only mean that the salvation-event celebrated in these psalms was of such an order that it could be regarded as the true culmination
of the Old Testament dispensation as a whole."

64. As similarly noted by Jacque Dupont, "Le Magnificat come discours sur Dieu" *NRT* 102
(1980): 321–43, here 339–42.

65. These associations are also represented in the four passages from the LXX that offer
the closest parallels to the expression τῷ θεῷ τῷ σωτῆρί μου. Each connect the idea of God
as Savior with God's forgiveness and triumph over Israel's enemies. See the surrounding context
of Hab 3:18; Ps 24:6-7 (LXX); Isa 12:2; Mic 7:7.

66. Dupont, "Magnificat," 339; Nolland, *Luke 1:1—9:50*, 76.

67. Tannehill ("The Magnificat as Poem," *JBL* 93 [1974]: 263–75, here 274) comments
regarding Mary and Jesus: "Thus the mighty God's regard for a humble woman becomes the sign
of God's eschatological act for the world. In that small event this great event lies hidden. The
humble mother, the gift of the child, become images which resonate with all of the meaning of
that child for men in God's eternal purpose."

68. Farris, *Hymns*, 188n123.

69. Ibid., 122.

70. Ibid.

71. Ibid.

72. Thomas Hoyt (*The Poor in Luke-Acts* [Duke University Divinity School Diss.; Ann Arbor:
University Microfilms International, 1974], 50–51) similarly finds that even in the psalter "both
religious and secular connotations are present and intertwined in words which mean economic
want as well as religious 'poverty.'" As is often noted by scholars, Luke is especially concerned to
emphasize the danger of wealth and frequently identifies relief to the poor and socioeconomic
justice as fundamental elements of God's saving activity. See Luke 3:10-14; 4:18-19; 6:20-26;
9:10-20; 12:13-34; 14:7-24; 16:19-31; 18:18-28.

73. See especially Edouard Hamel, "Le Magnificat et le Renversement des Situations," *Greg*
60 (1975): 55–58, 76–77. See also Hoyt, *Poor*, 183; Brown, *Birth*, 363; Marshall, *Luke*, 84; Nolland, *Luke 1:1—9:50*, 72, 76; Farris, *Hymns*, 124.

74. Green, *Luke*, 100; Hamel, "Magnificat," 72.

CHAPTER 4: Birth Pangs (Luke 1:57—2:40)

1. François Bovon (*Das Evangelium Nach Lukas: 1 Teilband, Lk. 1,1-9,50* [EKKNT; Zürich:
Neukirchen-Vluyn: Benziger Verlag, Neukirchener Verlag, 1989], 70), John Nolland (*Luke
1:1—9:20* [WBC 35a; Dallas: Word, 1989], 79), Joseph A. Fitzmyer (*The Gospel According to
Luke (I–IX): Introduction, Translation, and Notes* [AB 28; Garden City, N.Y.: Doubleday, 1981], 380),
and Raymond A. Brown (*The Birth of the Messiah: A Commentary on the Infancy Narratives in Matthew
and Luke*, rev ed. [New York: Doubleday, 1993], 369) report that while there are precedents for
naming a son after a father (Josephus, *Ant.* 14:10), naming after a grandfather is better attested
(1 Macc 2:1-2; *Jub.* 11:15; Josephus, *Life*, 1.5). Joel B. Green (*The Gospel of Luke* [NICNT; Grand
Rapids: Eerdmans, 1997], 109n8) provides additional examples but concludes that neither practice of naming a son after father nor after grandfather was well established in Jesus' day. In contrast, Darrell L. Bock (*Luke 1:1—9:50* [Baker Exegetical Commentary on the New Testament

3a; Grand Rapids: Baker, 1994], 166–67) takes these same references as indication that both practices were customary, and equally so.

2. Harold K. Mouton, ed., *The Analytical Greek Lexicon Revised* (Grand Rapids: Eerdmans, 1977), 294; also noted in Mark A. Coleridge, *The Birth of the Lukan Narrative: Narrative as Christology in Luke 1–2* (JSNTSup 88; Sheffield: JSOT, 1993), 106n2.

3. It is disputed whether v. 66c (καὶ γὰρ χεὶρ κυρίου ἦν μετ᾽ αὐτοῦ) belongs to the direct discourse of the inhabitants of Judea or is a comment by the narrator. However, the past tense (ἦν) as well as the fact that summarizing or clarifying remarks are characteristic of Luke (for example, 2:50; 3:15; 7:39; 16:14; 20:20; 23:12) suggest the latter. The omission of the verb in several Western witnesses (D it[d, ff2, l, q, 26] syr[s]) is judged by Bruce Metzger (*A Textual Commentary on the Greek New Testament*, 2nd ed. [New York: American Bible Society, 1994], 110) as of no consequence for the original reading which included ἦν and was altered when copyists failed to recognize that the phrase was an observation made by the evangelist.

4. See Brown, *Birth*, 369; Fitzmyer, *Luke*, 381; John Nolland, *Luke 1:1—9:20* (WBC 35a; Dallas: Word, 1989), 33, 79; Green, *Luke*, 109; Bovon, *Luke*, 71.

5. As Coleridge (*Birth*, 109) comments: "There has been no hint in the narrative that Zechariah has been struck both deaf and dumb; and it would be crude tactics indeed on the narrator's part to make Zechariah deaf just for the moment so that he cannot hear Elizabeth's words and can therefore offer independent confirmation."

6. BAGD, 267.

7. For example, Brown (*Birth*, 369) argues: "It would be banal to assume that Zechariah had informed her about the angel's command to name the child John (1:13). Zechariah was mute, and the reader is probably meant to think that Elizabeth's decision was a spontaneous and marvelous confirmation of God's plan." I disagree for the reasons I indicate below.

8. Old Testament parallels would include accounts surrounding the births of Jacob, Esau, Moses, and Samuel. Joseph B. Tyson ("The Birth Narratives and the Beginning of Luke's Gospel," *Semeia* 52 [1990]: 103–20, here 103) lists biographies of Plato, Alexander the Great, and Apollonius of Tyana as examples of Greco-Roman parallels.

9. On the role of kinship in the ancient Mediterranean world, see Bruce J. Malina, *The New Testament World: Insights from Cultural Anthropology* (Louisville: Westminster John Knox, 2001), 134–43.

10. So also I. Howard Marshall, *The Gospel of Luke: A Commentary on the Greek Text* (NIGTC 3; Grand Rapids: Eerdmans, 1978), 89, and Coleridge, *Birth*, 111.

11. Green, *Luke*, 111–12.

12. By itself, the image of a "horn of salvation" (κέρας σωτηρίας) may not imply a messianic figure. It can serve simply as a reference to God's mighty rule. The closest Old Testament parallels come from 2 Sam 22:3 and Ps 18:2, each of which apply the designation to God in a nonmessianic context. Yet its coupling with "in the house of his servant David" clearly casts it against a background of messianic expectation. Precedents for the use of "horn" imagery in a messianic context are found at the conclusion of Hannah's Song in 1 Sam 2:10; Pss 88:25 (LXX); 131:17 (LXX); and Ezek 29:21. Similarly, Stephen Farris (*The Hymns of Luke's Infancy Narratives: Their Origin, Meaning and Significance* [JSNTSup 9; Sheffield: JSOT, 1985], 95) points out that the fifteenth benediction of the Shemoneh Esreh in the Babylonian version reads: "Cause the shoot of David to shoot forth quickly and raise up his horn by your salvation. . . . Blessed are you, Lord, who causes the horn of salvation to shoot forth."

13. Most commentators claim that messianic imagery is again being invoked in v. 78b: ἐπισκέψεται ἡμᾶς ἀνατολὴ ἐξ ὕψους (lit: "that which springs up from on high will visit us"). In the LXX, the noun, ἀνατολή, translates the Hebrew צמח ("branch, shoot") and in some texts refers to an awaited messianic redeemer (Isa 11:1; Zech 3:8; 6:12). The verb ἀνατέλλω is used of a rising sun or star in Num 24:17 and Mal 3:20 (LXX/MT). Both of these images, that of a branch (ἀνατολή) and that of rising (ἀνατέλλω) sun or star were common messianic designations in the intertestamental period and in contemporary Judaism. Among the Dead Sea Scrolls, the "Branch" of Isa 11:1-10 and the rising Star (and Scepter) of Num 24:17 played a major role in expressions of messianic expectation. There is also evidence that the two images represented by the verbal ("rising star") and noun ("shoot") form of the word began to converge in the period contemporary to the New Testament. Both Philo (*On the Confusion of the Tongues* 14.60-63) and Justin Martyr (*Dialogue with Trypho* 100.4; 106.4; 121.2; 126.1) saw the term ἀνατολή as messianic and also associated it with the image of a heavenly light. Similarly, *t.Jud.* 24:1, 5b-6, even though the Greek translation utilizes different terminology for "Shoot," appears to combine both images in reference to the awaited Messiah:

> And after this time there shall arise for you [ἀνατέλλω] a Star from Jacob in peace:
> And a man shall arise [ἀνατέλλω] from my posterity like the Sun of righteousness.
> . . . Then he will illumine the scepter of my kingdom, and from your root will arise
> the Shoot [πυθμήν], and through it will arise the rod of righteousness for the nations,
> to judge and save all who call upon the Lord.

In light of the prominent place of ἀνατολή and ἀνατέλλω in messianic imagery prior and contemporary to its use in the Benedictus, most consider the presence of the noun form here to be a messianic allusion (Brown [*Birth*, 374], who sees such a combination of images already present in Num 24:17; Douglas R. Jones, "Background and Character of the Lukan Psalms," *JTS* 19 [1968]: 39; Marshall, *Luke*, 95; Farris, *Hymns*, 140). Several additional observations support this understanding of the image. First, the appearance of κεράς as a messianic symbol at the start of the canticle, which in its LXX precedents and in contemporary Judaism was commonly paired with ἀνατολή and/or ἀνατέλλω, adds noteworthy support to this view. Psalm 131 (132):17 reads: "There I will cause a *horn* to *sprout up* [ἐξανατέλλω (LXX)] for David," and Ezek 29:21 states, "On that day I will cause a horn to sprout up [ἀνατέλλω (LXX)] for the house of Israel." In addition, the light imagery employed in v. 79a and associated with the rising ἀνατολή is a clear allusion to Isa 9:2 (9:1—LXX/MT; cf. Isa 49:9), which is part of a larger passage announcing the reign of a messianic figure who will establish an era of endless peace (see 9:6-7; cf. Luke 1:79b). Third, the parallel instance in vv. 68b-69 of God's saving act defined in terms of messianic deliverance supports the occurrence of this same progression of thought at the close of the hymn, where "that which springs up from on high" is presented as a manifestation of God's mercy (v. 78a). Finally, while the light imagery of v. 79 leads most translations to render ἀνατολή as "dawn," the common association of the noun form with "Branch" suggests that the merging of the two images found in Philo, *Testament of Judah*, and Justin Martyr is present here as well.

14. See H. Schürmann, *Das Lukasevangelium I. Kommentatar zur Kap 1,1-9,50* (HTKNT 3; Freiburg: Herder, 1969) 90–91; Fitzmyer, *Luke*, 379, 85–86; Farris, *Hymns*, 139; Green, *Luke*, 118.

15. Nolland, *Luke 1:1—9:50*, 89.

16. This same focus on forgiveness (manifested in his call to repentance) and conflict characterizes John's own preaching ministry as described by Luke in 3:1-20.

17. Nolland, *Luke 1:1—9:50*, 79.

18. Coleridge (*Birth*, 121) states: "That the horn of salvation will bring salvation through forgiveness implies that the real enemy is not the aggressive neighbour whose military pressure disallows peace, but the sin which disallows peace of another kind. This is the one piece of substantially new information given to the reader in the episode, and the significance of it for the direction and shape of the entire Lukan narrative is hard to overestimate."

19. As Fitzmyer (*Luke*, 384) astutely notes: "On the lips of Zechariah, it [the reference to enemies] scarcely refers to the Roman occupiers of Palestine, but rather to all the forms that hostility to the chosen people took over the ages. In the Lucan setting of the canticle the 'enemies' would include all those who resist or refuse to accept the new form of God's salvation-history." Nolland, *Luke 1:1—9:50*, 87, Green, *Luke*, 114–15, and Bock, *Luke 1:1—9:50*, 182–83, similarly resist a spiritualized understanding of Luke's reference to enemies.

20. See Luke 3:18-20; 4:16-37; 6:6-11, 20-26; 10:13-16; 11:37-54; 12:1-12; 17:20-37; 22:1—24:53; Acts 4:1-31; 5:17-42; 6:8—8:3; 12:1-24; 16:6—17:9; 19:1-41; 21:27—28:31.

21. As Green (*Luke*, 122, 23) suggests, the census "was a penetrating symbol of Roman overlordship." For a helpful discussion of how the census would be perceived by many Jews as a particularly egregious instance of oppressive Roman hegemony, see Richard A. Horsley, *The Liberation of Christmas: The Infancy Narratives in Social Context* (New York: Crossroad, 1989), 33–38.

22. Helpful overviews of the debate can be found in Fitzmyer, *Luke*, 400–5, Nolland, *Luke 1:1—9:50*, 99–103; and Bock, *Luke 1:1—9:50*, 903–9.

23. As similarly noted by Brown, *Birth*, 415; Fitzmyer, 393; Green, *Luke*, 121–22.

24. The description of Jesus wrapped in bands of cloth (ἐσπαργανωμένον) may be an allusion to Wis 7:3-6, which emphasizes the humble beginnings of every king:

> And when I was born, I began to breathe the common air, and fell upon the kindred earth; my first sound was a cry, as is true of all. I was nursed with care in swaddling cloths [ἐν σπαργάνοις]. For no king has had a different beginning of existence; there is for all one entrance into life, and one way out.

If indeed in view, the passage fits well with Luke's portrayal of Jesus as both a lowly and exalted figure, and joins the use of the manger and strips of cloth as a sign throughout the passage that reminds us of the humble origins of this exalted one.

25. Bock's (*Luke 1:1—9:50*, 208) description of Joseph and Mary's lodgings is representative of most recent commentators: "The mention of the feed trough does suggest that Jesus was born in an animal room of some sort. But what kind of animal room was it and why were the child's parents there? The passage tells us that they were there because (διότι, *dioti*) there was no room for them at the καταλύματι (*katalumati*, public shelter). Κατάλυμα suggests that a formal inn is not in view here. . . . Rather, κατάλυμα seems to refer to some type of reception room in a private home or some type of public shelter. Since this place was full, refuge was sought elsewhere."

26. Perhaps my gap-filling activities as a reader are a little overactive here, but I imagine that most travelers making use of such public shelters or the close quarters of a guest room would prefer not to have a laboring woman and newly born infant camping out next to them.

27. In a review of passages of the LXX in which the term σημεῖον is used, Charles H. Giblin ("Reflections on the Sign of the Manger," *CBQ* 29 [1967]: 87–101, here 90–95) has insightfully observed that with biblical texts whose formulation approximates that of Luke 2:12, "the sign is intrinsically proportioned to the message which precedes it and may be expected to exemplify or develop that message, thus contributing to an understanding and realization of that message." In light of this precedent, Luke, it seems, has the sign further articulate the significance of what has just been announced: the giving of the sign in Luke 2:12 follows immediately upon the angel's proclamation of Jesus as "Savior, the Messiah Lord," and offers additional description that characterizes Jesus' mission and person as both exalted and lowly.

28. Green, *Luke*, 130–31.

29. The reversal in play here may be directed not only at Rome, but also at Jerusalem and the temple. Green (*Luke*, 131) states: "Given the respect assigned earlier to the Jerusalem temple and particularly to its sanctuary as the *axis mundi*—the meeting place between the heavenly and the earthly, the divine and human—this appearance of the divine glory is remarkable. God's glory, normally associated with the temple, is now manifest on a farm! At the birth of his son, God has compromised (in a proleptic way) the socio-religious importance of the temple as the cultural center of the world of Israel. Luke thus puts us on notice that the new world coming is of a radically different shape than the former one, that questions of holiness and purity must be asked and addressed in different ways, and that status and issues of values must be reexamined afresh."

30. Translation from S. R. F. Price, *Rituals and Power: The Roman Imperial Cult in Asia Minor* (Cambridge: Cambridge University Press, 1984), 54.

31. As Horsley (*Liberation of Christmas*, 32–33) comments, "Any reader or hearer of this story in the Hellenistic-Roman world, particularly in Palestine, would have understood here a direct opposition between Caesar, the savior who had supposedly brought peace, and the child proclaimed as the savior, whose birth means peace. Luke clearly understands Jesus to be in direct confrontation with the emperor, for here finally is the birth of the messiah in the city of David that the stories and particularly the songs in Luke 1 are proclaiming and eagerly anticipating."

32. Some have argued that the expression χριστὸς κύριος, which occurs nowhere else in the New Testament, was an alteration of the original reading χριστὸς κυρίου. However, this reading has only weak textual support (β r¹ syʰᵖᵃˡ Tat Ephr), and as Metzger (*Textual Commentary*, 110) explains: "It was to be expected that copyists, struck by the unusual collocation, should have introduced various modifications."

33. Mark L. Strauss, *The Davidic Messiah in Luke-Acts: The Promise and Its Fulfillment in Lukan Christology* (JSNTSup 110; Sheffield: Sheffield Academic Press, 1995), 116.

34. Ibid. Instead, Strauss argues that κύριος functions epexegetically to refer "to messianic lordship—the authority and dominion which Christ deserves and possesses."

35. R. Hann, "Christos Kurios in PsSol 17:32: 'The Lord's Anointed' Reconsidered," *NTS* 31 (1985): 620–27. Χριστὸς κύριος also occurs in Lam 4:20 (LXX), but this is generally regarded as a mistranslation. See Hann, "Christos Kurios," 622. Hann is preceded in his judgment that χριστὸς κύριος is the original reading and was coined as a royal title parallel to

Hellenistic usage by R. B. Wright (*The Old Testament Pseudepigrapha*, ed. James C. Charlesworth [New York: Abingdon, 1985], 2.667–68, n. z.

36. To be sure, the pronouncement of Jesus as κύριος elsewhere in Luke-Acts also draws a connection to Jesus' designation as Messiah (e.g., Acts 2:36; 10:36). However, these same passages also indicate that the proclamation of Jesus as "Lord" is not to be seen simply as an aspect of his messianic identity, but exists alongside and complements the proclamation of Jesus as Messiah: "Let all the house of Israel therefore know assuredly that God has made him both Lord and Christ, this Jesus whom you crucified" (2:36); "You know the word which he sent to Israel, preaching good news of peace by Jesus Christ (He is Lord of all)" (10:36). Thus, in much the same way that Luke's portrayal of Jesus as the exalted Divine Son in 1:31-35 significantly recasts his designation as the awaited Davidic ruler, so, too, does Luke's reference to Jesus as κύριος in these passages further suggest a closeness of relation between Jesus and God that transcends most traditional, messianic imagining. This is contrary to the view of Strauss (*Davidic Messiah*, 116 [see above]), who stresses that Jesus' Davidic messiahship is the only context for understanding the title and, in my opinion, overlooks the full implications of Luke's proclamation of Jesus as κύριος here in the infancy narrative.

37. Scholars are divided over whether the references παντὶ τῷ λαῷ ("all the people") and ἐν ἀνθρώποις εὐδοκίας ("among those whom God favors") should be understood as referring only to faithful Jews or inclusive of Gentiles as well. Most commentators take the expressions "all the people" and "among those whom God favors" as references only to Israel. It is typically pointed out that Luke often utilizes the phrase "all the people" without any emphasis on πᾶς in a universalistic sense, and that with the exception of Acts 15:14 and 18:10 the normal use of the singular λαός refers to Israel (Luke 3:21; 7:29; 8:47; 18:43; 19:48; 21:38; 24:19; Acts 4:10; 13:24). Stephen G. Wilson (*The Gentiles and the Gentile Mission in Luke-Acts* [SNTSMS 23; Cambridge: Cambridge University Press, 1973], 34–35) infers from this evidence that, "thus, while admitting that a reference to the new people of God, both Jews and Gentiles, is possible in 2:10, we conclude that it is unlikely." Wilson is followed in his judgment by the majority of commentators, including Brown (*Birth*, 402); Marshall (*Luke*, 109); Coleridge (*Birth*, 139 n.2); Nolland (*Luke 1:1—9:50*, 107); Bock (*Luke 1:1—9:50*, 215), contra Green (*Luke*, 134n54).

Yet, it should also be pointed out that in each of the occurrences of the phrase throughout Luke-Acts it is the *context* that establishes who is in view. For Luke, there is nothing intrinsic to the phrase itself that indicates that it is to refer exclusively to Israel, as evidenced by its use to indicate both Jews and Gentiles in Acts 15:14 and 18:10 and by the use of the qualifier "of Israel" in Acts 4:10 and 13:24 where the context would otherwise not indicate those to whom the expression refers. Moreover, there are several reasons for perceiving that in this passage Luke introduces what he will much more directly relay in the following episode (2:32): the salvific significance of God's act of salvation in Jesus for both Jews *and* Gentiles. First, as discussed above, Luke's casting of this episode against a background of world history has already implied a universal significance for Jesus' birth. Second, the couplet parallelism of v. 14 places the realm of ἐν ὑψίστοις ("in the highest") in apposition to ἐπὶ γῆς ("upon the earth"), with the implication that Jesus' birth is proclaimed as an event that has an impact on both heavenly and earthly reality. This expansive spatial imagery suggests that the peace accomplished in Jesus' advent is cosmic in scope. Third, the presentation of Jesus as the true Lord and Savior in contrast to Caesar clearly implies that Jesus' sovereignty *and* salvific rule extend beyond the borders of his relatively small homeland and similarly encompass "all the world."

38. For a more complete articulation of the view that the αὐτόπται καὶ ὑπηρέται ("eyewitnesses and ministers") to whom Luke refers in 1:2 includes characters of his infancy narrative, please see Karl A. Kuhn, "Beginning the Witness: The αὐτόπται καὶ ὑπηρέται of Luke's Infancy Narrative" *NTS* 49 (2003): 237–55.

39. Representing a fairly common perspective, Brown (*Birth*, 429) and Fitzmyer (*Luke*, 397) deny that the response of the shepherds to the angelic announcement is to be associated with the apostolic task of proclaiming the faith portrayed at the end of Gospel and throughout Acts. Fitzmyer states concerning the shepherds: "They are not to be regarded as eyewitnesses whom Luke decades later contacted in order to get the story. Their function is that of showing spontaneous trust in the heavenly message." Similarly, Brown goes on to say that "they are the forerunners, not of the apostles, but of future believers who will glorify God for what they have heard and will praise God for what they have seen." It seems to me that both Fitzmyer's and Brown's assessments draw too sharp a distinction between "praising" and "proclaiming" as if for Luke the former cannot include or be paired with the latter. Rather, the opposite of this dichotomy is presented here in this episode, as Luke draws an intentional connection between the shepherds' spoken testimony to what God has revealed *and* their act of glorifying God as *both* comprising a faithful response to God's good news announced by the angels. First of all, verbal cues underline the shepherds' role as those who proclaim to others what God has revealed to them. Hearing of the angel's message (v. 15) and seeing what the angel had announced (v. 17a) leads to their "making known" (γνωρίζω [v. 17]) and "telling" (λαλέω [v. 18]) those gathered around the manger what the Lord had "made known" (γνωρίζω [v. 15]) and "told" (λαλέω [v. 17]) to them. The shepherds are clearly portrayed as bearing witness to the announcement they have received. Their hearing and seeing are also given as the very reason for their praise in v. 20: the shepherds return "glorifying and praising God, *for all they had seen and heard, as it had been told them*" (v. 20). As ones who have received "the good news of a great joy" (v. 10), they both bear witness to what God has revealed to them and erupt with thanksgiving and praise. Other examples of Luke drawing a close connection between proclaiming and rejoicing include the "triumphal approach" (19:36-40) and the worship of the disciples in the temple (24:52-53) right after having been commissioned by Jesus as witnesses (24:48).

In contrast to Fitzmyer and Brown, other commentators have long emphasized the shepherds' role as those who eyewitness and proclaim the amazing events taking place before them. Frederick Danker (*Jesus and the New Age According to St. Luke: A Commentary on the Third Gospel* [St. Louis: Clayton, 1972], 61) calls them the "first evangelists." Darrell Bock (*Luke 1:1—9:50*, 221–22) adds, "The shepherds reflect a vibrant faith, where the sequence is God's word, faith, and then testimony. When God's word comes to pass, testimony should follow (2.17). . . . The full understanding by people will come later. But for now to the voices of the angels is added the testimony of humans."

Likewise, Eduard Schweizer (*The Good News According to Luke*, trans. D. E. Green [Atlanta: John Knox, 1984], 51) similarly concludes, as I argue above, that Luke portrays both the shepherds' spoken witness to what God has revealed and their act of praising God as together comprising a faithful response to the announcement of the angelic host, and moreover one that initiates the Christian mission to the world.

But this chain of events evokes a countermovement, the coming of the hosts of heaven to proclaim to "all the people" the "Lord" anointed by God, who in turn cause a band of shepherds to set forth. This leads to the formation of a first community, *praising God and proclaiming his mighty acts* (emphasis mine), from which there will then arise a movement back to Rome (Acts 28:14-31).

40. Several scholars have suggested that the references to Jesus being wrapped in strips of cloth (σπαργανόω) may be a proleptic allusion to the wrapping of Jesus' body in a "linen cloth" (σινδών) in Luke 23:53. For example, Luke Timothy Johnson (*The Gospel of Luke* [Sacra Pagina 3; Collegeville, Minn.: Liturgical, 1991], 53) wonders:

> Is there perhaps another dimension to the odd details enumerated by Luke? Can the threefold, deliberate phrasing in the Greek of "wrapped him in swaddling cloth strips, placed him in a manger, because there was no place" perhaps anticipate the same threefold rhythm of "wrapped him in a linen cloth, placed him in a rock-hewn tomb, where no one had yet been laid" (23:53) so that birth and burial mirror each other?

Whether or not Luke intended such a connection via the reference to swaddling, Theophilus and most of Luke's readers know how the rest of the story unfolds (see 1:4) and would likely make a connection between the humble circumstances surrounding Jesus' birth and his humiliation on the cross.

41. Bruce Malina, *The New Testament World: Insights from Cultural Anthropology* (Louisville: Westminster John Knox, 2001), 52.

42. Green (*Luke*, 132) adds, "The announcement of birth is directed to shepherds rather than to parents, and thus to 'outsiders' in a double sense—that is, to persons who are outside the circle of Jesus' family of origin and are persons of low regard. This portends the considerable ramifications of his birth, which cannot be conceived as a family affair, and may also anticipate the redefinition of 'family' in Jesus' ministry (see Luke 8:19-21; 9:57-62; 12:51-53; 14:26).

43. Bock, *Luke 1:1—9:50*, 216.

44. Luke's treatment and understanding of the Israelite customs of purification and presentation of the firstborn son are widely debated by commentators, some of who claim that Luke misunderstood the customs and others who argue that Luke merely combined them for the sake of convenience. For a review of the discussion, see Bock, *Luke 1:1—9:50*, 234–37. Despite the difficulties Luke's account presents, however, the intent is clear: to present Mary and Joseph as faithful adherents to the law.

45. Brown (*Birth*, 467–68) notes that Anna, whose lengthy widowhood of eighty-four years Luke emphasizes, is also portrayed by Luke in terms that correspond to the ideal widow of the Pauline churches, as described in 1 Tim 5:3-16. Like Anna, to be enrolled as a widow, one must be over sixty years of age and of one husband. Also similar to Anna, the ideal for the widow is to continue "in prayers and supplications day and night" (1 Tim 5:6).

46. Green, *Luke*, 143.

47. Brown, *Birth*, 450.

48. In taking the infant Jesus into his arms and proclaiming, "My eyes have seen your salvation" (v. 30), Simeon speaks of Jesus in a manner that once again invites us to see a convergence between Jesus and Yahweh, though one more so of mission than of person. The compact phrase

Notes

succinctly summarizes one of the most crucial ideas of Luke's birth narrative. Once again, Jesus is proclaimed as the very embodiment of God's awaited deliverance. His coming marks the advent of God's promised redemption for Israel and all peoples.

49. For a helpful listing and reproduction of these texts from Isaiah, see Brown, *Birth*, 458.

50. Green, *Luke*, 147.

51. Scholars disagree over whether "for revelation to the Gentiles" and "glory for your people Israel" are to be seen as mutual manifestations of the "light" that is in apposition to salvation (v. 30) or whether "light" refers only to the revelation for the Gentiles, hence: "a light for revelation to the Gentiles, and glory for your people Israel" (with both "light" and "glory" in apposition to the "salvation" of v. 30). Yet in either case the meaning is essentially the same, since with both readings all of v. 32 is a manifestation of the salvation "God has prepared before all peoples" (v. 30-31). I opt for "light" as the subject of all of v. 32 for two reasons: (1) this reading better appreciates the symmetry of the phrase (φῶς εἰς + accusative [ἀποκάλυψιν] modified by genitive [ἐθνῶν] + accusative [δόξαν] modified by genitive [λαοῦ σου Ἰσραήλ]; and (2) Acts 26:23 similarly refers to the salvific significance of light (φῶς) for both Israel and the Gentiles.

52. Isaiah 49:6b reads: "It is too light a thing that you should be my servant, to raise up the tribes of Jacob and to restore the survivors of Israel; I will give you as a light to the nations, that my salvation may reach to the end of the earth."

53. John J. Kilgallen, "Jesus, Savior, the Glory of Your People Israel," *Bib* 75 (1994): 305–28.

54. Ibid., 313–20.

55. Luke Timothy Johnson (*The Literary Function of Possessions in Luke-Acts* [SBLDS 39; Missoula: Scholars, 1977], 91) states: "What makes the prophecy of Simeon so important as a key to the following narrative is that it directs us to see in the story of Jesus a story of a people divided over the prophet, a division in which some are to rise and others are to fall." So also John O. York, *The Last Shall Be First: The Rhetoric of Reversal in Luke* (JSNTSup 46; Sheffield: JSOT, 1991), 113–16.

56. Simeon's prophecy alludes to Jesus' rejection as preordained by God. BAGD (s.v., 426 2. b.) lists "be appointed, set, destined" for the figurative use of the verb, κεῖμαι.

57. Recall the similar juxtaposition of seemingly contradictory details associated with Jesus in the angel's announcement to the shepherds: Jesus is proclaimed as Savior, who is "Messiah Lord," and then described as wrapped in swaddling clothes and laid in the manger (2:11-12).

58. Scholars commonly identify the description of Jesus as σημεῖον ἀντιλεγόμενον ("a sign to be spoken against") as well as the reference to the "rising and falling of many" is an allusion to the "stone texts" tradition. Consisting of a conflation of Isa 8:14-15; 28:16; and Ps 118:22, these texts had been combined in early Christian tradition (see Rom 9:32-22; 1 Pet 2:6-8) into a messianic prophecy to help explain Jesus' rejection by his fellow Jews. In light of this allusion, it is instructive to note that the parable of the tenants in the vineyard (Luke 20:9-19) is the only other place in the Gospel where the evangelist employs the stone tradition. There he also uses it to speak of Jesus' rejection, and in a parable that rather transparently addresses Jesus' impending death at the hands of the unfaithful of Israel. Similarly, in Acts 4:10-11 Luke again uses the image in connection to Jesus' rejection and crucifixion.

59. For a review of the many interpretations of this puzzling statement, see Brown, *Birth*, 462–63; and Bock, *Luke 1:1—9:50*, 248–50.

60. Marshall, *Luke*, 123. So also Nolland, *Luke 1:1—9:50*, 121–22.

61. Brown, *Birth*, 688.

172

62. Ibid., 463–64.

63. Ibid., 465. Brown is followed in this interpretation by Fitzmyer, *Luke*, 430; and Bock, *Luke 1:1—9:50*, 250.

64. Brown, *Birth*, 343.

65. The placement of the parenthetical remark in the Greek is obscured by the NRSV, which pushes it to the end of the oracle, rather than immediately following the reference to Jesus' rejection.

66. Recall that the depiction of "the beautiful and ugly, the desperate and hopeful" was identified as a literary device used to evoke an emotional response in readers back in chapter 3. This is, I believe, the first clear instance of it in the infancy narrative.

67. This also coheres well with the narrative to follow, the bulk of which (from 9:51 onward) presents the movement of the narrative toward Jerusalem, the locale not only of Jesus' passion but also his resurrection.

68. On the tragic character of Luke-Acts, see Robert C. Tannehill, *The Narrative Unity of Luke-Acts*, 2 vols (Minneapolis: Fortress Press, 1990), especially his summary on 2:1–8.

CONCLUSION: From Scripture's Heart to Ours

1. For a helpful listing of various proposals concerning Luke's primary aims, see Darrell L. Bock, *Luke 1:1—9:50* (Baker Exegetical Commentary on the New Testament 3a; Grand Rapids: Baker, 1994), 14–15.

2. Luke Timothy Johnson, *The Gospel of Luke* (Sacra Pagina 3; Collegeville, Minn.: Liturgical, 1991), 10. So also David Tiede, *Prophecy and History in Luke-Acts* (Philadelphia: Fortress Press, 1980). See also the essays of David Moessner, ed., *Jesus and the Heritage of Israel: Luke's Narrative Claim upon Israel's Legacy* (Harrisburg: Trinity, 1999).

3. Robert C. Tannehill, *The Narrative Unity of Luke-Acts*, 2 vols. (Minneapolis: Fortress Press, 1990), 2:2.

4. This view has been promoted by Richard Horsley (*The Liberation of Christmas: The Infancy Narratives in Social Context* [New York: Crossroad, 1989]) and Joel Green (*The Gospel of Luke* [NICNT; Grand Rapids: Eerdmans, 1997]; see esp. 9, 23–25).

5. Gregory E. Sterling, *Historiography and Self-Definition: Josephus, Luke-Acts, and Apologetic Historiography* (NovTSup 64; Leiden: Brill, 1992); Philip Esler, *Community and Gospel in Luke-Acts: The Social and Political Motivations of Lucan Theology* (SNTSMS 57; Cambridge: Cambridge University Press, 1987).

6. Larry Hurtado, *Lord Jesus Christ: Devotion to Jesus in Earliest Christianity* (Grand Rapids: Eerdmans, 2003), esp. 27–153.

7. Hurtado (*Lord Jesus Christ*, 349–407) points to numerous indications of such debate between Christians and non-Christian Jews, especially as reflected in the Johannine traditions. See also Raymond Brown, *The Community of the Beloved Disciple: The Life, Loves, and Hates of an Individual Church in New Testament Times* (New York: Paulist, 1979), and John Ashton, *Understanding the Fourth Gospel* (Oxford: Clarendon, 1991), 121–380.

8. For a more thorough challenge to a "monological" view of Scripture and the proposal of an alternative approach that sees Scripture as both embodying a collection of inspired testimony and inviting an ongoing, sacred dialogue among believers, please see Karl Allen Kuhn, *Having Words with God: The Bible as Conversation* (Minneapolis: Fortress Press, 2008).